HOW FIRM A FOUNDATION:

LEADERS

OF

THE

LITURGICAL

MOVEMENT

*Compiled and
introduced by
Robert L. Tuzik*

LITURGY
TRAINING
PUBLICATIONS

ACKNOWLEDGMENTS

Some of the essays in this book appeared first in the pages of *Liturgy 80* magazine.

Printed in the United States of America.

Edited by Elizabeth Hoffman
Design by Jane Kremsreiter
Cover design by Carolyn Riege
Cover art from *Orate Fratres* 13, no. 11, 1939. Used with permission of The
Liturgical Press, Collegeville, Minnesota.

CONTENTS

FOREWORD

EWARE OF BOOKS that begin with apologies! Beware of this book! It needs its apologies.

We apologize for leaving some people out. For example, Annibale Bugnini. He ought to be here. Martimort ought to be here. Charles Buswell and the Southwest Liturgical Conference ought to be here. Conception Abbey in Missouri ought to be here. Every reader will have a few additions and every reader will be right. The selection is arbitrary with decisions made by those of us who don't ourselves have the picture all together.

In defense, we had to get started. We wanted to focus on the liturgical movement in the United States, so the emphasis went there. We soon recognized the importance of including the European leaders. We also had to deal with some cutoff point. Just the dead? Just those who worked before Vatican II (that was our guide in the first volume of this series, a book filled with quotes from many of these people)? That seemed not to work for this second book. So we have included the dead and the elderly, though a few in their 60s have gotten in. Arbitrary? Certainly.

We apologize next for the varieties of approach you will find in these pages. We knew of no one person who knew about all these people. Robert Tuzik turned first to some of the candidates for advanced degrees in liturgy at the University of Notre Dame. Then he went in search of other authors, some with firsthand knowledge of their subjects. That led not only to varied writing styles but to great differences in how the authors chose to approach their stories. Some were heavy on dates and took a chronological approach to their task. Others worked more from impressions and a desire to communicate the contribution made to the liturgy by their people. Some used lots of footnotes, some none.

Might an able editor with much time have created consistency? Yes, and the reader may well wish for such an editor. Our decision was to let the diversity hold sway. You must open the book expecting to hear from a whole crowd of storytellers, some more to your liking than others.

We apologize for what is needed most but is not here: the wholeness of a pattern. We have not woven these lives into a cloth. We have left the threads to be threads. Some you can tie together yourself, but more help is almost certainly needed.

Happily some of the people in this book have been celebrated in full-length biographies in the past few years (Bethune, Botte, Diekmann, Mathis and Michel, for example) and there have been some studies of this or that aspect of the movement. But we seem to be a ways from the whole story well told.

What we do not apologize for, then, is what you do hold in your hand: some of the stories, diversely told, of some of the people. All of us who believe in the importance of renewing the liturgy in the church need to know about these men and women. We need to know how they saw things, how they worked and helped each other, how they brought about beginnings. We need to know their mistakes also. These are people of great diversity. Some you would love to know. Others are hard to take. What else could we expect? We build on their "firm foundation," and we will build better if we know them and, in many cases, if we know their writings.

In the end, it is not an apology we have but an invitation to meet some unusual people, a marvelous company.

■ *Gabe Huck*

INTRODUCTION

Whence the Liturgical Movement?

I N THE SIXTEENTH CENTURY, the Council of Trent set out to reform the liturgy by returning to the "ancient rite and norms of the Holy Fathers." The conviction then developed in the Roman church that the way the liturgy was given in the 1570 missal was as close to the pristine tradition of the church as possible.

During the eighteenth and nineteenth centuries, historical studies made some people aware that the liturgy found in the 1570 missal was certainly not this "ancient rite" but was, in fact, based on a 1474 missal, which at best reflected the tradition of the Roman Curia in the thirteenth century.

While the 1570 missal did correct many abuses of the time (e.g., overemphasis on the veneration of the saints, lack of reverence in celebrating the eucharist), it froze the liturgy in a style dominated by the clergy. Private Masses (celebrated by a priest with only a server or at best a few people present) came into general use only around the year 1200. At these Masses, the priest took over all the roles of deacon, lector, choir and people. Sung parts were dropped or read; everything was done at the altar and most of it was done quietly. The format of the private Mass became the pattern of celebration accepted by the 1570 missal as normative for the church.

In eighteenth-century France, liturgical reforms advocated or made during the Enlightenment period were associated with Gallicanism (the tendency to see the French church as independent of Rome) and Jansenism. In fact, some eighteenth-century French Catholics called for the vernacular in the liturgy, for using only one altar, for having only one community Mass on Sunday, for restoring the offertory procession, for encouraging people to receive communion with greater regularity and for having communion under both kinds. When Prosper Guéranger, the abbot of Solesmes in the mid-nineteenth century, called for the use of the 1570 Roman Missal in order to bring stability back to the French church, any liturgical reforms associated with Gallicanism and Jansenism were largely lost.

In eighteenth-century Germany, the stress was on communal celebration, promoting congregational singing in the vernacular at low (and sometimes even at high) Mass. Some of these songs were paraphrases of Mass prayers (a German "Gloria Hymn" or "Sanctus Hymn"), thus fostering a better understanding of the liturgy. They criticized the too-frequent requiem Masses and called for the reform of the breviary, more frequent reception of communion and communion under both kinds.

In the nineteenth century, two Tübingen theologians greatly influenced the future leaders of the liturgical movement: Johann Adam Möhler (1796–1838) and Matthias Joseph Scheeben (1835–1888). Möhler's books, *The Unity of the Church* (1825) and *Symbolism* (1832), pioneered a new ecclesiology based on an organic conception of church as the body of Christ and an ecumenical openness to learning from the insights of Protestant theologians.

Matthias Scheeben's works, *Nature and Grace* (1861) and *Mysteries of Christianity* (1865) built on Möhler's thought. Scheeben was part of a movement in the church to redefine the responsibilities of membership in the church in the light of the data surfacing in biblical and patristic scholarship.

The movement toward restoring active participation to the laity received tremendous help from Pope Pius X. In 1903, he issued the document *Tra Le Sollecitudini*. One line in particular became the rallying cry of the liturgical movement in this century: "The foremost and indispensable font of the true Christian spirit is the active participation in the holy mysteries and in the public and solemn prayer of the church."

With this endorsement, a freer discussion of the agenda of liturgical renewal could be conducted. This was the beginning of the modern era of the movement. Within two decades, liturgical weeks gathered large numbers of interested scholars, liturgical and social activists, and pastoral leaders.

The liturgical movement in Europe was joined with a dynamic social action movement (e.g., the Catholic Youth Movement in Germany or the Young Christian Workers in Belgium), whose goals were an activist understanding of membership in the church based on our baptism and a reform of the structures of society.

The European leaders of the liturgical movement set out to do more than move furniture and have people sing chants at Mass. They wanted to reform the way people lived as church. They came to understand the liturgy as a celebration of what it means to be, to become and to build up the church. They wanted to rescue popular piety from its preoccupation with worship before the tabernacle to a style of worship that would relate the liturgy to life. They wanted the liturgy to become the source of the life of the church, the source of the lay apostolate.

We owe gratitude to these leaders. They often labored under difficult circumstances. At times, the Catholic leaders were criticized as being heretical or too "Protestant" and the Protestant leaders were criticized as being too "Catholic." Nonetheless, they persevered and the work they began is still changing the way we live and worship as a church.

The American liturgical movement learned from and adapted what arose first in the European church through Lambert

Beauduin, Pius Parsch, Romano Guardini, Joseph Cardijn and other scholarly and pastoral leaders.

Like the European movement, the American liturgical movement was concerned with the pastoral effectiveness of the liturgy. Goals went beyond singing congregations and renovated churches. The movement was about a revolution in spirituality, in Christian life.

Much of the credit for making available to the American church the scholarship and pastoral practices of the European movement goes to Virgil Michel, a monk of St. John's Abbey in Collegeville, Minnesota. Having studied under Lambert Beauduin at the College of Sant' Anselmo in Rome, Michel returned to the United States to found the Liturgical Press and *Orate Fratres*. Until his early death in 1938, Michel was himself the center for all those who rallied to his call for liturgical renewal.

In 1928, architects and artists on the East Coast founded the Liturgical Arts Society. This attempted to open the eyes of the American church to the best church art and architecture from different parts of the world.

The American liturgists embodied the insights of the biblical and patristic movements. They saw identity in Christ as crucial to the church's understanding of itself. Participation in the liturgy and the liturgical year were the church's "matchless" means of transforming us into other Christs, responsible for completing his mission on earth. The apostolate was seen as the extension of the altar, of the self-giving celebrated in the eucharist.

In 1940, almost 30 years after the first Belgian Liturgical Week, the first Liturgical Week in North America was held in Chicago. These annual gatherings were to achieve in the United States what the Liturgical Weeks had achieved in Europe: a renewed consciousness of the importance of baptism, the priesthood of the laity, the connection between liturgy and social justice, and excitement and support among those in the movement. A hallmark of the American liturgical movement was its insistence on the necessary connection between liturgy and life, liturgy and social justice.

It soon became obvious that the United States had to provide academic training for the future leaders of liturgical renewal. This began in a small way with the summer programs in Chicago and New York in the early 1940s. Michael Mathis of the University of Notre Dame then took up this challenge and organized the first summer school of liturgy at Notre Dame in 1947.

At the 1946 Liturgical Week in Denver, the St. Jerome Society was organized to promote the study of greater use of the vernacular in the liturgy. After *Mediator Dei* in 1947, this group changed its name to the Vernacular Society, encouraging "the use of the mother tongue in conjunction with several of the rites."

Those are the broad strokes of the movement. Much of this and of what followed, in Europe and in the United States, is told in this book (see especially the chapter on the years between *Mediator Dei* and the *Constitution on the Sacred Liturgy*). The work of renewal, after the *Constitution*, has been under way for a generation. The liturgical movement now goes far beyond Europe and the United States. Ecumenical forces have been joined. Problems impossible to foresee have influenced the course of the reform.

The liturgical movement continues.

■ *Robert L. Tuzik*

CHRONOLOGY

This chronology is far from exhaustive. It is intended only to place the persons whose stories are told here in relation to one another and in relation to some elements of the developing liturgical renewal.

1833   Prosper Guéranger restores monastic life and liturgy at the French abbey of Solesmes

1841   Guéranger's *L'Année liturgique* is published

1899   Edmund Bishop writes his essay on "The Genius of the Roman Rite"

1903   Pius X issues a *motu proprio* on music and liturgy, *Tra Le Sollecitudini*

1907   Lambert Beauduin joins the Benedictine community of Mont César (in Belgium); the prior of the community is Columba Marmion

1909   Beauduin's address to the Malines Congress on Catholic Action inaugurates a new era of the liturgical movement; Beauduin begins the publication of *Questions liturgiques*

1910	First Liturgical Week is held (Mont César)
	Quam Singulari, on children's communion, is issued by the Congregation of the Sacraments
1913	Reform of the breviary is announced by the Congregation of Rites
1916	Justine Ward and Georgia Stevens found Pius X Institute of Liturgical Music at Manhattanville College
1921	Beauduin begins teaching at Sant' Anselmo in Rome where one of his students is Virgil Michel from St. John's Abbey in Minnesota
	Odo Casel, monk of Maria Laach in Germany, publishes the first of the 15-volume *Jahrbuch für Liturgiewissenschaft*
1922	Pius Parsch of Klosterneuburg in Austria publishes the first pages of what would become *Das Jahr des Heiles (The Church's Year of Grace),* as part of his *Volksliturgisches Apostolat,* "popular liturgical apostolate"
	First decree on the dialogue Mass from the Congregation of Rites
1923	Walter Frere, English liturgical scholar, is consecrated bishop of Truro
1926	Virgil Michel begins publication of *Orate Fratres*
	William Busch begins writing articles for *Orate Fratres;* he will continue to contribute until 1951
1927	Romano Guardini becomes the director of the German Catholic Youth Movement and its center, Burg Rothenfels, becomes the place of liturgical, social and artistic development; here the liturgical movement changes from a monastic to a lay movement

1928   *Divini Cultus,* apostolic constitution promoting participation through the singing of chant by the assembly, is issued

Liturgical Arts Society is founded; Maurice Lavanoux begins publication of their journal, *Liturgical Arts;* he will serve as editor until the magazine ends publication in 1972

1929   Virgil Michel organizes a Liturgical Day to conclude the first summer school in the liturgy held in the United States

1932   Joseph Stedman publishes the first edition of *My Sunday Missal*

1933   First edition of *Christian Life and Worship* by Gerald Ellard

1934   Adé Bethune is commissioned by Dorothy Day to do pictures for the *Catholic Worker;* later Bethune will illustrate editions of Ellard's *Christian Life and Worship* and Stedman's *My Sunday Missal;* later still she will edit *Catholic Art Quarterly* and *Sacred Signs*

1935   English-language edition of Guardini's *The Spirit of the Liturgy* is published

1936   Reynold Hillenbrand named rector of St. Mary of the Lake Seminary in Chicago where he will bring together education in liturgy and social issues

H. A. Reinhold comes to the United States; his "Timely Tracts" will appear in *Orate Fratres/Worship* until 1957

Bernard Laukemper brings in national speakers for a parish liturgical week at his parish, St. Aloysius, in Chicago

1937   Evelyn Underhill publishes her study *Worship* on the prophetic, formative and mystical qualities of liturgy

1938   Godfrey Diekmann becomes editor of *Orate Fratres* at the death of Virgil Michel

1939   Guardini is dismissed by the Nazis and Rothenfels is
        confiscated

1940   Martin Hellriegel becomes pastor at Holy Cross in St. Louis;
        the parish will become a model where liturgy serves as the cen-
        ter of all activity and prayer

        First Liturgical Week in North America is held in Chicago with
        more than 1200 in attendance; among the presentors: Reynold
        Hillenbrand, Godfrey Diekmann, Mary Perkins Ryan (on "Lay
        Persons Using the Breviary")

        Founding of the Grail Movement in the United States at
        Doddridge Farm, Libertyville, Illinois; moved to Loveland,
        Ohio, in 1944.

1941   First National Summer School of Liturgy, Chicago

        Founding of the Gregorian Institute of America (GIA) by
        Clifford Bennett

1943   Pius XII issues *Mystici Corporis* and *Divino Afflante Spiritu*

        Centre de Pastorale Liturgique founded in Paris by Roguet and
        others

        Gregory Dix at the Anglican Abbey of Nashdom finishes *The
        Shape of the Liturgy*

        Therese Mueller writes *Our Children's Year of Grace*

1945   *La Maison Dieu* begins publication

1946   Founding of the St. Jerome Society (became known as the
        Vernacular Society in 1948); their periodical, *Amen,* will pro-
        mote the cause of English in the liturgy

1947   Pius XII issues *Mediator Dei*

In Paris, Joseph Gelineau begins to put into parish practice his theories about vernacular singing of the psalms

Michael Mathis begins the first summer school of the Notre Dame liturgy program; the finest European scholars make this a center of learning and publication

Balthasar Fischer becomes first person to hold the chair of liturgy in the theology school of Trier (Germany)

1948   Publication of Josef Jungmann's *Missarum Sollemnia (Mass of the Roman Rite)*, written during his academic exile under the Nazis

First authorization for bilingual editions of the *Roman Ritual*

1949   Pierre-Marie Gy begins four decades of teaching (most will be at the Institut Supérieur de Liturgie of the Institut Catholique de Paris)

1950   First German National Liturgical Congress; participants ask that the bishops request the Easter Vigil be moved to evening

Alexander Peloquin becomes music director at the cathedral in Providence; his *Mass of the Bells* will be published in 1972 and his *Lyric Liturgy* in 1974

1951   Revisions of the Easter Vigil approved for experiment

First International Liturgical Study Week at Maria Laach attended by leading European liturgical scholars

Frank Kacmarcik begins designing *Worship* (formerly *Orate Fratres*)

1952   Louis Bouyer teaches in the summer program at the University of Notre Dame; his lectures are published as *Liturgical Piety*

1953   Third International Liturgical Study Week is held in Lugano (Italy), attended by scholars and by members of the hierarchy

Scripture scholar Bernard Botte begins summer school for seminary professors of liturgy

1954   Bilingual version of the *Roman Ritual* approved for the United States

1955   Restored rites approved for Holy Week

Pius XII publishes encyclical *Musicae Sacrae Disciplina*

1956   The First International Congress of Pastoral Liturgy is held in Assisi; 1200 participants

Botte and others found the Institut Supérieur de Liturgie in Paris where future scholars from all over the world will study

1958   Congregation of Rites issues *Instruction on Sacred Music and the Liturgy* with concern for active participation, including the simultaneous reading of the scriptures by lay readers in the vernacular

Readings and hymns in the vernacular allowed during Holy Week in India

United States bishops create a Commission for the Liturgy

1959   John XXIII announces the Second Vatican Council

New England Liturgical Committee founded

1960   Frederic Debuyst begins 20 years as editor of *Art d'Église*

Publication of Reinhold's *Bringing the Mass to the People*

1962   Southwest Liturgical Conference holds the first of its annual study weeks

1963   Godfrey Diekmann joins Frederick McManus as second
English-speaking *peritus* on the conciliar liturgical commission

Formation of the International Commission on English in the
Liturgy by Paul Hallinan, archbishop of Atlanta, and other
bishops from English-speaking countries

December 4, *Constitution on the Sacred Liturgy* ratified by
Vatican II

1964   Frederick McManus is appointed secretary of the Bishops'
Commission on the Liturgical Apostolate

Theophane Hytrek and others found the Church Music Association of America

Omer Westendorf's World Library of Sacred Music publishes
the *People's Mass Book*

With Gerard Sloyan as president of the Liturgical Conference,
the St. Louis Liturgical Week celebrates Mass in English for the
first time; the music includes Clarence Rivers' "God is love"

1965   Gelineau, Huijbers and others form Universa Laus for the
study of liturgy and music

Robert Hovda begins 13 years as an editor at the Liturgical
Conference, writing *Living Worship* essays and creating the
Manual of Celebration

1966   Publication of Alexander Schmemann's *Introduction to Liturgical Theology*

1969   Reformed Roman rites of marriage, funerals, order of Mass
and general instruction, baptism of infants, lectionary and
calendar

1971   Balthasar Fischer directs the Roman commission preparing the
Directory for Masses with Children, published in 1973

Reformed Roman liturgy of the hours and the rite of
confirmation

1972   Reformed order of Christian initiation of adults and pastoral care of the sick

Music in Catholic Worship issued by United States Bishops' Committee on the Liturgy

1973   First meeting of the North American Academy of Liturgy

1974   Reformed rite of penance and eucharistic prayers for Masses with children and of reconciliation

1978   *Environment and Art in Catholic Worship* published by the United States Bishops' Committee on the Liturgy

1982   *Pastoral Care of the Sick: Rites of Anointing and Viaticum* is published for use in the United States

1988   *Rite of Christian Initiation of Adults* is published for use in the United States

1989   *Order of Christian Funerals* and *Book of Blessings* are published for use in the United States

EUROPEAN
LEADERS

PROSPER GUÉRANGER

Founder of the Modern Liturgical Movement

P ROSPER LOUIS PASCAL GUÉRANGER (1805–1875) was born in an era shaped politically, culturally and religiously by the Enlightenment, as well as by post-Revolutionary secular and ecclesiastical politics in France. The struggle to resuscitate that nation, the church's "eldest daughter," provided the context for practically everything that this herald of the liturgical movement represented.

It was Guéranger himself who first used the expression "liturgical movement" to describe the revival of liturgical studies and the growing interest in understanding and improving liturgical practice. "Let us hope," he wrote in 1851, "that the liturgical movement which is expanding and spreading will awaken also among the faithful the meaning of the Divine Office, that their attendance at it in church will become more intelligent, and that the time will come when, once more imbued with the spirit of the liturgy, they will feel the need to participate in the sacred chants."[1] Guéranger lived to see this hope at least partially realized.

From Diocesan Priest to Benedictine Abbot

As a young priest, Guéranger lamented the disunity within and among French dioceses because of the multiplicity of liturgical usages. Because the decrees of the Council of Trent never had been promulgated in France, French bishops claimed the right to make many liturgical decisions for their dioceses. The widely differing texts and practices are contained in the so-called "neo-Gallican" missals and breviaries of the seventeenth and nineteenth centuries (to distinguish them from the particular diocesan usages of medieval France). While serving as a chaplain to religious from Rome, Guéranger came to know and appreciate what he considered to be the surpassing treasures of the Roman missal and breviary and even obtained permission to use the latter in place of his own diocesan breviary of Le Mans.

Thus, it is not surprising that Guéranger's growing love for the Roman liturgy and for its ultimate overseer, the papacy, would lead him to meet and collaborate with like-minded thinkers such as the priest Félicité de Lamennais, an articulate spokesperson for the independence of the French church and for its dependence on papal leadership. Guéranger believed that complete allegiance to the pope in liturgical matters would rid the liturgy of the arbitrariness and errors that he found so detrimental to the life of the church in France.

Guéranger set out to make his love for the Roman liturgy visible, audible and tangible in a particular setting: the restored St. Peter's Abbey at Solesmes. In 1833, he and several associates began to live a communal life there based on the Rule of St. Benedict. Guéranger explained that he chose the Benedictine way of life precisely because of the importance it placed on the celebration of the Divine Office in choir and because of the possibility of undertaking serious study of the liturgy with an eye to its renewal. Guéranger's monastery at Solesmes served as a kind of showcase for the proper celebration of the Mass and Divine Office and as a workshop for the pursuit of liturgical scholarship. Anyone could come and see what revived communal life and prayer looked like in a country where they had all but disappeared. It was Guéranger's hope that where the individualism and rationalism of the Enlightenment had led to an unraveling of Christian faith and practice, the monastic life and the liturgical life would help bind things up again.

Primacy of Liturgical Prayer

While concerning himself with the worship and work of monks, Guéranger did not ignore the faith of laypersons. He believed that they should be shaped and strengthened by the sacraments. This meant seeking a sacramental theology and liturgical spirituality that the Enlightenment had rejected. According to Guéranger, the spiritual heart of the Christian life was the liturgical prayer of the church, the Mass and the Divine Office. These were to be preferred to the age's very popular but individualistic extraliturgical devotions (for example, devotions centered on the Blessed Sacrament or the Blessed Virgin Mary). Guéranger promoted the liturgical prayer of the church as a source and model of all prayer.

Guéranger's goal of forming monks and other Christians through the liturgy led him toward recovering patristic texts and collecting and editing Gregorian chant. This goal lay behind two of Guéranger's more significant writings.

Institutions liturgiques (1840, 1841 and 1851) is a three-volume history of liturgical tradition from ancient Israel to Guéranger's time. In it he describes in detail the development of Western liturgical practice and he critiques missals, breviaries and other liturgical books. Because Guéranger believed that the church's public prayer was meant to be the outward sign of the church's unity, he argued that the Roman rite was of necessity *the* legitimate rite because of its antiquity, universality, authority and eloquence. Guéranger's views sparked a controversy within the French church that ended with the return of all its dioceses to the Roman rite by 1875. Yet for him, unity did not mean uniformity in every detail and he lamented the loss in the Roman books of the few treasured remnants of ancient Gallican liturgies that had been retained in the French books.

To recover the practice (and even the concept) of daily prayer shaped by the liturgy, the first volume of *L'Année liturgique (The Liturgical Year)* was published in 1841. This series later was translated into English and other languages. The work, original in form and structure, is a 5,000-page meditative commentary on the texts and prayers of the Mass and the Divine Office for each day of the year. Historical sketches, sermons of the Fathers, poetry and hymns from Eastern and Western liturgical sources, along with explanations of ceremonies, draw the reader into the mysteries of Christ during the various liturgical seasons and feasts.

Guéranger's purpose in these volumes was to deepen comprehension of liturgical texts, especially the scriptures, which he saw as the chief requirement for renewed participation. "This liturgical prayer," he wrote in the preface, "would soon become powerless were the faithful not to take a real share in it. . . . It can heal and save the world, but only on the condition that it be understood. Be wise, then, ye children of the Catholic church, and obtain that largeness of heart which will make you pray the prayer of your mother."[2] Cuthbert Johnson declares that "these words could be taken, without exaggeration, as the signal which marks the beginning of the modern liturgical movement."[3] Guéranger advocated a return to the liturgy as the true source of spiritual life. He believed that people needed the liturgy and the liturgy needed the *whole* people of God to celebrate it.

Today we easily accept Robert Taft's maxim that "all liturgy celebrates the paschal mystery." Guéranger was the first author in modern times to use the term "paschal mystery" (in his commentary on the Easter season), thus illustrating his grasp of this reality's importance in the life of every Christian. His was the contemporary-sounding insight that in the liturgy, Christ's saving mysteries are actualized for the life of the people of God. "His teaching upon the church as the Mystical Body, the centrality of the paschal mystery, the doctrinal character of the liturgy, and his insistence upon the need to study the texts of the liturgy, all these ideas were absolutely original in the nineteenth century."[4]

The Legacy of Guéranger

The influence of Guéranger's liturgical theology, scholarship and practice extended far beyond the walls of Solesmes to German abbeys like Beuron and to French parish churches. Guéranger's legacy of monasteries and parishes transformed into vibrant centers of liturgical energy has been well chronicled by R. W. Franklin in *Worship* magazine.[5] Clearly, the chief means to renewal of community life, then as now, was liturgical formation and active participation on the part of all. For example, celebration of the Divine Office by the entire parish, albeit in a rather monastic manner, was a goal of pastors who were influenced by Guéranger.

Abbot Guéranger once remarked: "Imitate the patience of God and do not demand autumn fruits in springtime."[6] This was a principle by which he himself lived and guided others. His budding efforts to make the liturgy the "people's work" once again bore mature and wholesome fruit in the decades leading to the *Constitution on the Sacred Liturgy* of Vatican II.

■ *Michael Kwatera*

NOTES

1. Prosper Guéranger, *Institutions liturgiques,* Vol. 3 (Paris: Julien, Lanier et Ce, Éditeurs, 1851), 170–71. My translation.

2. "General Preface," *The Liturgical Year,* Vol. 1: Advent, trans. Laurence Shepherd (Westminster MD: The Newman Press, 1949), 5–6.

3. Cuthbert Johnson, *Analecta Liturgica 9: Prosper Guéranger (1805–1875): A Liturgical Theologian: An Introduction to His Liturgical Writings and Work,* Studia Anselmiana 89 (Rome: Pontificio Ateneo S. Anselmo, 1984), 350.

4. Ibid., 370.

5. R. W. Franklin's articles in order of publication in *Worship* magazine: "Guéranger: A View on the Centenary of His Death," 49 (1975), 318–28; "Guéranger and Pastoral Liturgy: A Nineteenth Century View," 50 (1976), 146–62; "Guéranger and Variety in Unity," 51 (1977) 378–99; "The Nineteenth Century Liturgical Movement," 53 (1979), 12–39.

6. Letter of Guéranger to Dom Maurus Wolter, May 5, 1863, quoted in Johnson, *Analecta Liturgica 9,* 421.

LAMBERT BEAUDUIN

The Vision Awaits Its Time

WHEN ONE HEARS the word "movement" used to describe a phenomenon of human history, one is tempted to envision a throng of humanity rather than the faces of the individual human beings in the throng. Any discussion of what is called the "liturgical movement," however, must center on the individuals whose energies and visions have fueled and directed this movement of the Spirit in all the communions of the church. Among these men and women we find Lambert Beauduin, OSB, whose epitaph at Chevetogne reads: "Monk, Presbyter, Man of the Church."

Christened Octave, Beauduin was born near Liége in Belgium on August 5, 1873. His family was well-to-do, liberal in political issues and deeply religious. Octave's father gathered the family and domestic servants for daily evening devotions and the children frequently engaged in "playing church."[1] From his father, Beauduin inherited a strong sense of political duty (although his father disliked clerical involvement in political affairs).

Following his ordination in 1897, Beauduin was assigned to teach in the minor seminary that he had attended as a boy. But his attraction to service in the world was strong, so in 1899 he volunteered for service as a Labor Chaplain.[2] Beauduin's first interests in this ministry appear to have been the result of a concern for social activism, but by 1902 he became more evangelical in his view of the priestly ministry among the workers: "One is a priest to give the truth and divine grace to people through the liturgical rites, preaching, the celebration of feasts and retreats."[3]

The movement into which Beauduin had entered encountered increasing political and ecclesiastical opposition. Beauduin left the Labor Chaplains and, after a period of spiritual reflection, entered the Benedictine monastery of Mont César. It is indicative of his lifelong commitment to action in the church at large that he took the name Lambert at his profession in 1907: Lambert is the patron saint of Liége, Beauduin's home diocese and the diocese of his ordination.

In his first years at Mont César, Beauduin came under the tutelage of an Irish monk, Columba Marmion (1858–1923), who at that time was prior of the monastery. Beauduin thus came to appreciate the liturgy of the church. Although reluctant to discuss the stages of his own spiritual development, Beauduin would admit to Marmion's influence as well as his reading of Guéranger on liturgical prayer and the lectures of B. Destrée (then master of novices) on the chanting of the office. In *Liturgy, the Life of the Church* (written in 1914), Beauduin reveals something of his reaction to private devotions:

> The charge that liturgical piety is the enemy of private devotion . . . rests on a misunderstanding. It is true that the former is, in this domain, traditional, discreet, even extremely reserved. The sickly desire that is ever in quest of pious novelties justly affrightens the liturgical mentality; the latter is the enemy of all devotionalism and glories in that. But far from destroying traditional and authentic private devotions, it gives them an increase of vigor and strength. A stranger to all fashions and to all fads, imbued with sane doctrine, pure and unalloyed, broad and generous, the liturgy, having become the principle food of the Christian soul, will transform the private devotion, give it a new impetus, a new intensity, while at the same time keeping it in its proper place.[4]

Beauduin's nascent commitment to the liturgy came to flower during 1908–1910. Sometime prior to 1909, Beauduin was said to have burst into the class he was to teach and to have exploded, "I've just realized that the liturgy is the center of the piety of the church!"[5] In 1909, Beauduin presented a paper on the liturgy at Malines and in November, the journal *Questions liturgiques* (later *Questions liturgiques et paroissales*) began publication with Beauduin as editor. In June of 1910, the first Liturgical Week was held at Mont César. The goal of the early liturgical movement was "to restore Christian spirituality [and] the means proposed was the restoration of the parochial High Mass on Sunday, with full participation."[6]

From 1909 until 1921, Beauduin was the heart and soul of the Belgian liturgical movement. Such activity was not welcomed in all quarters and Beauduin's critics were many. In response to his critics, Beauduin wrote his only monograph, *La piété de l'église* (*Liturgy, the Life of the Church*, English edition, 1926), published on the eve of World War I. In a memorable chapter entitled "The Sad Consequences of the Present Condition," Beauduin enumerates the results of the failure to maintain the liturgy as the center of true Christian piety: individualism, abandonment of prayer, deviations of piety, the secular spirit and the lack of hierarchical life. Later in the book, Beauduin gives his goals for the liturgical movement:

1. Active participation of all Christian people in the Mass by understanding and following the rites and texts.

2. Emphasis on the importance of the High Mass, Sunday services and liturgical singing by the faithful.

3. Preservation and the reestablishment of Sunday Vespers and Compline as parish celebrations.

4. Acquaintance and active association with the rites of the sacraments received and assisted at, and the spread of this knowledge to others.

5. Fostering a respect for and confidence in the church.

6. Restoration of the Liturgy of the Dead to a place of honor and combating the dechristianization of the cult of the dead.[7]

Behind these goals for liturgical renewal lay Beauduin's own reflection on his experience of and attitudes toward the liturgy prior to his "awakening":

> You'll excuse my frankness, but the missal was for me a closed and sealed book. And this ignorance extended not only to the variable parts [of the Mass], but even to the unchanging parts and principally to the canon. . . . Even the great and perfect acts of worship, the principal end of the Mass, of participation in the sacrifice in communion with the body of the Lord, the spiritual offering of our good acts . . . in short, none of the great realities that the eucharistic liturgy constantly puts into act, not one dominated my eucharistic piety. . . . Visits to the Blessed Sacrament had a more vital role in my piety than the act of sacrifice itself.[8]

In 1921, Beauduin was appointed to serve as professor of fundamental theology at Sant' Anselmo. These years saw the awakening of Beauduin's awareness of the Christian East. He developed plans for a biritual monastery of Benedictine monks (to be located at Amay) who, by their knowledge and love of both Latin and Eastern rites, theology and piety, would serve as a witness to the East and foster eventual unity. By 1926, he had received permission to begin a monastery with five novices. Within a month of opening its doors, Amay received canonical status from the Congregation for the Oriental Church. *Irénikon,* a journal devoted to the study of the Eastern church, began publication the same year. Beauduin's vision of the unity of the church extended westward as well; contacts with Anglicans during World War I had quickened his interest in and participation (by correspondence) in the Malines Conversations.[9] Opposition to his openness to Anglicanism and to his work at Amay (both from Benedictine superiors and curial officials) resulted in Beauduin's eventual ecclesiastical exile from Belgium.

I t was during the period of Beauduin's professorship at Sant'
Anselmo that his influence was transported to the North
American continent. A young American monk, Virgil Michel,
came to Rome to study. He quickly absorbed the teaching of
Beauduin and was inspired to begin the liturgical apostolate on
his return to the United States.[10]

From 1931 to 1951, Beauduin was forbidden to return to
Amay or Mont César or to enter Belgium. During this period,
he served as a chaplain to two convents in France. He traveled
widely and wrote frequently. In 1943, he was among the
founders of the Centre de Pastorale Liturgique in Paris. In
1944, Beauduin renewed an old friendship with the papal nun-
cio to France, Angelo Roncalli (later John XXIII).

Beauduin's exile ended in 1951 and he returned to the monastery he had founded (now located at Chevetogne). There he
lived in an active retirement, despite the crippling effects of
rheumatoid arthritis, until his death on January 11, 1960.

At his death, Beauduin knew that his vision slowly was coming to fruition. Chevetogne was thriving; Roncalli had been
elected pope and called a council; the liturgical movement was
alive and well on all fronts. Although Beauduin did not live to
see it, the Anglican archbishop of Canterbury would visit both
the pope and the ecumenical patriarch in 1960. Beauduin was,
as his American biographer said, "a prophet vindicated."

In that biography, Sonya Quitslund states: "Beauduin had an
insatiable thirst for unity. At first envisaged in rather narrow
lines and somewhat hesitantly, unity soon became the predominant passion of his entire life."[11] His commitment to liturgical
renewal was part of this passion. In the liturgy, the faithful
were united with one another, the congregation with the church
and the church with Christ. Furthermore, Beauduin was aware
that the purpose of the incarnation, death, resurrection and
ascension of Christ and the descent of the Spirit was, and is, to

lead humanity to the Father. Thus, unity with Christ in the liturgy serves to draw humanity closer to the one whom Christ called "Abba." In this bosom, humanity would find its unity.

Beauduin's contribution to the life of the church is substantial. Several of the journals he founded still are important means of research and communication. The monastery of Chevetogne continues to witness to Beauduin's vision of ecclesial unity. The fullness of that vision still awaits its time.

■ *Richard G. Leggett*

NOTES

1. Sonya Quitslund, *Beauduin: A Prophet Vindicated* (New York: Newman Press, 1973), 3. Much of the biographical information in this paper is taken from this important work.

2. Ibid., 5: "[The Congrégation des Aumoniers du Travail] conceived late in 1894 and officially begun on March 25, 1895, offered an apostolate based on direct contact between priest and worker."

3. Ibid., 7.

4. Lambert Beauduin, *Liturgy, the Life of the Church,* trans. Virgil Michel (Collegeville: The Liturgical Press, 1926), 16–17.

5. Quitslund, *Beauduin,* 16.

6. Ibid., 19.

7. Beauduin, *Liturgy, the Life,* 44–46.

8. Quitslund, *Beauduin,* 10–11.

9. The Malines Conversations were a series of meetings between Anglican and Roman Catholic theologians between 1921 and 1925 under the presidency of Cardinal D. J. Mercier, archbishop of Malines.

10. Jeremy Hall, *The Full Stature of Christ: The Ecclesiology of Virgil Michel, OSB* (Collegeville: The Liturgical Press, 1976), 12.

11. Quitslund, *Beauduin,* 241.

PIUS PARSCH

Evangelist
of the Liturgy

HE POST—WORLD WAR I INTEREST in liturgy found a twofold expression: the ever-increasing research into liturgical history and the growing desire of lay-persons to become better instructed in liturgical matters. Theodor Klauser notes, "It so happened that for both of these purposes, the right people were found at the right centers and at the right time."[1] In German-speaking lands, the "right people" were Romano Guardini (1884–1968) at Rothenfels and Pius Parsch (1884–1954) at Klosterneuberg.

Born at Olmütz, Moravia, Parsch became a canon of St. Augustine at the Austrian monastery of Klosterneuberg in 1904. There he took the name Pius in honor of Pope Pius X, with whom he came to share a great love of the Bible and a desire for the people's active participation in the liturgy. He was a student at Klosterneuberg until his ordination in 1909 and thereafter taught pastoral theology.

The Popular Apostolate

During World War I, Parsch served as chaplain with the Austrian army. While celebrating Mass with the soldiers, he sadly realized how little of it they understood and he was much disturbed by their passivity. In his wartime experiences, he discovered the two ideas that were to dominate his later years, the Bible as the people's book and the liturgy as the people's work: "I realized that we must bring our people to the very fountainhead of God's word."[2] Parsch believed that the biblical and liturgical movements were different but complementary facets of the same apostolate.

With the encouragement and resources provided by his superiors, Parsch started a publishing center he called the *Volksliturgisches Apostolat.* This name, "Popular Liturgical Apostolate," clearly announced his main purpose: "It was not for research, neither for monastic or academic liturgical forms, much less for liturgical reform. His energy was spent in an apostolate for the Christian people, to bring them to both interior and exterior participation in the liturgy."[3]

First, people had to be provided with suitable liturgical texts. Toward this goal, Parsch produced a host of booklets containing the words and music and sometimes commentaries for the services. He published numerous explanations of the liturgy. All of this made his monastery a liturgical center of Austria and all German-speaking lands. A monthly review, *Bible and Liturgy* (intended chiefly for priests), and a weekly paper, *Live with the Church* (intended chiefly for the nonordained), enjoyed great popularity.

While liturgical reforms may not have been Parsch's primary goal, he was not afraid to suggest a variety of them. He expressed a preference for restructuring the liturgical year so that it would begin with the then pre-Lent Sundays of Septuagesima (three Sundays before Ash Wednesday); in this way, there would be "a year of supernatural life beginning with Easter and its preparatory season and concluding with the final union and marriage to Christ at Epiphany." But his pastoral sensitivity made him "shy away from this radical departure for fear that such a great break of custom would only confuse."[4]

In remarks on "Communion and the People" in *The Liturgy of the Mass,* Parsch offered several practical suggestions: "a greater stress on the meal aspect of holy communion" (which Parsch suggested might result from the use of leavened bread); reintroduction of communion under both kinds; communion from hosts consecrated at each Mass (not those taken from the tabernacle); omission of the people's Confiteor before communion (a duplication, according to Parsch); revival of the communion chant (a refrain sung between psalm verses, "perhaps even in the vernacular").[5] Indeed, Parsch's very early campaign for increased use of the vernacular achieved some success in the partly vernacular Ritual granted to Austria in 1935 and in the still more radical version granted to Germany in 1950.

In Parsch's day, the Easter Vigil was celebrated on Holy Saturday morning, even though its texts referred to night and darkness. As early as 1934, he discussed the reform of this liturgy and its restoration as a night service. "At that date the notion was widely opposed as a shocking novelty, but increasing numbers of priests came to see its intrinsic reasonableness. It became a 'live issue' in the periodicals of Austria and Germany, and then spread to France, Belgium and Holland."[6] In 1951, this major goal of the liturgical movement was approved on an experimental basis by Pope Pius XII; it was made the centerpiece of the revised Holy Week liturgy in 1955.

The Church's Year of Grace

Parsch considered the vital celebration of the liturgical feasts and seasons to be necessary nourishment for the Christian people. "One may ask," he noted, "if it is worth the trouble to consider the church year as a school of formation and to discover the cultural value thereof. To this one might reply that the liturgical movement has the duty and the task to do so, because this apostolate has once again discerned and unfolded the beauty of the church year."[7] What began in 1922 as Parsch's slim booklet of 30 pages of commentary on the Sunday Masses assumed permanent form in a book of about a thousand pages: *Das Jahr des Heiles* (1929). It was translated into many languages and was published in English between 1953 and 1959 by the Benedictines of St. John's Abbey in five volumes as *The Church's Year of Grace*. This explanation of texts and ceremonies of the liturgical year may have "won more adherents to the liturgical movement than any other book ever written,"[8] including Michael Mathis, founder of the liturgical studies program at the University of Notre Dame.

Parsch believed that celebrating the seasons of the liturgical year was a practice for everyone, not only for those whom Carl Dehne calls "people living under a rule, or with privileged information and highly developed liturgical tastes."[9] He explained that "the church year is a very definite segment in the life of the mystical Christ. Our Savior lived an earthly life of some 33 years, but the mystical Christ will live, I know not how many millenia. He will live as the life of my soul, I know not how many decades."[10] Every liturgical year is "a term in the school of God."[11] Thus, we are learners in the liturgy's school as long as we live.

Parish Eucharist

Like other great pioneers of the liturgical movement, Parsch insisted on the essential and intimate connection between liturgy and scripture. He believed that people could be brought to an understanding of the liturgy only by a knowledge of scripture and he identified the *parish* as the center of liturgical renewal. For him, the doctrine of the Mystical Body was the basis of the two great movements in the church of his day, "the liturgical movement and the apostolate of Catholic action. The parish cannot remain aloof from either of these movements. In fact, these must find the milieu and the locality in which to exert their redeeming influences in the parish."[12] Thus, "the celebration of the Holy Sacrifice, without question, should hold the central place in the life of a parish. . . . Indeed, the Sunday Mass is the very heartbeat of a parish."[13]

For those who seek to shape their parish into a "community," Parsch provides the key: "To rebuild the parish truly into a unified family of God, with but one heart and soul, this eucharistic celebration must be the starting point."[14] The zeal and earnestness with which the parishioners participate in this celebration Sunday after Sunday "will be the gauge of their religious fervor and family spirit. The entire parish is one body in Christ."[15] No matter how vibrant the parish's other activities may be, the heart of them all is the eucharist: *"The center, the source, the focus of this growing parish communion will always be the altar, the eucharistic sacrifice-banquet."*[16]

Parsch underscored this belief in a highly audible way by developing the *Betsingmesse,* a logical combination of two forms already in use—the dialogue Mass and hymn-singing during Mass. The complete structure of the Mass was preserved and highlighted, but congregational participation in the Latin responses and vernacular hymnody was maximized. Parsch commented that his proposed reforms were "impelled not by profitless disaffection, but by an ardent love of holy church. I long to see this jewel in her crown, the eucharist, shine forth in as perfect a setting as is possible."[17] Many liturgists believed that the *Betsingmesse* was the most satisfactory form of the people's active participation possible at that time.

Parish Communal Prayer

Yet Parsch did not minimize the importance of the other major form of the church's worship, the Divine Office. He prepared an introduction to the daily prayer of the church for clergy and laypersons in which he declared that "all Christians have the duty, or rather the right, to pray together as a community. In this matter the priest has not the slightest advantage over the layperson. Our confident expectation is that the time will soon come when not a few Christians, entire families and parishes, will join in and maintain the church's prayer."[18] Parsch encouraged parishioners to assemble morning and evening and to "pray the Office in the name of the whole community. And naturally, as head of the community, the pastor will, and should participate in this prayer in the vernacular tongue."[19] Parsch's hope for daily morning and evening prayer has yet to be realized in most parishes. The United States bishops recently have stated that "this is an area which calls for much more attention on the part of pastors and prayer leaders in our Catholic communities."[20] "You may think these ideas utopian," Parsch observed, "but I can assure you that all this is quite possible," and he offered the example of his parish of St. Gertrude in Klosterneuberg. The custom of daily Lauds before the morning community Mass "has become so entrenched in the parish that it is an essential part of our worship."[21]

Biblical/Liturgical Spirituality

Parsch's liturgical work stemmed from his promotion of the scriptures but eventually overshadowed it. Yet, for him, liturgy remained the necessary and best commentary on scripture and scripture the very heart of the liturgy.

Speaking to the members of the North American Academy of Liturgy in 1984, Lutheran liturgist Gordon Lathrop suggested that Pius Parsch "might be for us a paradigm for this close relationship between liturgical renewal and the biblical movement."[22] Parsch realized that "the scripture lived and sparkled in the liturgy" and he "began his great liturgical work so that the Bible might speak more clearly in the parishes."[23] This life-giving union of scripture and liturgy is Parsch's challenging legacy to all who love the word of God proclaimed and enfleshed in the eucharist.

■ *Michael Kwatera*

NOTES

1. Theodor Klauser, *A Short History of the Western Liturgy,* 2d ed., trans. John Halliburton (Oxford: Oxford University Press, 1979), 122.

2. Pius Parsch, *The Breviary Explained,* trans. William Nayden and Carl Heogerl (St. Louis and London: B. Herder, 1952), Foreword.

3. T. Schnitzler, "Parsch, Pius," *New Catholic Encyclopedia* (New York: McGraw-Hill, 1967).

4. Pius Parsch, *The Church's Year of Grace,* trans. William Heidt (Collegeville: The Liturgical Press, 1957), 1:11.

5. Pius Parsch, *The Liturgy of the Mass,* 3d ed., trans. and adapted by H. E. Winstone, with an introduction by Clifford Howell (London and St. Louis: B. Herder, 1957), 311.

6. Ibid., Clifford Howell, Introduction.

7. Pius Parsch, *Sermons on the Liturgy for Sundays and Feasts,* trans. Philip T. Weller (Milwaukee: Bruce Publishing Co., 1953), Introduction, viii-ix.

8. Parsch, *The Liturgy of the Mass,* Howell, Introduction, ix.

9. Carl Dehne, "Roman Catholic Popular Devotions," *Christians at Prayer,* ed. John Gallen (Notre Dame: University of Notre Dame Press, 1977), 91.

10. Parsch, *The Church's Year of Grace,* 5:135.

11. Ibid., 5:136.

12. Pius Parsch, *Is This My Parish?,* trans. Wilfrid Tunink (Conception MO: Conception Abbey Press, 1950), 20.

13. Ibid., 23.

14. Ibid., 37.

15. Ibid., 38.

16. Ibid., 40. Emphasis is Parsch's.

17. Parsch, *The Liturgy of the Mass,* Foreword, xii.

18. Parsch, *The Breviary Explained,* 6.

19. Ibid., 448.

20. National Conference of Catholic Bishops, *The Church at Prayer: A Holy Temple of the Lord,* No. 35 (Washington DC: United States Catholic Conference, 1984), 18.

21. Parsch, *The Breviary Explained,* 449.

22. Gordon W. Lathrop, "A Rebirth of Images: On the Use of the Bible in Liturgy," *Worship* 58 (1984), 291.

23. Ibid.

ROMANO GUARDINI
The Teacher of Teachers

THROUGHOUT HIS LIFE, Romano Guardini was a man of frail health. In addition, he had to endure—as had his mother—severe depressions that led him at one time to the brink of suicide. Nevertheless, he valued this lifelong predicament because it gave him depth and ballast.[1]

Compared with other pioneers of the liturgical movement who pursued a predictable academic career and spiritual path, Guardini's life was an odyssey in every respect. When it ended after 83 years and word of his death reached Rome, 30 bishops with their advisers—attending a session in Rome of the commission to implement Vatican II's *Constitution on the Sacred Liturgy*—rose to sing the *De Profundis*.[2]

Guardini (1885–1968) was one of the leading figures of European thought (*Geistesleben*—the life of mind and soul together) in the twentieth century. He put his mark on at least three generations of Christians in the era leading up to Vatican II. For the centennial of his birth in 1985, the West German government acknowledged his immense importance to our century by issuing a commemorative postal stamp. Each year, the public is reminded of this great philosopher of religion when, with much media fanfare, the Romano Guardini Prize is awarded by the Catholic Academy of Bavaria.

Guardini was born in Verona, Italy, the oldest of four brothers. When he was one year old, his parents immigrated to Mainz, Germany, where his father continued to run a family business. His mother objected strongly and persistently to the move and kept the boys and herself away from all outside influences. In his moving and sometimes shocking auto-biographical notes, intended for publication only after his death, Guardini says that he never experienced a feeling of happiness during his childhood.[3]

Insecurity in choosing a career led Guardini first to study chemistry in Tübingen for two semesters, then economics in Munich and Berlin for three semesters. Both left him untouched. In Berlin, now 21 years old, he felt an attraction to the priest-hood, but his father was unsupportive and his mother undermined all efforts in this direction. Nevertheless, he began studies in theology in Freiburg. There he faced a dilemma: To the same degree to which he converted his parents to accept his vocation, he himself developed an aversion to the priesthood. Later, he identified this as a subconscious revolt against the necessary sacrifices expected of a priestly life.

Finding the Liturgy

He changed universities again and went to Tübingen where he experienced the happiest and most fruitful time of his early life. "My innermost being became alive."[4]

Part of this was because of his professor of dogmatics who was accustomed to accept a few students for confession. After arrival at an appointed time, the professor would walk with the student up and down in his large study, letting the student say whatever came to mind: things scientific, practical, religious, moral. Eventually, the teacher would put on his stole, ask for a synopsis of what had gone before, then give absolution. Guardini writes that this man freed him of his scruples.

He experienced what a wonderful, life-giving power the sacrament of penance is when administered in the right spirit.

A second factor during his Tübingen studies was his contact with the Benedictine abbey of Beuron, where he experienced the creative strength that grew out of the strict monastic discipline. He became acquainted with the Beuron art, which was at its height, and, above all, he took part in the liturgy. "It was as if a mystery permeated the entire church, holy and sheltering at the same time." From this moment on, he understood the nature of liturgy. "I took liturgy deep into my thoughts, and my thoughts were circling constantly around one thing: the church, this mysterious reality which is rooted so deeply in the present while, at the same time, being the guarantor of things eternal."[5] At this point, still a university student, he wrote two books, *The Spirit of the Liturgy* and *Liturgical Education*. These had a deep effect on the liturgical movement in the United States. The depth of young Guardini's insight is evident in the closing words of *The Spirit of the Liturgy:*

> In the liturgy the Logos has been assigned its fitting precedence over the will. Hence the wonderful power of relaxation proper to the liturgy, and its deep reposefulness. Hence its apparent consummation entirely in the contemplation, adoration and glorification of divine Truth. This is also the explanation of the fact that the liturgy is apparently so little disturbed by the petty troubles and needs of everyday life. It also accounts for its infrequent attempts at direct teaching and direct inculcation of virtue. The liturgy has something in itself reminiscent of the stars, of their eternally fixed and even course, of their inflexible order, of their profound silence, and of the infinite space in which they are poised. It is only in appearance, however, that the liturgy is so detached and untroubled by our actions and strivings and moral position. For in reality it knows that those who live by it will be true and spiritually sound, and at peace to the depths of their being; and that when they leave its sacred confines to enter life they will be full of courage.[6]

Responsible Teaching

It was the time of Modernism and the promulgation of the encyclical *Pascendi Domini Gregis* and the lists of errors. The great number of condemnations created deep distress among those professors who were affected and also among their students. Guardini's professor of dogmatics, however, "picked up what burdened their mind, lifted up what others had smothered by the weight of their authority or what was intimated by the pathos of unconditional faith, and spoke frankly and openly. That set us free." But they feared for their teacher's career and future. In the context of these times, Guardini would later speak of "the frequent sin of orthodoxy." He recognized then the duty and the obligation to voice critical objection openly when the church was in danger of suffering damage.

After studying only at universities, Guardini finally entered the seminary at his hometown of Mainz. Here, that "obligation to criticize" almost cost him admission to ordination. Writing about it after 35 years, he still could not overcome his anger: "The lectures only covered the conventional. There was no attempt to educate an independent judgment or a viable ability to act responsibly. Authority and obedience were not only the basis for everything, they *were* everything. The consequences were predictable: The education rested on a system of mistrust and supervision of every minute detail."[7] As punishment for his critical observations, his ordination was postponed by half a year to May 1910.

More Detours

He now was anxious to start teaching school, but his Italian citizenship kept him from doing so. In Germany, teaching religion, like any other subject, required becoming an employee of the state. "For my father the idea of giving up my

Italian citizenship was incomprehensible. He refused the papers that allowed the necessary steps to be taken. But eventually he had to see that it didn't work any other way." Guardini became a German citizen more than a year after his ordination.

He also began his pastoral work. From the very onset, he considered the Mass as the focal point and attentively celebrated it with great care. People complained that it took too long. But he argued that if the Mass meant nothing to the priest himself, it could mean nothing to the people. And that would certainly happen if he were forced to hurry—for whatever reason. He felt helpless when he was obliged to say Mass for two years before the exposed Blessed Sacrament while the parishioners were reciting the rosary.

In these situations, Guardini devoted most of his energy to preparing his homilies. He realized that for each homily he needed a "fuse," a burning question that interested him personally. He followed the liturgical year, but chose his subjects based only on his own questions embedded in themes of the feasts and seasons. During this time, he discovered the creative element for his preaching: not only that the words and sentences and structure had to be beautiful, but that the homilist had to use the same language from the pulpit that he used in the words and deeds of his personal life. This required a training in self-discipline, so that when *speaking* one always would *say* something and that this "something" would be said with accuracy. The sermon then would naturally be good.[8]

This very ability "to say something" he later would develop to such perfection that people came by the thousands to hear him wherever he was speaking. Coupled with his gift came a constant fear about whether he would be able to give his parishioners or listeners what they really needed: "The bread of truth given into their being, as it really was."

During his years as associate pastor, he became aware that preaching and public speaking were his special calling. Therefore, he went to Freiburg for postgraduate studies and was promoted to doctor of theology with a dissertation on *The*

Teaching of St. Bonaventure on Salvation: A Contribution to the History and System of Teaching Salvation.[9] His concept of "salvation" was not to save Christians from the world, but rather to place the world back into the hands of a good God.

His intense desire to be an effective agent in this struggle toward salvation found an outlet when, in 1915, Guardini became director of the Juventus organization, a large community of Catholic high school students in Mainz. For five years, he led the young people with astonishing creativity, embracing all the sciences and arts, coupling a joyful enthusiasm with academic brilliance and clarity. Most contagious, though, was his love for the church and her liturgy. Challenging the young people to struggle for the truth, he warned them not to use faith and trust as an easy substitute. As their leader he always walked beside them, helping them to ask the right questions. They granted him authority; he never had to claim it.

Setting a Course of Action

These early years were a foundation; they set up the constellation under which he would attain greatness during the second part of his life. In a later book, *Power and Responsibility,* he would write about the course he set for himself:

> Do everything that is to be done with respect for the truth, and do it in freedom of spirit, in spite of obstacles within and without, and in the teeth of selfishness, laziness, cowardice, popular opinion. And do it with confidence!
>
> By this I do not mean to follow a program of any kind, but to make the simple responses that always were and always will be right: Not to wait until someone in need asks for help, but to offer it; to perform every official act in a manner befitting both common sense and human dignity; to declare a truth when its "hour" has come, even when it will bring down opposition or ridicule; to accept responsibility when the conscience considers it a duty.[10]

While Guardini was working with the Juventus organization, he visited for the first time the Benedictine abbey of
Maria Laach. The then abbot, Ildefons Herwegen, asked to
publish his *Spirit of the Liturgy* as the first volume of the
planned series *Ecclesia Orans* that was to popularize the liturgy. At Maria Laach, Guardini also received encouragement
to prepare himself to seek a chair in Catholic dogmatics at
the University of Bonn. After preparing from 1920 to 1922,
he became a member of the Catholic theological faculty
there.[11]

During this time, he also was coeditor with Odo Casel of
the *Handbuch für Liturgiewissenschaft* (a compilation of the
scientific study of liturgy). From that time stems a quote:
"The surest way to completely miss the voice of Christ is to
study liturgy as a science."

The Catholic Youth Movement

Guardini made his first contact with the Catholic Youth
Movement in Germany in 1922 during a congress of
the Quickborn at Burg Rothenfels. The Quickborn (the
word was *Jungbrunnen,* which literally means "fountain of
youth") Association of Catholic Youth was founded in 1910.
Its aim was to infuse the whole of life, literature and art
with the Catholic spirit. In 1927, Guardini became its director and all his wonderful powers erupted into creativity.

Burg Rothenfels, a castle above the Main River, was the
center of the growing youth movement. Under Guardini's
guidance, it became an academy for character formation
and a cultural center that attracted many young Catholic
intellectuals. There they met, lived in community, learned
and debated and were inspired to develop in their own work
a vision of a cultural renewal of society. That vision included
the sacramental life of the church with the social consequences that this life entails.

Many thousands of young people came and Guardini's "Workweeks" were so successful that the Nazis not only planted spies, but actually moved four 100-member units of the paramilitary FDA[12] into the castle compound during the mid-1930s. Teaching, debating and celebrating liturgies were difficult against the sound of boots and the bellowing of nationalistic songs. These constant activities in the courtyard severely affected the atmosphere, but they pointed to the urgency of the undertaking.

The young people lived lives of abstinence and total dedication to each other; the doctrine of the Mystical Body formed the theological *a priori* for their behavior. They began to see body, mind and soul functioning as a unit. They learned how things worked together as they took part in debates, in music, choreographed dances, choral speech groups and especially in the liturgy. Guardini intensely developed their "cult-ability" *(Kult-Fahigkeit)* by developing their individual and corporate personality. The question of interior readiness for a cultic action occupied him constantly, especially because people developed the how-to of liturgy without ever asking the question "why?" and without consciously nurturing the culture that is a prerequisite of liturgy.

From Rothenfels, Guardini's influence on the liturgical movement was enormous. It clearly changed, on a large scale, from a monastic to a lay movement. Young people, bored with a bourgeois world, came, caught fire and went back to their youth groups in their hometowns to effect the changes that would bring liturgy and life together.

Rudolph Schwarz, 1897–1961, later a renowned church architect, describes in his autobiography these celebrations with their extraordinary climate of active unity that characterized them.[13] Schwarz was the architect whom Guardini chose, "the only genius in my entourage," to convert the sixteenth-century castle into the center for the youth movement. Schwarz designed the chapel and also the "hall of knights" where liturgy was celebrated for large groups. Both were in the same style: The walls were white; daylight, or candlelight in the evening, provided the main decorative element. The altar was not placed against the back wall as was common at that time, but forward toward the people who sat on small black cubes arranged around it on three sides. The presider was seated behind the altar and so closed the circle. With this arrangement, Guardini reintroduced and applied the very old concept of the *circumstantes* of the early church's eucharistic celebration. The *missa recitata* was the most frequent style of celebration; because many of those attending knew Latin, a most lively exchange was possible.

The work at Rothenfels ended in 1939 when the building was confiscated by the Nazis.

Guardini's Preaching and Teaching

Because of an asthmatic condition, Guardini preached with a low voice. Often the assembly had to strain to hear him and by so doing, preacher and people together became partners. His preaching usually was arranged in themes: One at a time, he would treat such subjects as the gestures of kneeling, standing, using holy water. This particular cycle was published as *Von Heiligen Zeichen* and appeared soon in several translations. When the English translation, *Sacred Signs,*[14] became available in the United States, people treated this small volume as if they had discovered a rare treasure. The impact on the liturgical renewal was lasting, for this book showed that while the externals may be performed properly according to the rubrics, interiorization may not have occurred yet. Guardini's writing gave the reader a sense of wholeness, of completeness, of knowledge for how things fit together. One began to understand that there is an inner meaning to all ritual action and that the study of rubrics alone was insufficient to capture the spirit of the liturgy.

All the while Guardini was involved in the youth movement and in his writing, he also pursued a teaching career. In 1923, Guardini had been called to Berlin. He had gained such widespread fame (his *The Spirit of the Liturgy,* for example, saw twelve editions within five years) that there was a saying, "When Guardini speaks, Europe's elite is listening." In response to such acclaim, the Ministry of Culture created for him a chair of "Philosophy of Religion and Philosophy of Life" at the University of Berlin. This was a triumphant beginning; here he remained a respected and famous teacher until the Nazis stripped him of that position in 1939.

During his teaching period, he perfected his own philosophical method and style, which he developed in his book *Der Gegensatz*[15] *(The Contrast):* to present opposites as complementary sides of the same reality and to bring these polarities into balance. He calls this constellation of opposites the root of his entire life's work and the most ancient mystery of all existence. Titles of his books based on such lecture cycles serve as examples: *Power and Responsibility, Freedom, Grace and Destiny* and *World and Person.*

In his years in Berlin, he showed his mastery of interpretation when he presented the literary cycles of Dante, Holderlin, Dostoyevski and Rilke. He filtered their works through his own creative center and presented them from a Christian perspective. Those who had an ear for it thought they heard him speak about the key concern in his life, the liturgy, yet he never used such terms in the literary presentations.

The War Years

Present at Guardini's Masses was the Catholic elite of Berlin. To outsiders this might have seemed a little like an exclusive club with an esoteric leader. Guardini never was able to deal with simple people and they could not relate to him either. Therefore, in an almost scrupulous sense of responsibility as a priest-teacher, he invited leaders of thought in practically all fields to be present and then to carry his message of renewal to their people. He understood his prime responsibility to be a teacher of those who, through their own work in many fields, would teach others.

Participating in this Mass was like a catacomb experience. One had to walk a few steps down into the low-ceilinged room and had to stand shoulder to shoulder in an unspoken sense of solidarity. As Guardini unfolded the mystery of redemption, a deep sense of joy and peace helped the assembly face the Nazi pressure. One of the themes that Guardini developed during these Masses was that of the person of Jesus. These addresses first resulted in *The Living God*[16] and then grew into the classic, *The Lord,*[17] which Guardini named, next to *Holderlin,* as his favorite among his more than 60 books. Thanks to the Chicago publisher, Henry Regnery, who went to see Guardini in Germany to gain publishing rights, the work received a splendid English translation and saw eight printings in eight years; it had a tremendous influence on educated Catholics in the United States.

Although many individual bishops in Europe were Guardini's friends, the hierarchy as a whole never encouraged or as much as acknowledged him. An air of mistrust prevailed for most of his life, probably because he so influenced young people and the intelligentsia. Yet the search for truth he so embodied and encouraged was not an invitation to rebellion but to total honesty and integrity within the framework of church teaching.

If this made the German hierarchy uncomfortable, it infuriated the Nazi officials to the point that they removed him from his chair and confiscated his life's work, Burg Rothenfels. Because of the quick action of the Burg administrators in destroying implicating material, Guardini escaped arrest and the likelihood of being sent to the concentration camp. This was a time when the Third Reich had spelled out its own *Weltanschauung* and to proclaim any other philosophy of life was subversive.

The loss of his large audience in Berlin and Rothenfels and the uncertainty of his own future deeply depressed Guardini. His concern for the many young people who felt academically and spiritually deprived kept him in Berlin for most of the war years. Rather than be evacuated, he resumed giving his lecture cycles at the Jesuit church to large audiences who came despite air-attack warnings and regular blackouts. He also lectured for the Catholic speakers service, but without ritual involvement and in secular garb, so that everybody would feel welcome, believers and nonbelievers alike.

Toward the end of the war, as the bomb attacks on Berlin became more frequent, Guardini's energy waned and he finally took refuge in a friend's parish house in the south of Germany. Cut off from all contact and direct inspiration from friends and students, he spent two humble years at his desk and produced his often sad and shocking auto-biographical notes. When the war was over, he was called again to teach, first in Tübingen and eventually, for 20 more years, in Munich.

Guardini's Legacy

He had played the role of the prethinker and generator in the liturgical movement and throughout his life he suffered the isolation that came with this prophet's vocation. The implementation of the work proclaimed by Vatican II was beginning when Guardini died. There was hope that seeds he had planted now would germinate worldwide. Karl Rahner said about him: "It is a widely known fact that the

Rothenfels experience was the immediate model for the liturgical reforms of Vatican II. Seldom was the origin of a spiritual movement of worldwide dimensions, a movement of immeasurable depth of soul and spirit, as historically traceable to almost one single person as in the case of Guardini."[18]

■ *Regina Kuehn*

NOTES

1. Romano Guardini, *Vom Sinn der Schwermut (The Significance of Depressions)* (Mainz: Grünewald, centennial ed., 1985).

2. Eleventh plenary session of the Concilium ad Exequendam Const. de S. Liturgia, Oct. 6, 1968.

3. Romano Guardini, *Berichte über mein Leben (Reports about My Life),* trans. Regina Kuehn (Düsseldorf: Patmos, 1985), 61.

4. Ibid., 80.

5. Ibid., 88.

6. Romano Guardini, *The Spirit of the Liturgy* (New York: Sheed and Ward, 1935), 210.

7. Guardini, *Berichte.*

8. Ibid., 97.

9. Romano Guardini, *Die Lehre des Heil. Bonaventura von der Erlosung.* Dissertation published in 1921.

10. Romano Guardini, *Power and Responsibility: A Course of Action for the New Age* (Chicago: Henry Regnery, 1961), 103–4.

11. *Systembildende Elemente in der Theologie Bonaventuras.* Habilitations-Schrift, 1922 (Leiden: Brill, 1964).

12. FDA: *Freiwillizer Deutscher Arbeitsdienst.* Between 1933 and 1935, this Voluntary German Work service was employed to build roads and waterways. For all information about Rothenfels, see Hanna-Barbara Gerl, *Romano Guardini 1885–1968* (Mainz: Grünewald, 1985), 153–247.

13. Rudolph Schwarz, *Kirchenban (Church Architecture)* (1960), 37–46.

14. Romano Guardini, *Sacred Signs* (Several English translations and publishers, including a recent edition: Wilmington DE: Michael Glazier, 1979).

15. Romano Guardini, *Der Gegensatz* (Mainz: Grünewald, centennial ed., 1985).

16. Romano Guardini, *The Living God* (Chicago: Henry Regnery, 1962).

17. Romano Guardini, *The Lord* (Chicago: Henry Regnery, 1962).

18. Karl Rahner, ceremonial address at the academic celebration of Guardini's 80th birthday.

ODO CASEL

Theologian
of the Mystery

N MANY WAYS, Dom Odo Casel (1886–1948) was not so different from his comrades in the first wave of the liturgical reform.[1] Like Guéranger, Beauduin and many other pioneers of the liturgical movement, Casel was a Benedictine. A monk of the abbey of Maria Laach, he personally was responsible for much of its liturgical genius. Also like other pioneers, he was a proponent of Mystical Body theology,[2] expanding it toward previously unexplored horizons (pushing it, some said, well over the brink). Casel even has ministry to and reform work with religious women in common with other liturgical reformers.

Despite these similarities, Casel was a unique figure. It has been said that he was singularly responsible for removing the theological shackles of the post-Reformation Roman church. He was at least a thinker not to be ignored and both the hierarchy and the scholars cast suspicious and even condemnatory glances in his direction. Because of these denunciations, the liturgist H. A. Reinhold confessed to have lost nights of sleep "worried sick over the master."[3] Casel, by contrast, seems to have weathered the controversy well.

Perhaps "the master" came into conflict with the hierarchy and the theological establishment more than did other early proponents of the liturgical movement because of his peculiar concerns. He was not suspect because of his liturgical experimentation, but because his thought was believed by some to be unorthodox, even heretical. A jaundiced eye was cast as well on those who accepted or elaborated Casel's teachings.

The Roots of His Thought

Casel was born September 27, 1886, in Koblenz-Lützel in western Germany. After preparatory schools, he attended the University of Bonn. There he came to know Ildefons Herwegen, monk of Maria Laach, through whose influence Casel was to embrace the monastic life. He began the novitiate at Maria Laach in 1905, making his profession in 1907. After philosophical study in his own monastery, he studied theology at the international Benedictine house in Rome, Sant' Anselmo, and in 1911 he was ordained a priest by the archbishop of Trier.

Casel wrote two doctoral theses. The first was submitted to the faculty at Sant' Anselmo in 1913. It concerned the eucharistic doctrine of Justin Martyr and subsequently was published in serial form. On its completion, Casel was sent immediately to Bonn (thanks to the prodding of Herwegen) to study philosophy and classical philology. There he produced his second doctoral thesis, concerning mysticism and Greek philosophy. These two dissertations established the patterns for Casel's subsequent scholarship.

Hundreds of articles and a number of books came from the pen of Casel during the next 30 years.[4] Among them, his two volumes in the *Ecclesia Orans* series are lauded as his most important contribution to the advancement of liturgical renewal. Originally published in German and later in French, the books might be titled in English *The Memorial of the Lord in the Ancient Christian Liturgy* and *The Liturgy as a Mystery*

Rite. His thought was substantially developed in the 15 volumes of *Jahrbuch für Liturgiewissenschaft* (1921–1941), an important liturgical journal that Casel himself edited.

Mystery-theology

He called his system *Mysterientheologie,* mystery-theology. It attempted to explain how the divine is present in Christian worship: in Casel's terms, the "mystery-in-the-present," the *Mysteriengegenwart.*[5] Drawing from the witness of both the early church and Hellenistic religious traditions—the areas of his dissertations—Casel proposed that in the liturgy, the mystery of Christ (which is Christ himself) actually is made present again. This mystery is not simply grace, nor a memory of Christ in the minds of believers, nor in the case of the eucharist only the presence of Christ in the bread and wine. Rather, Christ's historical life as well as his glorified life is made present for the liturgical assembly, which can experience its impact anew. Exactly how this is possible, neither Casel nor his disciples were able to say. Casel, in fact, resisted asking the question because he believed that it intruded into an aspect of the divine life beyond the proper limits of human inquiry.[6] He was satisfied with asserting, on the basis of his understanding of scripture, tradition and liturgical writings, that Christ is present in his historical and glorified reality in the liturgy. By celebrating the church's rites, including the Liturgy of the Hours and sacramentals, contemporary Christians transcend time and are brought into transformative contact with Christ. Because Jesus' life reached its culmination in the paschal mystery—his passion-death-resurrection—it is in these events that the church especially knows him in its common prayer.

Some theologians, in an attempt to explore Casel's teaching, suggested that it was the *effect* of Jesus' life that was made available in the sacraments: Sacraments thus can be seen as channels of divine life, of grace. This, however, was not what

Casel intended and he was insistent in his own position. He claimed that the Mystery that the rites make present is not a substance, sentiment or state of being before God. The sacramental Mystery is Jesus himself.[7] Referring to a quote from the *Apostolic Constitutions,* "This [martyr] died with Christ in suffering death, the others die with him in the *typos* of his death," Casel explained:

> That indicates that baptism does not confer only an image, a pure and simple figure of the death of Christ, but that the death of the Lord becomes a reality in [the one baptized], that it [the death] is accomplished in a "mystical" fashion, under the external image of the sacrament, just as the witness of the blood carries the death of the Lord in all its natural reality.[8]

This theory has far-reaching implications for the liturgy. For example, because Christ lives in mystery in the entire Mystical Body, the liturgy is seen as an act of the whole church.[9] In the liturgical prayer of *all* the gathered church, not only in the work of its ministers, the liturgical reactualization of Christ's life is accomplished.

Sources of His Ideas

Casel concerned himself with theory far more than with practice, except as it was affected by his theology of *Mysteriengegenwart.* Casel drew his position from four sources. The first three—Jewish tradition, Christian scriptures and early church writers—were universally accepted (although Casel's interpretation of them was not). However, the fourth source—Graeco-Roman traditions—brought vehement criticism.[10] He dared to claim that pagan religions have something to say about the Christian cult.

Casel's opponents were many. Some sought to prove that he was not in accord with Aquinas, even though Casel claimed to be. Others mastered the Caselian system well enough to question its lack of internal consistency. And some merely dismissed the whole affair as absurd. The one issue that most captivated the critics was the seeming dependence of *Mysterientheologie* on the pagan mystery religions. Since the death of Casel, it has been shown that he approached the study of Graeco-Roman mystery cults with a certain naïveté and actually imposed Christian and New Testament concepts on them. At the time, however, his critics were not concerned with how well Casel understood the ancient religions in themselves. Their fear was that Casel was subordinating the church's sacraments to pagan rites. By investigating the similarities between pagan ceremonies and Christian rites, Casel appeared to doubt that Jesus had instituted the sacraments and that Christianity was unique among religions. He seemed to be undermining the Christian cult rather than restoring it.

Mediator Dei and the Constitution on the Sacred Liturgy

M *ediator Dei* was written just one year before Casel's death. His opponents saw him condemned on its pages. He, however, saw the encyclical as his vindication. After Casel's death, a friend wrote that both affirmation and renunciation could be found in *Mediator Dei,* but that the gentle condemnations were not of Casel's own thought but of his disciples' theories that misconstrued Casel's intent.[11] More impartial witnesses suggest that, in fact, the document skirts the issue. Its Latin is carefully constructed to capture the tenor of Caselian thought while denying some of its specific tenets. The papacy, it seems, wanted nothing to do with this battle of theologians.

Neither did Vatican II. It did not "directly take a position on questions discussed among Catholic theologians; that is not the function of a council."[12] Casel's thought nonetheless can be shown to have had a profound influence on the documents that were written for Vatican II, especially its liturgy constitution.[13] The *Constitution* understood the liturgy not as an act of the ordained only, but as an act of all those assembled; it recognized that Christ is present in every act of the liturgy, not only in the so-called sacramental moments; it emphasized that Christ is present in the liturgy not merely as abstract grace but as a living person; and further, it acknowledged that he is present among his people in several ways, not only in the eucharistic bread and wine. In these examples, we hear echoes of Casel's thought.

The Nuns at Herstelle

During the days when the battle over Casel's orthodoxy raged most fiercely, Abbot Herwegen assigned Casel to the peaceful work of resident spiritual director and chaplain of the Benedictine nuns in Herstelle. Although Herstelle had been founded as a Benedictine house, it bore but little resemblance to a classical monastery.[14] The community was dedicated to perpetual adoration and the ceremonies surrounding the Blessed Sacrament eclipsed everything else liturgical. In place of the psalms of the Divine Office, the nuns recited eucharistic devotional prayers. In their chapel, nuns were chained voluntarily for a given period each day to a "pillar of scourging" in commemoration of the scourging of Jesus. This sort of piety was far from the liturgical life of a Benedictine monastery.

In matters of governance, the Holy Rule of St. Benedict mandates the election of abbots for life. Yet the nuns at Herstelle held annual elections of an abbess. The one elected always was the same: the Virgin Mary, whose image was annually led through the ceremony of abbatial enthronement. The earthly superior at Herstelle was a prioress, not an abbess.

Some of the nuns, realizing that their life was not in line with the Benedictine tradition, sent to Maria Laach for help. Herwegen undertook the task of lifting the obligation of perpetual adoration, imposing the canonical Office and having an abbess elected and bestowed with pontifical insignia. After these canonical tasks had been accomplished, Abbot Herwegen sent Casel to continue the education of the nuns in the ways of monasticism. Many of those who wrote obituaries of Casel referred to the place of his death as "Dom Odo's Herstelle." Clearly, he was thought to have had a profound impact on the community. The nuns themselves verified the assessment, referring to him as their "mystagogue."

"Death is Conquered, Glory Fills You"

The circumstances of the death of Odo Casel could not have been more fitting or remarkable. Casel, who had sought to give back to the church a belief that Christ in the paschal mystery was present in every liturgy, died as he proclaimed that resurrection. He had just intoned the *Exsultet* at the Easter Vigil liturgy at the convent at Herstelle. One commentator remarked that if such an event were recorded in a medieval biography of a saint, moderns would disregard it as pious fantasy.[15] It was not.

It was in light of the wonder of Casel's death that the sisters of Herstelle concluded the obituary of their mentor:

> His whole life was beset with bodily suffering and given to untiring labor in sacred science; his passing over into the eternal Pentecost took place by the grace of God during the great night of the Pasch. *Deo gratias.*[16]

■ *Patrick Malloy*

NOTES

1. The details of Casel's life are recorded in Burkhard Neunheuser, "Biographie," *La Maison Dieu* 14 (1948), 11–14; H. A. Reinhold, "Timely Tracts: Dom Odo Casel," *Orate Fratres* 22 (1948), 366–72; and Osvaldo Santagada, "Dom Odo Casel," *Archiv für Liturgiewissenschaft* 10 (1967), 7–9.

2. See Odo Casel, *Le Mystère du culte dans le christianisme: richesse du mystère du Christ,* 2d ed., *Lex Orandi* 38 (Paris: 1964), 46 ff.

3. Reinhold, "Timely Tracts," 371.

4. See the bibliography compiled by Eloi Dekkers in *Ephemerides Liturgicae* 62 (1948), 374 ff., and the more complete one of Santagada in *Archiv für Liturgiewissenschaft* 10 (1967), 10–77. The latter includes works both by and about Casel and a topical index of Caselian thought.

5. See Dennis O'Callaghan, "The Theory of the *Mysteriengegenwart* of Dom Odo Casel: A Controversial Subject in Modern Theology," *Irish Ecclesiastical Record* 90 (1958), 246–62.

6. Burkhard Neunhauser, "Odo Casel in Retrospect and Prospect," *Worship* 50:6 (1976), 500–1.

7. See Casel, *Le Mystère du culte*, 16–19.

8. Ibid., 32. My translation.

9. Jean Hild, "L'Encyclique *Mediator Dei* et le mouvement liturgique de Maria Laach," *La Maison Dieu* 14 (1948), 16.

10. An overview of the many criticisms leveled against Casel and a defense of his positions is offered by Eloi Dekkers, "La liturgie, mystère chrétien," *La Maison Dieu* 14 (1948), 22 ff.

11. Hild, "L'Encyclique," 16.

12. Neunhauser, "Odo Casel," 493.

13. Ibid., 493–96. This is demonstrated extensively in "Casel's Theology and the Second Vatican Council" and "The Mystery of Worship."

14. Reinhold, "Timely Tracts," 366–69.

15. Pie Duployé, (no title), *La Maison Dieu* 14 (1984), 10.

16. Quoted in Reinhold, "Timely Tracts," 366.

JOSEF JUNGMANN

*Laying a Foundation
for Vatican II*

 ORN A MILLER'S SON on November 16, 1889, Josef Andreas Jungmann became perhaps the greatest liturgical scholar of his day. From 1895 to 1901, Josef attended the elementary school in Sand, a small Austrian village. Studies in the *gymnasium* at Brixen followed from 1901 to 1909. For four additional years, Josef attended the seminary in Brixen. There he studied with Franz Josef Doelger, met Pius Parsch and mastered Latin and Greek. The educational methods employed at the seminary Josef found boring. The liturgy there he found equally dull.

Soon after his graduation from the seminary in 1913, Jungmann and his elder brother, Franz, were ordained diocesan priests at Innsbruck. Four years of work followed as an assistant pastor in the villages of Niedervintl and Gossensasz, work responsible at least in part for the pastoral orientation of his eventual liturgical research. Late in life, Jungmann fondly remembered his pastoral assignments. With great delight he would describe the events on Ascension Day when he had to hoist a statue of Christ into the rafters of the church.

In 1917, Jungmann entered the Society of Jesus. One year later, he traveled to Innsbruck to begin studying philosophy. Granted the title Doctor of Theology in 1923, Jungmann visited Munich for two additional semesters of study. In August of 1924, he returned to Innsbruck to prepare his *Habilitationsschrift,* a second dissertation required of those who wished to become full professors. Some 40 years later, this thesis would appear in English as *The Place of Christ in Liturgical Prayer.*

Teacher and Scholar

From 1925 until 1938, when the Nazis closed the theology department, and again from 1945 until 1963, when he reached the age of mandatory retirement, Jungmann taught pastoral theology, catechetics and liturgy at the University of Innsbruck. During this same period, he edited the journal *Zeitschrift für katholische Theologie.*

Jungmann's work helped to prepare the way for the liturgical reforms of Vatican II. Named to the German Liturgical Commission in 1940, Jungmann became in 1945 a member of the Austrian Liturgical Commission. He addressed several important liturgical congresses: Frankfurt (1950), Munich (1955) and Assisi (1956). Not surprisingly, Jungmann was widely regarded in the late 1950s as perhaps the most outstanding liturgical scholar in the German-speaking world and was named in 1960 to the conciliar preparatory commission. He then served as an honored *peritus* at Vatican II and as a consultor for the Consilium, the commission entrusted with implementation of the *Constitution on the Sacred Liturgy.*

Within the Consilium, Jungmann exercised great influence, this almost despite himself. Diffident and shy, he often was surprised to discover that others deferred frequently to his informed liturgical good sense. Explained Charles Riepe: "The conclusions from his scholarship were often so obvious that Father Jungmann himself never really had to draw them." Mastery of his field, regard for others' accomplishments, a wonderful ability to separate the essential from the secondary, all this with an extraordinary modesty, won Jungmann many admirers. Neither a fighter nor a propagandist, he was merely, wrote Johannes Hofinger, "a confessor of his well-substantiated convictions."

Dr. Balthasar Fischer, who is himself one of the great scholars and teachers of our generation, says of Jungmann, "I owe everything to him, everything I have been as a professor of liturgy." Fischer believes that Jungmann's special talent consisted in "letting the past teach an understanding and right evaluation of the present and point to the right solutions for the future." Solid historical research was for him "the indispensable tool" for a right assessment of the present condition of the Christian community. "If he were alive today," Fischer insists, "I'm certain that he would remind us that thorough liturgical research remains indispensable for the understanding and the further organic development of the liturgy." (Quotations are taken from a March 1986 letter from Dr. Fischer.)

Jungmann's "deep faith" and "imperturbable adherence" to the church did not prevent him "from seeing clearly unhealthy trends and developments of the past in Christian worship and preaching. At first, many considered him to be unorthodox," Fischer explains. Soon, however, "the weight of his incontestable reasons and also his modest and prudent presentation" achieved admiration. "Without the work of Father Jungmann, the liturgical reform as initiated by the Council could not have been possible."

Though hindered by deafness and loss of sight, Jungmann continued to study and write until his death. His last book, a study of the history of Christian prayer, appeared in 1969. In his last letter to Hofinger, penned a few weeks before he died on January 26, 1975, he wrote: "I live now in the infirmary like a hermit between time and eternity, happily waiting for the hour when the Lord will come and knock."

In addition to some 800 book reviews, Jungmann produced 304 books and articles. In his first book, the dissertation *The Place of Christ in Liturgical Prayer* (German, 1925; English, 1965), he examined the worship of the church and called for a renewal of devotional prayer. A second significant work, *The Liturgy of the Word* (German, 1938; English, 1966), investigated the nature of liturgical celebration outside the sacramental liturgy.

By his own admission, Jungmann's greatest interest was the religious instruction of children. In his *The Good News Yesterday and Today* (German, 1936; English, 1962), a work so visionary that its publication was suspended soon after it appeared, he advocated a new direction for the catechetical movement, one which favored reinvigorated preaching and worship. Here, wrote Richard Laurick, Jungmann "anticipated much of what the liturgical movement would later implement, such as the centrality of the paschal celebration as the focal point of the entire church year." Perhaps no other book did as much to prepare the way for the pastoral renewal accomplished at Vatican II.

During the academic exile that Hitler imposed, Jungmann prepared his most important book, the two-volume *Missarum Sollemnia* or *Mass of the Roman Rite* (German, 1948; English, 1950). Work on this scholarly masterpiece began at Vienna in 1939. Jungmann had to search with great difficulty for new sources of books and texts that were destroyed by the Nazis. The manuscript was completed during October of 1945 at Hainstetten where Jungmann had served for three years as the chaplain for a convent of sisters. Publication was delayed until 1948.

The response to *Missarum Sollemnia* was swift and enthusiastic. Writing in *Orate Fratres* (January, 1949), H. A. Reinhold commented that "there has been quite a bit of guesswork concerning the historical aspects of the Mass and the development of its parts. . . . Jungmann frankly states where . . . the path gets lost in the jungle. The recitation or singing of the Canon aloud, the practice of an introit procession, the solitary *Oremus* at the offertory and its contradictory explanations . . . are answered with a final and scholarly authority based on good evidence." "Probably more than any other single book," wrote Balthasar Fischer, "*Missarum Sollemnia* prepared the way for the conciliar reform of the liturgy."

In 1949, Jungmann came to the United States to teach in the summer liturgy program at the University of Notre Dame. His lectures were published as *The Early Liturgy to the Time of Gregory the Great* (English, 1959; German, 1967).

At least two translations of works by Jungmann, *The Mass: An Historical, Theological and Pastoral Survey* (1976) and *Christian Prayer through the Centuries* (1978), appeared after his death in 1975. In the former book, Jungmann summarized the historical development of the liturgical forms of the eucharist, highlighting along the way the theological and pastoral implications of these forms. The latter work, a study on private prayer, represented a historical investigation of extraliturgical prayer.

■ *Robert Peiffer*

GREGORY DIX
Salutary Gadfly

C ANON A. M. RAMSEY, Regius Professor of Divinity at the University of Cambridge, wrote these words of tribute to Dom Gregory Dix after his death in 1952: "He was one of the best loved figures in the Church of England in recent years. . . . Convocation has lost a leader in debate, and the bishops a salutary gadfly; theology has lost the spur of a penetrating mind, and lovers of stories one of the best of raconteurs. And a host of people have lost a friend and counselor, wise and witty, loving and loyal. It will be hard to do without him."[1] When looking at Dom Gregory Dix, we see the monk of Nashdom Abbey, the insightful, intuitive scholar. He was an important writer: *The Shape of the Liturgy* has influenced in one way or another nearly every post–World War II revision of the eucharistic liturgy and his theories continue to excite discussion. As the previously mentioned account makes clear, a complex, lively personality stood behind the scholarship, influencing friend and foe alike, always leaving a lasting impression.

George Eglington Alston Dix was born at Woolwich, England, on October 4, 1901, the son of Dr. George Henry and Mary Jane (Walker) Dix. Nothing further is known of his parents, except that his father eventually was ordained a priest and was interested in English literature and theology. Young George Eglington showed interest in these subjects as a King's Scholar at Westminster and also seems to have taken a great interest in acting.

Dix was a "man about campus" during his time as a history student at Merton College, Oxford. He was the coxswain of the college crew team and exhibited an "impish sense of humor and sheer naughtiness," according to Canon A. H. Couratin.[2] In 1923, he graduated from Oxford. According to the brothers of Nashdom Abbey, Dix went to the university originally intending to read for the bar; what changed his mind is unknown.[3]

After graduation, Dix was appointed a lecturer in modern history at Keble College, Oxford, where he also served as chaplain after his ordination as priest in 1925. In 1926, he resigned his position and entered the novitiate at the Anglican Benedictine community at Pershore (later to move its location and become Nashdom Abbey), where he took the name Gregory.[4]

The early times at Pershore were eventful. Dix was sent to help at St. Augustine's College, Kumasi, Gold Coast (now Ghana), a seminary for Anglican clergy. While in Africa, however, he developed appendicitis and other ailments. He was so sick that it was thought that he would be unable to carry on his work. The sickness was a blessing in disguise, for he was sent back to England and spent the years 1929 to 1936 throwing himself with vigor into the study of patristics and other serious reading. This period of study would provide the groundwork for Dix's "fat green book" (as he liked to call *The Shape of the Liturgy*).

In 1937, he published an edition of *The Apostolic Tradition of St. Hippolytus,* the first fruit of his long period of patristic study. This translation into English of the famous church order contained not only full critical notes on each chapter of the document but also a succinct discussion of all the pertinent witnesses to the text. Dix also administered St. Michael's Parish in

Beaconsfield, where his brother, Father Ronald Dix, had worked until he left to become a chaplain in His Majesty's Forces. Dom Gregory Dix remained in charge of the parish until September 1941, after which he retired to one of the guest cottages at Nashdom and spent the next 14 months writing *The Shape of the Liturgy.*

In 1946, Dix participated in a series of discussions concerning the proposed union of the Church of England and the Church of South India. He was opposed to the union, voicing Anglo-Catholic misgivings over the proposed joint understanding of ministerial orders. In 1944, he published a booklet entitled *The Questions of Anglican Orders* at the request of the Bishop of Oxford, who wanted to "answer" Anglicans who were upset by the South India Unity Scheme and who were threatening to join the Roman Catholic Church. *The Theology of Confirmation in Relation to Baptism,* emphasizing the importance of confirmation as the liturgical locus of the reception of the Spirit, appeared in 1946.

Four years after its publication in 1945, *The Shape of the Liturgy* was accepted as a thesis for the doctor of divinity degree at Oxford (1949). In 1948, Dix became claustral prior of Nashdom Abbey. While lecturing in the United States in 1950, he became ill and returned to Nashdom, where he died of cancer on May 12, 1952. After a requiem Mass at St. Mary Magdalene, Oxford, he was buried at Nashdom. A friend said of him:

> He was an acute ecclesiastical politician, a brilliant pamphleteer, a superb raconteur. Possessing a great gift of self-dramatization, he could act himself into any part he chose, but underneath he remained a spiritual person.[5]

Dix's Scholarship

In *Gregory Dix: Twenty-Five Years On,* Kenneth Stevenson notes the recurring features of Dix's scholarship: (1) interest in the continuity between Judaism and Christianity; (2) commitment to the patristic period, even to the point of perhaps becoming a "patristic fundamentalist"; (3) seeing the medieval and reformation periods in close relation; and (4) "spreading his nets further than his data."[6] Dix also was a lucid writer, as E. C. Ratcliff remarks about *The Shape of the Liturgy*: "It's an extraordinary thing to find a book that reads like a novel, but is in fact a serious contribution to scholarship."[7] Many reviewers have noted that Dix often worked as much by brilliant guesswork as by intense study of the patristic texts and that in *The Shape of the Liturgy* what often begins as a hypothesis early in the book ends up as documented fact.

Dix's Hypotheses: Recent Critiques

In recent years, some of Dix's theses have been criticized. Two areas of critique will be discussed here: the main thesis of *The Shape of the Liturgy* and the "historicization" of Christian worship in the fourth century.

The Shape of the Liturgy is Dix's most well-known work and many of its hypotheses are taken as liturgiological gospel today. Dix's main thesis is well known: The seven actions of Christ at the Last Supper that the eucharistic liturgy recall (taking the bread, taking the cup, blessing the bread, blessing the cup, breaking the bread, giving the bread, giving the cup) were eventually reduced to four: taking, blessing, breaking, sharing. This fourfold action forms the core of every eucharistic liturgy in Christianity, no matter how obscured the central actions might be by later accretions. Some reviewers have noted that Dix's emphasis on the offertory rite (a result of identifying the action of "taking" with the offertory) was incorrect, in light of recent research on the origins of the offertory, particularly in the Eastern Christian eucharistic rites. Thus, much of the popular "theology of the offertory" that developed in many churches in the 1960s and 1970s partially as a result of Dix now has been discarded or qualified.

Some question the very premise of Dix's magnum opus, asserting that the diversity of traditions in the early church nullifies any search for a common "core" of the early eucharistic liturgy, whether in the old form of "the" original text or texts the apostles used or in the more nuanced common "shape" of the liturgy. In an age when some scholars question the gospel accounts of the Last Supper, it seems impossible to construct an entire theory of the historical development of the eucharist based on these accounts.

Another of Dix's misconceptions was the idea of the "historicization" of the liturgy. Dix saw the fourth century as a time when the original unitive, eschatological, communal celebration of the Christian mystery was shattered into a large number of historical commemorations of each phase of the mystery of salvation. In other words, history replaced eschatology and the individual (particularly in the monastic office) replaced the communal. Both Thomas Talley and Robert Taft have shown, however, that an interest in history was present in Christian worship from the beginning and that Dix's opposition of an "eschatological" eucharist with the "sanctification of time" in the monastic office is wrong.[8]

Yet Dix also had a gift for inspired guesswork. For example, his theory concerning the origins of the liturgy of St. James in large part has been corroborated recently by John Fenwick.[9] Certainly, Dix's influence on post–World War II revision of the eucharistic rite is undeniable (beginning with the Church of South India's eucharistic liturgy of 1950). Even if his theory of the "shape" of the liturgy was not entirely correct, it formed much contemporary understanding of the eucharist. That so many across the denominational spectrum today describe liturgy in terms of action and that writers persist in using the phrase "sanctification of time" are at least in part a tribute to Dix's popularity and lasting influence.

Through his "fat green book" and other writings, Gregory Dix continues to play an active role in the field of liturgical studies to this day, ultimately calling us (despite his antiquated language) to an all-embracing vision of liturgy and life:

> Over against the dissatisfied "Acquisitive Man" and his no less avid successor, the dehumanized "Mass Man" of our economically focused societies insecurely organized for time, Christianity sets the type of "Eucharistic Man"—man giving thanks with the product of his labors upon the gifts of God, and daily rejoicing with his fellows in the worshiping society which is grounded in eternity. This is man to whom it was promised on the night before Calvary that he should henceforth eat and drink at the table of God and be a king. That is not only a more joyful and more human ideal. It is the divine and only authentic conception of the meaning of all human life, and its realization is in the eucharist.[10]

■ *Grant Sperry-White*

NOTES

1. "Dom Gregory Dix: Originality of the Mind," *Times of London* (May 19, 1952), 9.

2. A. H. Couratin, "Dix, George Eglington Alston, Dom Gregory," E. T. Williams and Helen Palmer, *The Dictionary of National Biography, 1951–1961* (Oxford: Oxford University Press, 1971), 301.

3. *The Jubilee Book of the Benedictines of Nashdom* (London: The Faith Press, 1964), 71.

4. Couratin, "Dix, George Eglington Alston," 301. Nashdom (Russian for "our house") was founded in 1914 at Pershore and moved to Nashdom in 1926. See Peter F. Anson, *The Call of the Cloister* (London: SPCK, 1955), 183–92.

5. Ibid., 301–2.

6. Kenneth W. Stevenson, *Gregory Dix: Twenty-Five Years On*, Grove Liturgical Study No. 10 (Bramcote Notts: Grove Books, 1977), 36–38. This booklet is a basic resource in understanding the contemporary reception and critique of Dix's work.

7. Ibid., 38.

8. Robert Taft, "Historicism Revisited," *Beyond East and West: Problems in Liturgical Understanding* (Washington DC: The Pastoral Press, 1984), 15–30; Thomas J. Talley, "History and Eschatology in the Primitive Pascha," *Worship* 47 (1973), 212–21.

9. For a summary of Fenwick's London Ph.D. dissertation on the topic, see John R. K. Fenwick, *Fourth-Century Anaphoral Construction Techniques,* Grove Liturgical Study 45 (Bramcote Notts: Grove Books, 1986).

10. Dom Gregory Dix, *The Shape of the Liturgy,* with additional notes by Paul V. Marshall (New York: Seabury Press, 1982), xx–xxi.

EVELYN UNDERHILL

The Sacrifice of a Humble and Contrite Heart

F ONE WERE TO READ an account of the foremost liturgists of the twentieth century, it is doubtful that the name Evelyn Underhill would appear. She wrote no technical nor academic treatise on any specific liturgical subject nor did she edit any obscure manuscript from whose pages light was shed on some stage of Christian liturgical development. Her contribution consists in this: Evelyn Underhill prayed. From that prayer and from her study of the mystic tradition emerged insights that have guided readers for three-quarters of a century and an understanding of the role of the liturgy in the formation of the Christian that places her among the leaders of liturgical renewal in the Anglican communion.

If one considers her beginnings, Evelyn Underhill is not a likely candidate for the role of a liturgical pioneer.

> Looking back to her childhood, Evelyn Underhill says frankly, "I was not brought up to religion." Her parents were not churchgoers. Her father said he had had too much of "school-chapels" as a boy; possibly he did not meet the right sort of people while he was young. They were not hostile to religion, but it did not count for much in their lives.[1]

She was born on the eighth of December, 1875. Her father, Arthur Underhill, eventually rose to prominence in English legal circles and was rewarded with a knighthood for his services to his profession and his English ancestry. Travel was a regular aspect of the Underhills' family life, whether as a threesome, a twosome (mother and daughter) or, after Evelyn's marriage, a foursome.

Finding a Church

Her "conversion" from agnosticism to Christian faith was a gradual one. During her early adult years, Underhill was attracted to various mystical movements in English society, most of these movements theistic but not exclusively Christian. As she drew closer to explicit Christian faith, it was the Roman Catholic communion that seemed to beckon as a spiritual home. Reasons for this attraction are easily discovered. First, Underhill had drawn from her experience in non-Christian mystical movements a strong belief in the power of ritual.[2] Second, exposure at an early age to the religious art of Italy resulted in Underhill's sincere appreciation of the central images of the Roman Catholic tradition, especially those images that focus on sacrifice and on the sacramentality of creation. Third, as a historian of mysticism and as a mystic herself, Underhill found in Roman Catholicism a community of support that she could not find to the same extent in her native Anglicanism.

Despite these compelling reasons, however, she did not take the step of being received into the Roman Catholic communion. The first decade of the twentieth century was a period in her life in which she maintained the discipline of a Roman Catholic life while remaining outside its eucharistic communion.

As to prayer and meditation, since we have no other indication we must assume that she set aside a period in the morning when in principle she attempted a set meditation. . . . She also went to Mass regularly in Roman Catholic churches. . . . She seems in this respect to have behaved in all intents and purposes as one of the Catholic faith, keeping the festivals and fasts of the church together with the calendar of saints, using established devotions including the Way of the Cross and the rosary, genuflecting before the tabernacle. She, like von Hügel, had a special penchant for Benediction. . . . We also learn from a letter of Ethel Ross Baker that she accumulated in these years a collection of pious amulets, of "holy medals."[3]

The reasons for her hesitation are as clear as those that compelled her toward the Roman Catholic communion. Her fiancé, Hubert Stuart Moore, like her father a lawyer, was adamant in his opposition to her becoming a Roman Catholic.[4]

During the period of her engagement to Moore, 1906 to 1907, there was an increase in public statements by officials of the curia criticizing the theological movement known as "modernism." For Underhill, these statements came at an unpropitious time. She required an ecclesial community in which she could maintain intellectual freedom and honesty.[5] Despite her strong attraction to Roman Catholicism, Underhill turned away.

Mysticism

The year 1911 marks a watershed in Underhill's life. Two events merit closer examination. The first is the publication of her book, *Mysticism;* the second is the beginning of her relationship with Baron Friedrich von Hügel, the lay Roman Catholic theologian whose influence was widespread in the early decades of the twentieth century. In *Mysticism,* Underhill ranges throughout the whole mystical repertory of East and West, Christianity and non-Christian religions. From this she derives four characteristics of the mystic consciousness: (1) Mysticism is practical, not theoretical; (2) mysticism is an entirely spiritual activity; (3) the business and method of mysticism is love; (4) mysticism entails a definite psychological experience.[6] She is guided by the Flemish mystic Ruysbroeck who speaks of the mystical life as "not the passage of one life to another, but the *adding* of one life to another: the perpetual deepening, widening, heightening and enriching of human experience."[7]

> Throughout *Mysticism* Evelyn is aware, indeed her whole treatment is guided by the supposition that falling in love with God usually absorbs the whole human personality into a process of organic, cataclysmic development of which the three stages, purgative, illuminative, and unitive, give a rough and ready outline.[8]

She does not see the mystic path as restricted to a select few but as an invitation that all human beings receive, the invitation to love God as God, with no ulterior motives, and from that love will issue an experience of life as it is meant to be lived in the fullness of reality.

Initially, *Mysticism* was understood by Underhill to be a synthesis of Christian and non-Christian mystics. However, the book was reprinted and revised numerous times, the final edition occurring in 1940. Each edition marks a point in Underhill's journey.

> What is more satisfactory is to compare *Mysticism* and its revisions with other books and letters by the author. Here we can see the effect of these major "shifts" which led her from mysticism to spirituality, from an anti-historical approach to religion to an historical approach and from being strictly theocentric to becoming christocentric.[9]

In later years, Underhill remarked that there was much she would change were she to rewrite the book.[10]

The immediate effect of the publication of *Mysticism* was to make Evelyn Underhill a public figure and to bring her to the attention of Friedrich von Hügel. At first, their relationship was conducted through the medium of correspondence, von Hügel challenging Underhill to come to a greater appreciation of the institutional character of the Christian faith and to a greater precision in her theological language. Eventually, Underhill asked von Hügel if he would serve as her spiritual director, a responsibility he undertook for four years until his death in 1925. It is ironic to note that she asked him to be her spiritual director precisely at the time she had decided to remain an Anglican and to serve actively in its ministry. This seems to have had no ill effect on their relationship; on the contrary, there is every reason to suspect that the Baron was pleased that she had chosen to exercise her ministry within a historic branch of the Catholic Church.

The Spiritual: Clearing Time and Space

The year 1921 marks the invitation of Manchester College, Oxford, to Underhill to give a series of public lectures on the spiritual life.[11] These lectures are important for they mark the introduction of a new theme into the writings of Underhill. This focuses on the role of the liturgy in the spiritual lives of all Christians.

> Organized ceremonial religion insists upon it, that at least for a certain time each day or week we shall attend to the things of the Spirit. It offers us its suggestions, and shuts off as well as it can conflicting suggestions: though, human as we are, the mere appearance of our neighbors is often enough to bring these in. Nothing is more certain than this: First, that we shall never know the spiritual world unless we give ourselves the chance of attending it, clear a space for it in our busy lives; and next, that it will not produce its real effect in us, unless it penetrates below the conscious surface into the depths of the instinctive mind, and molds this in accordance with the regnant idea. If we are to receive the gifts of the cultus, we on our part must bring to it the very least what we bring to all great works of art that speak to us: that is to say, attention, surrender, sympathetic emotion.[12]

Underhill takes the then unusual position of suggesting that within the liturgical celebration one encounters the spiritual life of the living God. Her contemporaries in the Anglican communion had long been familiar with the moral and theological arguments for public worship, but the suggestion that the liturgy can be a mystical experience must have astounded them. She speaks of the ability of the liturgy to "tune us up" and to keep ourselves "supple" so that "we can prevent that terrible freezing up of the deep wells of our being which so easily comes to those who must lead an exacting material or intellectual life."[13] She concludes a section of the lecture on "Institutional Religion," which deals most specifically with the liturgy, as follows:

> If, then, the cultus did nothing else, it would do these two highly important things. It would influence our whole present attitude by its suggestions, and our whole future attitude through unconscious memory of the acts which it demands. But it does more than this. It has as perhaps its greatest function the providing of a concrete artistic expression for our spiritual perceptions, adorations and desires. It links the visible with the invisible, by translating transcendent fact into symbolic and even sensuous terms. And for this reason human beings, having bodies no less surely than spirits, can never afford wholly to dispense with it. Hasty transcendentalists often forget this; and set up spiritual standards to which the race, so long as it is anchored to this planet and to the physical order, cannot conform.[14]

In these words Underhill bids farewell to her past association with non-Christian mystics in English society and sets her feet clearly on the historic Christian path.

The Manchester College lectures begin the period during which Underhill entered a vibrant ministry of spiritual direction. Her association with von Hügel and, after von Hügel's death, Walter Howard Frere, the Anglican bishop of Truro in Cornwall, guided her as she herself began to guide many others. She was actively sought as a retreat conductor, her addresses frequently being published later in book form. Worship was a central part of these retreats. Eucharist was celebrated every morning before breakfast and evening prayer concluded the day.[15] Music played an important role in these retreats and Underhill personally chose the hymns to be sung.[16]

In *The Life of the Spirit,* Underhill speaks of the importance of hymnody in the liturgical life of the church:

> We do speak to ourselves—our deeper, and more plastic selves—in our psalms and hymns; so too in the common recitation, especially the chanting of a creed. We administer through these rhythmic affirmations, so long as we sing them with intention, a powerful suggestion to ourselves and everyone else within reach. We gather up in them—or should do— the whole tendency of our worship and aspiration, and in the very form in which it can most easily sink in.[17]

The Dimensions of Worship

Underhill's experience of liturgy and its role in the spiritual life finds its greatest expression in her 1937 book *Worship.* She drew on contemporary liturgical scholarship and her own spiritual insights.

> Where did she get her ideas from? The index is revealing. Jesus Christ gets by far the most citations; but von Hügel comfortably pushes St. Paul into third place. Augustine, Aquinas, and de Caussade walk side by side with Brilioth, Cabrol, and Frere himself. This is the mind of synthesis and synthesis is often a fruitful experience when the author in question is pioneering a work which attempts to bring different disciplines together.[18]

The book itself is divided into two parts: (1) the theological first principles of Christian worship and (2) brief accounts of various worship traditions. In her discussion of the theological first principles, she asserts that worship is "the only safe, humble and creaturely way in which people can be lead to acknowledge and receive the influence of an objective Reality."[19] This experience of "an objective Reality" has four characteristics: (1) "Ritual or liturgic pattern," (2) "Symbol or significant image," (3) "Sacrament, in the general sense of the use of visible things and deeds, not merely to signify, but also to convey invisible realities" and (4) "Sacrifice or voluntary offering."[20] She goes one step further and speaks of these elements as having "a marked social quality" and as having visible and invisible actions, "both real, both needed, and so closely independent that each loses its true quality if torn apart."[21]

Sacrifice is a recurrent theme in all of Underhill's writings and *Worship* is no exception. Repeatedly through the book the term or related terms surface as she tries to speak of the relationship that a human being has with the Holy One who is Creator:

> For sacrifice is a positive act. Its essence is something given; not something given up. It is a freewill offering, a humble gesture which embodies and expresses with more or less completeness the living heart of religion; the self-giving of the creature to its God.[22]

In the second part of the book, she focuses on a variety of worship traditions: Jewish, early Christian, Catholic (Eastern and Western), Reformed, Free Church and Anglican. In so doing, she echoes the opinion of the Anglican theologian, Frederick Denison Maurice:

> The fact that each of these types has its particular shortcomings, that each tends to exaggerate one element in the rich Christian complex at the expense of the rest, that all are liable to degeneration and are seldom found in their classic purity, is merely what our human contingency would lead us to expect.[23]

She attributes this tendency toward degeneration to the fact that the prophetic character of Christian worship sinks into the background:

Primitive Christian worship was therefore both sacramental and prophetic: and during the early centuries the church seemed to fluctuate between these ideals. The free and charismatic type with its accompanying difficulties and inconveniences— already manifest in the New Testament—gradually sank into the background of the Christian corporate life.[24]

It is therefore of great importance that representatives of these contrasting forms of worship should learn to regard each other with sympathy and respect, and even to practice that difficult degree of generosity, which is willing to be taught by those of whom we do not quite approve. This will only be possible when there is a clear understanding of the part each plays or should play in the total Christian response to God; and of the fact that this response cannot achieve its full and balanced reality and beauty, unless both order and sponta- neity, liturgy and liberty, the ministry of the word and the ministry of the sacraments, the work of the prophet and the work of the priest, give it of their best.[25]

Among her conclusions are these: Corporate worship is to be preferred to hieratic worship; Mass without communion is an incomplete act of worship; the loss of the intercessions from the Roman Mass is regrettable.[26]

From the vantage point of 50 years, the English liturgist Kenneth Stevenson gives an appreciative review of Underhill's work. While her work is very much dated, this is due not to the quality of her work but to the advance of liturgical studies since the publication of *Worship* in 1937. In concluding his review, Stevenson writes this:

Were Evelyn alive today, she would have welcomed the ways in which Easter prayers and spirituality have been used in West- ern liturgical reform; but she would also be chiding us for not taking worship (in its specific and less restrictive senses) seri- ously enough. Worship and spirituality belong together, and liturgy exists to serve both, in order to act as a vehicle for men and women to have a genuine sense of the transcendent and a vision of the redeemed humanity. The road to adoration, communion and cooperation, as Evelyn Underhill showed, is a fruitful one.[27]

In 1988, the Episcopal church in the United States added Evelyn Underhill to its calendar of saints (commemorated on the 15th of June, the day of her death), specifying the use of the proper preface for the dedication of a church that speaks of the "sacrifice of praise and prayer which is holy and pleasing in your sight." Her lasting influence on the Anglican communion is found in the wealth of spiritual teaching still to be gleaned from her writings and in the well-established retreat movement that gained considerable impetus from her leadership in the 1920s and 1930s.[28] In her liturgical writing, her emphasis on the corporate aspect of worship is one that still awaits fulfillment in many of our churches.[29]

■ *Richard G. Leggett*

NOTES

1. Olive Wyon, *Desire for God: A Study of Three Spiritual Classics* (London: Collins, 1966), 89.

2. Christopher J. R. Armstrong, *Evelyn Underhill (1875–1941): An Invitation to Her Life and Writings* (London: A. R. Mowbray, 1975), 38.

3. Ibid., 98.

4. Wyon, *Desire for God,* 90.

5. Ibid., 90.

6. Armstrong, *Evelyn Underhill,* 111.

7. Ibid, 185.

8. Ibid., 124.

9. Elizabeth Dalgaard, "The Churching of Evelyn Underhill," *Arc* 17 (Spring 1989), 43.

10. Wyon, *Desire for God,* 90.

11. Evelyn Underhill, *The Life of the Spirit and the Life of Today,* 7th ed. (London: Methuen and Company, Ltd., 1928). This series of lectures was first published in 1922.

12. Ibid., 137.

13. Ibid., 136, 137.

14. Ibid., 140.

15. Wyon, *Desire for God*, 95.

16. Armstrong, *Evelyn Underhill*, 265.

17. Underhill, *The Life of the Spirit*, 136.

18. See Kenneth Stevenson, "Re-Review: Evelyn Underhill's *Worship*," *The Modern Churchman* 28 (1986), 45–49.

19. Ibid., 17.

20. Ibid., 20.

21. Ibid., 22–23.

22. Ibid., 48.

23. Ibid., xii.

24. Ibid., 88.

25. Ibid., 91.

26. Armstrong, *Evelyn Underhill*, 283.

27. Stevenson, "Re-Review," 49.

28. *The Book of Common Prayer and Administration of the Sacraments and Other Rites and Ceremonies of the Church Together with the Psalter of David According to the Use of the Episcopal Church* (New York: The Church Hymnal Corporation, 1979), 381.

29. Stevenson, "Re-Review," 47.

EDMUND BISHOP

The Discipline
of History

I T IS ONLY WITHIN the last century and a half that
the historical-critical method has been applied to
the study of liturgy, in no small measure because of
the efforts of Edmund Bishop, an erstwhile monk
and self-taught English scholar. His influence on a
generation of European liturgical scholars cannot be underesti-
mated. By means of his articles and his collaborations with
other scholars, Bishop became the preeminent English liturgical
scholar of the late nineteenth and early twentieth centuries.

Born in Totnes, England, on May 17, 1846, Bishop was the
ninth of ten children in a home influenced by the Evangelical
movement in the Church of England. His religious education in
this tradition never entirely left him; even after his conversion
to Roman Catholicism, Bishop "never forgot the Prayer Book
Catechism, never abandoned the Evangelical attitude to Holy
Writ, and never understood English nonconformity."[1] During
his early education in England, Bishop was taught to keep
notebooks drawn from his reading and study; this habit provided him with a vast treasure house of data on which to draw
in his later scholarly work.

In 1860, Bishop was sent to Belgium to study at the same school at Vilvorde where his elder brothers had studied. Destined for a career in government service under the patronage of the Duke of Somerset, Bishop returned to England in 1861 and finished his education. In 1864, he was appointed a junior clerk in the Education Office and remained in that Office for 20 years. He used his time as a government clerk to develop new insights into the liturgical life of the church in the West even as he copied letters to schools, principals, school boards and bureaucrats.

With the position in the Education Office to support his personal needs and to finance his independent studies in the liturgy, Bishop embarked on his career. Already fluent in French and Latin, he taught himself German so he could read the most scientific liturgical research being published at the time. Bishop displayed a remarkable aptitude for learning new languages as his research horizons broadened. Later in life, he learned Hungarian and several Slavic and Scandinavian tongues.

Bishop had moved from the Evangelical attitude of his early years into an uncomfortable Anglo-Catholicism. His time in Belgium and his contacts with Roman Catholic scholarship brought him closer to a break with the Church of England. As late as April of 1867, Bishop still was a practicing Anglo-Catholic, but a trip to France in July brought him into contact with Abbé A. J. E. Malais, who became the agent of Bishop's conversion to Roman Catholicism. In August 1867, Edmund Bishop was received into the Roman Catholic church.

His mentors saw in him an able and apt scholar and supported him in his desire to study the liturgy. To them, however, liturgical studies consisted primarily in the collecting of rites and ceremonies from various periods and locales. Little did they know that Bishop could not and would not be confined to these parameters. His admission to the reading rooms of the British Museum in October of 1867 gave him access to the raw data on which he drew to develop a scientific understanding of the development of the liturgy in the West.

His first work focused on recovering a sense of the life of the great English Benedictine communities. In this, he was guided by his primary principle: "to copy fair what time hath blurred—redeem truth from his jaws."[2] To most English readers, this aspect of the religious life of England was unknown; Bishop sought to restore an understanding of this formative experience of Christianity in Great Britain to the public consciousness.

Bishop broke into the limelight in 1877 with his discovery of a collection of papal letters in the British Museum. Although they previously had been mentioned by scholars, it was Bishop who recognized that these 400 letters (a quarter of which date from the fifth and sixth centuries) were largely unknown. As was typical of much of his later work, the value of his discovery, published in the German *Neues Archiv,* was recognized in Europe and largely ignored by English scholars.

During the same period, Bishop became acquainted with the work of E. Ranke, a Lutheran scholar. Ranke taught him the importance of lectionaries and calendars in dating manuscripts and tracing the sources of influence on the liturgical manuscripts of Western Europe. This tool enabled Bishop in later years to develop a schema of the relationship between the various sacramentaries that has influenced subsequent study of this subject.

The eight years from 1878 to 1886 brought Bishop to the end of one phase of his life and to the beginning of a new one. He developed a strong sense of what it meant to be an "English" Catholic and emphasized his conviction that Roman Catholicism was not a foreign sect but the "old religion" of the English nation. To further this conviction, he aided in the preparation of an official calendar of saints for the Roman church in England and helped establish the Guild of Saint Gregory and Saint Luke "for the purpose of promoting the study of Christian antiquities and of propagating the true principles of Christian art."[3]

Downside Abbey

Bishop's sense of the character of English Catholicism can be seen most clearly in his attraction to the Benedictine life as it was being shaped by the community at Downside. In 1885, at the age of 39, he retired with a pension from the Education Office. He was free to turn where he would; he chose Downside. The next years were not happy ones for Bishop. Controversies within the Benedictine order and the discovery of some aspects of his own personality that made monastic life difficult —these dashed his dream of a Benedictine vocation to scholarship and he departed from Downside in 1892. At the age of 43, he was a retired bureaucrat and an ex-monk.

In 1889, Bishop had read Louis Duchesne's *Origines du culte chrétien* (English title, *Christian Worship: Its Origin and Evolution*) and was devastated by what he read. Duchesne's style and argumentation were skillful and persuasive, but he did not deal with the facts as Edmund Bishop knew them. Duchesne's account of the introduction of the Roman liturgical books into Gaul was impossible, his description of the relationship between the various books inaccurate and his discussion of the relationship between the Gallican and Mozarabic liturgies barely credible.[4]

Development of the Roman Liturgy

Bishop's life now became more devoted than ever to the scientific study of the history of the liturgy. By 1893, he could summarize his views on the development of the Roman Mass from the sixth to the tenth centuries: During the seventh century, Roman sacramentaries in an early form circulated in

Gallican and Irish circles. A revised form of that liturgy, traditionally ascribed to Gregory I, was introduced into France and Germany by Charlemagne at the end of the eighth century. To this "Gregorian" sacramentary a supplement was added, compiled from Gallican sources. This hybrid sacramentary (known as the "eighth-century Gelasian") was imported into Rome and became the basis for the Roman liturgy.[5]

Although certain points have been refined by subsequent scholarship, the basic shape of Bishop's view remains intact.

Bishop's discovery of the Gelasian sacramentary of the eighth century represented the manner in which he approached liturgical studies. He was reluctant to begin any project with an *a priori* thesis and to seek supporting evidence; he chose, rather, to examine all the evidence available and to develop a hypothesis in the directions dictated by the evidence.

"The Genius of the Roman Rite"

Bishop's scholarship confronts us with the painstaking study of the sources, but also with something else. He prized historical imagination as a valuable and necessary tool in liturgical studies. He wrote to a friend that he wanted to reread a particular manuscript "and bring before me that world, that atmosphere; and consult my (forgive the big words), my sensory impressions, my dramatic feelings, to consider quietly, at leisure, in regard to this or that or the other (in your article)— does it fit with my feelings about these people, with themselves as I seem to see them in their letters."[6]

April of 1899 saw the production of one of Bishop's most enduring essays, "The Genius of the Roman Rite." By "genius" Bishop means "a characteristic and distinguishing spirit that manifests itself in all that [a people] says and does, in its history and its literature; determining the character of both, and affecting the general character even of its thought."[7] He illustrates the genius of the Roman rite by comparing and contrasting the propers for various occasions in the Roman and Gallican traditions. This leads him to list the purely Roman elements of the text of the Mass as printed in the missal of Pius V. From there he gives a picture of the early Roman Mass as celebrated in the fifth century. He sums up his portrayal of the Roman rite in words that may have troubled some of his listeners:

> In fact, I think it would not be untrue to say that what is considered most picturesque, or attractive, or devout, or affective —in a word, what is most "interesting," as the saying is, in the services of our religion, just those things indeed which in the popular mind are considered distinctive of "Romanism," and which go to make up, in the main, what some people call the "sensuousness of the Roman Catholic ritual," form precisely that element in it which is not originally Roman at all, but has been gradually borrowed, imported, adopted, in the course of ages. Of course it would take a very long time to make a full survey and give historical evidence in each particular case. But I think that the general position is unassailable, . . . that the genius of the native Roman rite is marked by simplicity, practicality, a great sobriety and self-control, gravity and dignity; but there it stops.[8]

Bishop's view of the genius of the Roman liturgy seems to have colored the thinking of the bishops at Vatican II. In Article 34 of the *Constitution on the Sacred Liturgy,* one reads, "The rites should be distinguished by a noble simplicity; they should be short, clear, and unencumbered by useless repetitions; they should be within the people's powers of comprehension, and normally should not require much explanation."

Bishop's last years were spent in research on the epiclesis and in preparing a collection of his essays for publication by the Oxford University Press. These years also were marked by the increasing tokens of respect and affection given to him by liturgists throughout the world who saw Bishop as the master of the scientific study of the liturgy. Bishop died in 1917 and was buried at Downside among the monks whose life he had shared in and out of the cloister.

■ *Richard G. Leggett*

NOTES

1. Nigel Abercrombie, *The Life and Work of Edmund Bishop,* with a foreword by David Knowles (London: Longmans, Green and Co., 1959), 4.

2. Ibid., 30.

3. Ibid., 76, 102–3.

4. Ibid., 148–49. Bishop notwithstanding, Duchesne is still given as a resource in numerous reference works; see Cyrille Vogel, *Medieval Liturgy: An Introduction to the Sources,* trans. and rev. by William Storey and Niels Rasmussen (Washington DC: The Pastoral Press, 1986), 6, 107, 140, 274, 276; Robert W. Pfaff, *Medieval Latin Liturgy: A Select Bibliography,* Toronto Medieval Bibliographies, No. 9 (Toronto: University of Toronto Press, 1982), 14.

5. Abercrombie, *The Life and Work of Edmund Bishop,* 202–3.

6. Ibid., 259.

7. Edmund Bishop, *Liturgica Historica: Papers on the Liturgy and Religious Life of the Western Church* (Oxford: Oxford University Press, 1918; reprint ed., Oxford: Oxford University Press, 1962), 1–19.

8. Ibid., 12.

WALTER HOWARD FRERE

A Cowl among the Miters

Y ABIDING RECOLLECTION is of a great man who influenced for good all who came in contact with him. I remember with gratitude his charm, his cheerfulness, his courtesy, his humor; I respectfully admired the attainments of a scholar who never intruded his scholarship; but I suppose the central quality that made him so impressive a figure was his saintliness—a positive and active saintliness that illuminated his every word and action and combined, with the maximum consideration for others, an inflexible will and an almost terrifying singleness of purpose."[1]

With these words, an acquaintance of Walter Howard Frere described the monk who had become the first member of a religious order since the Reformation to be placed on the episcopal bench of the Church of England. Throughout his life, Frere was described as saintly; his enemies and those who shared his ideas found that the saint had a will of iron.

Frere was born on November 23, 1863, the second son of an English family famed for its clerical and academic members. His father was a clergyman, his mother the daughter of a clergyman. A quick glance at the *Dictionary of National*

Biography reveals several Freres occupying the pages. His cousin, Christopher Wordsworth, subdean of Salisbury Cathedral, was a noted liturgist and edited the three fine volumes of the Cambridge University Press edition of the Sarum Breviary.[2]

The first major crisis of Frere's life occurred in 1868 with the death of his father and was followed by that of his mother in 1870. Walter and his older brother already were away at school, but later in his life he said, "I sometimes think being an orphan is liable to make you a bit impersonal."[3] This distance was characteristic of Frere throughout his entire life. A custody battle in 1877 seems to have caused the young Frere to turn even more inward and develop a quietness that he possessed until his death. His biographer, C. S. Phillips, remarks:

> Some who knew Walter Frere well could not help suspecting that his boyhood had not been a particularly happy one. Here perhaps (given a nature proud, affectionate and sensitive, and inheriting the "Frere reserve") may be found to some extent the explanation of that intense reticence which not only made it intolerable for him to talk about himself, but also sometimes caused him to go out of his way to head others off from discovering his real grounds of opinion and action—a trait that puzzled not a few and, especially in his last years, diminished the influence that should have been his.[4]

In 1885, Frere distinguished himself by winning an academic award at Cambridge. He decided to pursue an ecclesiastical career and chose to attend Wells Theological College. His friends were surprised that he did not plan to study at Cuddesdon, a school with a high church tradition. When explaining his choice, Frere remarked that he had chosen Wells because "I don't want [Cuddesdon] to make a ritualist of me."[5] He was ordained a deacon in 1887 and a priest in 1889, serving as an assistant curate in the parish of Stepney. This was his only parish assignment during his entire ordained ministry.

Community of the Resurrection

In January 1891, Frere left Stepney and embarked on the path he was to walk for the remainder of his life. He decided to test his vocation in the newly formed Community of the Resurrection, a monastic order for men founded by Charles Gore, who later became bishop of Oxford. Frere professed his vows in 1892.

> Frere . . . told his friend Stewart at the time that he wanted to supply a Cambridge element in the undertaking, and that he felt that the country clergy needed help and that the parochial system was insufficient. Many years later he gave a further reason to another friend, Bernard Horner: "The thing that as much as anything brought me to the Community was the feeling that it was intolerable for me to possess money."[6]

The common assessment of Frere as a monastic is that this was his true vocation. E. K. Talbot gives the following consideration of Frere as the member of a religious order:

> Probably there were particular considerations that reinforced this central determination. Historical appreciation of the part played by the religious orders through the ages in raising and reanimating the life of the church, a spontaneous attraction of his spirit to the liturgical patterns of the Divine Office, a strong impulse to disencumber himself of personal possessions and to find contentment in simplicity, a resolve to fill his time with dedicated industry and to find in obedience the mortification of a will inclined to be imperious: All these may well have contributed to his submission to the religious yoke. But they were only elements comprised in a single purpose—to find freedom in the service of God under a religious rule.[7]

His brothers in the community must have recognized this commitment. After the appointment of Gore as bishop of Oxford, Frere was elected superior and remained in that office from 1902 to 1922 with a hiatus of three years (1913 to 1916).

In the second decade of the twentieth century, the Church of England, prodded by the growth of the Anglo-Catholic movement and of liturgical studies in general, began the process of revising the Book of Common Prayer. Frere was keenly involved in this effort by virtue of his extensive knowledge. In 1911, he published a book entitled *Some Principles of Liturgical Reform* in which he expressed his concerns over the manner the revision would be pursued:

> But principles come before details not only in order of importance and of general interest but also in order of logic and of time. Therefore, whether the church proceeds now to such a detailed revision, or whether it postpones that task and is content for the present with a very much smaller project, the principles which must govern revision, in whatever degree it is undertaken, need to be stated, criticized, amended, . . . and formulated as rules of conduct. Until this is done, all proposals to alter a rubric here and a phrase there, or to prune this and amplify that, are worse than useless. The best that can be hoped for them is, that proving abortive themselves, they may give place to something more thorough.[8]

When discussing the proposed project of revision, Frere came down early on the side of those who saw such a project as necessary for the well-being of the established Church. He commented:

> [A church] must be rich in its varieties and in the alternatives that it provides; it must also be ready to review its whole methods from time to time. A church that has not revised its plans of public worship for 250 years is of necessity face-to-face with a pressing problem, the solution of which is already long overdue.[9]

Despite Frere's articulate description of the need for liturgical revision, the proposed Prayer Book was defeated in the House of Commons twice, once in 1927 and, in revised form, in 1928.

By the time of the 1928 debate, Frere had withdrawn his support of the proposed Book, perhaps finding the revisions unacceptable.[10] Given the withdrawal of his support, it is ironic to note that, after its defeat in the House of Commons, Frere made use of the 1928 rite in his chapel at Truro.

His years of advocacy of liturgical reform brought him to the attention of Archbishop Davidson who proposed that Frere be made bishop of Truro, a small diocese in Cornwall. On the feast of All Saints in 1923, Walter Frere was consecrated bishop of Truro in Westminster Abbey. He remained in Truro until 1935. After retirement, Frere returned to the motherhouse of his community where he died on April 2, 1938, in the midst of those he loved and served.

Frere's Place in the Liturgical Renewal

As a liturgist, Frere is ranked among the greatest that the Church of England has produced. His works range from Reformation studies to the Russian Orthodox Church to the early Roman church. They remain among those works consulted by contemporary scholars. Gregory Dix, the author of the chapter on Frere as a liturgist in the Phillips biography, believed that Frere's greatest accomplishment was his two volumes on the early Roman gospel and epistle lectionaries. They are the fruits of more than 30 years of reflection and the sifting of minute bits of evidence: They remain authoritative.[11] Dix gives this appraisal of Frere:

> [Liturgists] fall, I think, the eminent among them, into two groups, divided not by a degree of greatness, but by a diversity of gifts. There are those to whom their successors turn naturally for texts and information . . . and there is another group . . . to whom one turns rather for their *apercus*, their general judgments. It is with the first group that Frere's name will live. True, he had a foot in either camp. He has left us one finished piece of specialized research on the Roman Mass lectionaries as near perfection as it is ever given to a mortal to

reach, whose conclusions will remain magisterial in their own field. But he has left behind him a whole shelf of standard editions of texts. At the difficult and laborious task of editing he was superbly competent—exactly faithful and of an excellent judgment, shrinking from no labor of index and table and analysis, yet always scrupulous to let the document speak for itself. Failing the discovery of radically new material, which in this part of the field is no longer very probable, these editions of his will be definitive. For centuries to come all students of medieval English *liturgica* will approach many of their most important documents under the guidance of Walter Frere. And they will be grateful.[12]

As a historian and liturgist, Frere never fell into the trap of perceiving a given past as the ideal against which all other ages must be measured. Frere's aim, in the words of A. Hamilton Thompson, was "truth, which ornamental or picturesque writing may distort or obscure."[13] This spirit is conveyed in remarks made to Orthodox Christians during his visit to Russia in 1914:

> The great task of Orthodox and Catholic Christianity is to discern in every age what part of its activity and power belong to that portion of itself which is permanent, unchanging and inalienable, and to maintain those inviolable; while at the same time giving free play to all those moving, progressing and developing forces within itself which life, just because it is life, exhibits in a continual state of energetic and purposeful change. The church must keep that which is fixed, fixed, and leave that which is free, free.[14]

At a time when many Anglo-Catholics were busily seizing on the latest continental Roman Catholic ceremonial fads, Frere, a leading spokesman for the Anglo-Catholic position in many other liturgical matters, was willing to take issue with his party within the Church of England. His advice rings true today.

> It is obvious to everyone who is familiar with church life, that ceremonial has been introduced in many quarters which is entirely unsuitable to our rites. The extreme form of this mistake

is seen when the zealous priest or layman comes home from abroad, from France or Italy or Germany, much impressed with something that he has seen done in church there; and then sets to work at once to introduce it in his own church, without considering, and perhaps without being capable of judging, whether it is suitable to our English rites. If he has sympathy with medieval services, it is perhaps on them that he draws rather than on foreign customs; but often with the same result, namely, incongruity.[15]

Frere made practical application of this approach. The use of the miter by bishops of the Anglican communion was still a matter of lively controversy during Frere's active career. In the midst of such turmoil, however, Frere could give an episcopal colleague some lighthearted advice on the proper use of the miter: "There are really only two rules: Don't pray in it and don't fuss with it."[16]

Few liturgists achieve what Frere achieved: Scholarship won him the respect of his peers and pastoral sensitivity won him the hearts of his brothers in religion and the people of his diocese. By virtue of these two characteristics, Frere was able to overcome 400 years of Anglican prejudice against the monastic movement and to restore its presence in the councils of the Anglican communion.

■ *Richard G. Leggett*

NOTES

1. C. S. Phillips et al., *Walter Howard Frere, Bishop of Truro* (London: Faber and Faber Limited, 1947), 172.

2. Ibid., 15.

3. Ibid., 16.

4. Ibid., 20.

5. Ibid., 27.

6. Ibid., 38.

7. Ibid., 44.

8. Walter Howard Frere, *Some Principles of Liturgical Reform: A Contribution towards the Revision of the Book of Common Prayer* (London: John Murray, 1911), vii–viii.

9. Ibid., 4–5.

10. Geoffrey J. Cuming, *A History of Anglican Liturgy,* 2d ed. (London: Macmillan, 1982), 171.

11. Phillips, *Walter Howard Frere,* 123. See also L. Edward Phillips, "The Problems of Terminology in Early Roman Lectionary Studies," The North American Academy of Liturgy, *Proceedings of the Annual Meeting of The North American Academy of Liturgy, San Francisco, California, 4–7 January 1988* (Valparaiso IN: North American Academy of Liturgy, 1988), 128–36.

12. Ibid., 146.

13. Ibid., 157.

14. Ibid., 197.

15. Frere, *Some Principles of Liturgical Reform,* 16–17.

16. Phillips, *Walter Howard Frere,* 118.

LOUIS BOUYER

Theologian, Historian, Mystagogue

L OUIS BOUYER'S CAREER has spanned not only several decades, it also has spanned several intellectual disciplines and churches. He is the author of scripture studies, a massive history of spirituality, a dictionary of theology, biographies and works on liturgy.[1] Bouyer is also a convert who began his ecclesiastical career as a Lutheran pastor and became a priest of the Oratory (a community of diocesan priests). His work has combined spirituality and liturgy in such a way that he has merited the term "mystagogue" from one author.[2] We will limit our discussion to Bouyer's work dealing specifically with liturgy and the liturgical movement. We begin with a brief account of his life and early work and move to a discussion of Bouyer's place in the liturgical movement and those works of Bouyer's that specifically treat liturgical topics.[3]

Life and Early Work

L ouis Bouyer was born February 17, 1913, in Paris. He grew up in a Protestant environment, eventually settling on the

Lutheran church because "there he saw most fully developed the integration between the prayerful study of the word of God and the eucharistic liturgy."[4] Bouyer's teachers in Paris during his study for the Protestant license in theology were the French Calvinist Auguste Lecerf and the Lutheran scholar Oscar Cullmann. Another early influence was the Russian Orthodox scholar Sergei Bulgakoff, whose "deeply sapiential form of the Christian vision" was to greatly influence Bouyer's later work.

Bouyer's first book, *Venez car tout est prêt* (1938), dealt with a liturgical topic: catechesis for Protestant children receiving first communion. In that same year, Bouyer's study of the gospel of John, *Le quatrième évangile*, was published. Bouyer dedicated the work to Cullmann. Erasmo Leivas-Merikakis sees in this first scholarly book of Bouyer's the articulation of one of his fundamental theological principles: a return to the sources, particularly the Word of God. Bouyer's thesis for the Protestant license in theology focused on the theology of the body of Christ in the writings of Athanasius of Alexandria. It was published in 1943 under the title *L'Incarnation et l'Église: Corps du Christ dans la théologie de Saint Athanase.* Another basic theme of Bouyer's subsequent work emerges from this study: an emphasis on the church as the concrete form of the body of Christ in the world.

Conversion

The exact date of Bouyer's conversion is unclear. In 1938, he still was writing as a Protestant, but by 1947 at the latest, he had become a Roman Catholic priest of the Oratory, had completed a doctor of theology degree at the Institut Catholique de Paris and had become professor of ascetical and mystical theology. Bouyer detailed his theological conversion in the 1955 book *De Protestantisme á l'Église (From Protestantism to the Church).*[5]

Bouyer saw his conversion not as a repudiation of what was true in the Reformation, but rather as a fuller affirmation of those principles. He writes:

> No sentiment of revulsion turned him from the religion fostered in him by a Protestant upbringing followed by several years in the ministry. The fact is, he has never rejected it. It was his desire to explore its depths, its full scope, that led him, step by step, to discover the absolute incompatibility between Protestantism as a genuinely spiritual movement stemming from the teachings of the gospel, and Protestantism as an institution, or rather complex of institutions, hostile to one another as well as to the Catholic church. . . . He saw the necessity of returning to that church, not in order to reject any of the positive Christian elements of his religious life, but to enable them, at last, to develop without hindrance.[6]

Bouyer and the Liturgical Movement

Three pieces of Bouyer's writings from the 1940s and the 1950s provide a clear picture of his understanding of the European liturgical movement, its goals and its weaknesses: two chapters from *Liturgical Piety,* based on a series of 24 lectures and six seminars he gave in the summer of 1952 at the University of Notre Dame[7] and a portion of a letter he wrote in 1943 to Father Duployé on the necessary steps toward liturgical renewal.

Bouyer devoted Chapters Four and Five of *Liturgical Piety* to a discussion of the European liturgical movements of the seventeenth century and the twentieth-century liturgical experiments in Belgium, Germany and France. In Chapter Four, Bouyer treats the liturgical projects of the Caroline Divines (for which he expresses much admiration) and critiques the pioneering work of Guéranger. Chapter Five includes an in-depth analysis of Beauduin's work at Mont César, praising Beauduin's vision in focusing on educating priests for the work of renewal.[8] Bouyer further lauds Beauduin for his "realism":

both in keeping in mind the actual men and women whom the work addressed and in its prudent refusal to propose changes in the liturgy. The work at Mont César was a "pure and strong rediscovery of living tradition as it is."

Bouyer describes the "high-brow" school of Maria Laach and its complement, Parsch's projects at Klosterneuberg. He expresses his admiration for Parsch's ability to reunite the liturgy with its source, the word of God. Then Bouyer discusses the recent liturgical movement in France, criticizing its use of the "para-liturgy" to the neglect of the worship of the local parish and its emphasis on missionary work among "modern pagans" to the exclusion of helping "faithful Christians in the church" to rediscover liturgy. Bouyer concludes the chapter with the admission that liturgical change is inevitable, but he asserts that "the only alternative to a deadly anarchy must be sought in a revival of the tradition itself. . . . Nothing will prove more effective for such a purpose than a return to the sources of tradition, a return entirely free of all archeologism."

A letter from Bouyer to Father Duployé dated October 8, 1943, shows Bouyer's personal understanding of the goals of the liturgical movement in France.[9] Bouyer begins by defining liturgy as the "spontaneous expression of the collective soul" of the church, disavowing both "archaeological" and "aesthetic" approaches to liturgy. He describes the steps necessary to "cultivate an understanding" of liturgy through a "popular biblical movement" (similar to Pius Parsch's work), "historical explanation" and "habitual union with the whole spiritual world in which [the texts] are bathed."

Bouyer describes a "definite first goal" for the movement: "the restoration of the parochial high Mass (or the solemn Mass when it is possible) as a Mass of communion, effectively assembling the whole local *ekklesia* for a truly collective act." Near the end of his letter Bouyer stresses the need for "clear vision" and cites the Belgian liturgical movement's "pushing . . . medieval adjuncts" (i.e., obscure ceremonial) as an example of an "unclear" effort of liturgical renewal.

Bouyer's own priorities for the liturgical movement clearly stand out in these three writings. Bouyer insists on the recovery of tradition and the simultaneous avoidance of archaeologism and on the strong biblical foundation of any adequate understanding of liturgy. As with other figures in the movement both in Europe and North America (for example, Pius Parsch and William Busch), Bouyer stresses the need for prudent restraint in proposing any changes in liturgical texts. He calls for the active participation of all in liturgical life. Finally, he insists on the unity of liturgy and spirituality in the everyday lives of those who participate in Christian liturgy.

Writings about Liturgy

Leivas-Merikakis correctly notes: "*Everything* in Bouyer's attitude and work bears a 'liturgical' character in the sense that it is the liturgy that takes everything else up into itself and transforms it: Theology here is a meditation of Christian revelation as it becomes liturgical act."[10] Here we will focus on five books: *Liturgical Piety, Eucharist, Christian Initiation, The Paschal Mystery* and *Rite and Man.*

Liturgical Piety (1954) and *Eucharist* (1968) stand out as Bouyer's historical-theological *tours de force* in the field of liturgical studies. The 19 chapters of *Liturgical Piety* cover the spectrum from Baroque and Romantic conceptions of the liturgy to an exposition of Casel's *Mysterientheologie* to historical discussions of the eucharist, initiation, the liturgical year, office, devotions and the relation between the Christian mystery and the world. Bouyer concludes with a brief history of the field of liturgical studies. In this one volume, Bouyer displays his mastery of both Protestant and Catholic liturgical literature as well as his knowledge of scripture and patristics. The book is not merely a showcase for scholarship, however; it is an analysis of Christian liturgy as celebration of the Christian mystery, the mystery of redemption through Christ. This theme unites the book's disparate chapters.

Eucharist traces the development of the eucharistic prayer in its many manifestations through history. Bouyer's precise description of the anaphora's origins in the prayers of the synagogue and the Jewish meal prayers has not won general acceptance and the early fixity of Jewish liturgical prayers in general has been disproved by Heinemann and others. In addition, Bouyer's assertion of the theological centrality of the Roman Canon has been challenged by other reviewers.[11] Yet, the sheer range of material Bouyer covers, as well as the number of hypotheses he suggests, has continued to make *Eucharist* a necessary resource for anyone studying the anaphora. Bouyer's ecumenical perspective emerges here as well, for unlike many historians of the eucharist, Bouyer seriously examines the eucharistic prayers of many Protestant traditions, including Taizé.

The Paschal Mystery (1945) and *Christian Initiation* (1958) belong to the same category of literature: theological and historical interpretation of liturgical rites. In both cases, Bouyer is concerned primarily with reaching the general reader and in guiding the reader in a journey of discovering the Christian mystery. In the Introduction to *Christian Initiation*, Bouyer states: "This book is intended for every Christian, actual or potential, as an initiation into Christian truth and life, which are inseparable."[12] In both volumes, Bouyer acts forcefully as mystagogue: In *Christian Initiation*, he leads the reader from "the discovery of the spiritual" through discovery of God, the divine word, the living church, the cross, resurrection, Christ, eucharist and new life, to "the discovery of eternal life." Bouyer begins *The Paschal Mystery* with an exposition of "The Christian Mystery" and its universality.

Rite and Man (1962) is a treatment of Christian ritual from the perspectives of the history of religions and depth psychology. The book is a response to the problem of the survival of

Christian sacramentalism in the late twentieth century and to
the challenge of adapting Christian liturgy to restore its meaning for people of today. According to Bouyer, "The sacred rites
are realities which cannot be known, much less reshaped, if
their roots in human nature and Christian tradition are never
really understood."[13] Bouyer discusses the relation of word and
sacrament, liturgical adaptation and the "concrete realization"
of liturgical adaptations. He emphasizes the importance of the
"meal-aspect" of sacrifice and argues that for signs to be able
to speak again, they must regain their reality: "The less sugges-
tive the hierophanies of water and eating are for modern man,
the more necessary it is that the saving bath should become a
real bath, that the sacred species should be recognized as those
of true bread and true wine."[14] Bouyer manifests his concern
for "returning to the living tradition" in *Rite and Man,* using
modern tools of analysis to understand those for whom liturgy
embodies the Christian mystery.

Conclusion

Louis Bouyer's liturgical writing uses the tools of historical
and theological scholarship to help Christians "return to
the sources," the "living tradition" that is to be reappropriated
by every Christian in her or his life. In many different ways,
Bouyer shows us the unfolding of the Christian mystery in the
liturgy. His liturgical writing, for all its command of historical
and theological sources, ultimately is pastoral and mystagogi-
cal in its orientation. This concern for the vocation of all
Christians to be comprehended by the mystery of Christ gives
Bouyer's liturgical work an ecumenical, even global perspective
that seldom is found in the writings of other figures in the liturgical movement.

Bouyer's citation on the occasion of his reception of an honorary Doctor of Laws degree from the University of Notre
Dame on May 7, 1964, sums up well the thrust of his work:

[He is] a theologian, a priest who has placed the best of his scholarship and intelligence to the service of the knowledge of God. He feels in his deepest life the transcending and transforming spirit of the liturgy of the church, and, forsaking both antiquarianism and sentimentality, has sought to bring it to bear, with the grace of good sense and the charity of true understanding, on the urgencies of our time.[15]

After the publication of *Liturgy and Architecture* in 1967, Bouyer's intellectual interests seem to have moved away from liturgy to systematic theology and the possibilities of the Eastern Christian traditions. In recent years, he has written two trilogies, one on creation and salvation and the other on the knowledge of God. While the theme of "mystery" still seems to be a hallmark of this later work, Bouyer's focus appears to be on the economy of salvation. A volume of memoirs reportedly is in progress.

■ *Grant Sperry-White*

NOTES

1. A bibliography of Bouyer's books can be found in: Erasmo Leivas-Merikakis, "Louis Bouyer the Theologian," *Communio* 16 (Summer 1989), 257–82, esp. 277–82.

2. Ibid., 270.

3. Ibid., 258–60. The following relies heavily on the treatment of Bouyer's early life.

4. Ibid., 258.

5. *Unam Sanctam*, No. 27 (Paris: Éditions du Cerf, 1955), trans. A. V. Littledale under the title *The Spirit and Forms of Protestantism* (Westminster: Newman Press, 1958).

6. Bouyer, *The Spirit and Forms of Protestantism*, trans. A. V. Littledale (Cleveland and New York: World Publishing Co., 1964), Introduction.

7. Michael A. Mathis, CSC, founder of the Summer School of Liturgical Studies at the University of Notre Dame, persuaded Bouyer to lecture at the Summer School a number of times in the 1950s and 1960s. In 1956, Bouyer lectured on "The Meaning of Sacred Scripture" and on "The Meaning of the Liturgy" in 1960.

8. Bouyer, *Liturgical Piety* (Notre Dame: University of Notre Dame Press, 1954), 61 ff. In 1964, Bouyer wrote a biography of Beauduin entitled *Dom Lambert Beauduin: Un homme d'Église* (Paris: Catermann, 1964).

9. Translated in *Communio* 16 (Summer 1989), 283–91.

10. Leivas-Merikakis, "Louis Bouyer the Theologian," 270.

11. See Robert M. Grant's review in *Worship* 43:10 (1969), 632–33.

12. Bouyer, *Christian Initiation,* trans. J. R. Foster (London: Burns and Oates, 1960), 7.

13. Bouyer, *Rite and Man* (Notre Dame: University of Notre Dame Press, 1963), 207.

14. Ibid., 211.

15. *Notre Dame Magazine* 17:2 (Spring-Summer 1964), 12–13.

FREDERIC DEBUYST

The Poetry
of the Domestic

I N 1980, AFTER 53 YEARS, the journal *Art d'Église* published its final issue. During the last two decades of the journal's life, Frederic Debuyst, OSB, edited *Art d'Église*—first from the Abbaye de Saint André in Bruges and later from the Monastère Saint André at Ottignies, Belgium. He imbued the magazine with a thematic perspective concerning church architecture that became synonymous both with the journal and his name. Every part of *Art d'Église* was permeated with the conviction that the early Christian house-church, the domestic model of church experience, is the font to which we must return for authenticity in our ecclesiastical architecture as well as our ecclesial experience. Debuyst often referred editorially to "the theme so familiar to our readers," implying that he did not need to reiterate the basic theme to pursue the content of his immediate focus, at whose foundation that familiar theme lay.

Ten years after its demise, the final 20 years of *Art d'Église* rest on library shelves around the world and Frederic Debuyst, the visionary and prophet, weary perhaps of crying in the wilderness, has turned his attention to other interests. The words of prophets have a way, however, of lingering and drifting, hovering somehow in the cosmos, refusing to be mutely bound

between the covers of musty journals. Debuyst found suste-
nance in philosophy, poetry, art, music—expressions of the
inquiring human spirit that beckon new audiences generation
after generation. New travelers look over their shoulders at
those who preceded them, rediscovering in the reflections of
their predecessors the capacity to enter into the most profound
center of their human nature, the place where joy and well-
being erupt. Debuyst's fervent hope that places of worship
might invite worshipers into the communion that is both notably human and eminently holy begs attention anew, even
though the author has collapsed his tent and moved quietly on
his journey.

The Paschal Meeting Room

Debuyst's widest forum was *Art d'Église,* but he also articulated his ideas in other periodicals, as well as in a 1968
book, *Modern Architecture and Christian Celebration.*[1] Here
he set forth the notions that he subsequently and relentlessly
returned to in *Art d'Église* from different perspectives.
Debuyst's context for Christian celebration is the notion of
feast—liturgy is a festive occasion.[2] His philosophical bent
leads him to describe one aspect of feast as Kantian "sublim-
ity," coupled then with the aesthetic category of "graciousness," which he compares with the music of Mozart. The
human phenomenon of feast is the matrix for the Christian
feast, the celebration of eucharist. At eucharist, the memorial,
the *anamnesis* of God's decisive interventions in the past and
the expectation of participation in the resurrection of Christ,
becomes the essential faith reality.

Debuyst names the place where that reality is celebrated the
"paschal meeting room."[3] Thus, he distinguishes between a
place that conveys the restrained joy and expectation of Christian festival and simply an ordinary meeting room. The
distinction is important, because the meeting-room concept

is a significant and radical notion that lends itself to abuse—
the place of worship as merely a gracious domestic living room.

Debuyst attributes his remarkable definition to the Dutch
bishop, Monsignor Bokkars, who in 1965 described a church
as "a kind of great living room, a place where the faithful
come together to meet the Lord, and one another in the
Lord."[4] For Debuyst, the meeting room must transcend the
merely bourgeois living room to become a meeting place red-
olent of domestic hospitality, of expectation, anticipation,
festival.

In both his book and in essays in *Art d'Église,* Debuyst
railed against the impulse toward monumentality in church
architecture. He lamented the all-too-common preference to
preserve the "traditional" image of churches with their imposing presences and symbolic sacredness, their exultation of
power.[5] He also lamented the movement toward all-purpose,
essentially secular spaces that he described as "nonchurches"
and even "nonarchitecture."

It is in the human dwelling place that Debuyst finds the middle ground, his so-called "third force," between traditional
monumentality and neutral, all-purpose "nonarchitecture." In
domestic houses, one finds a scale that honors and nurtures
human life. The house-church, that paschal meeting place of
early Christians, signified for Debuyst "the fundamental
human reality of the house joined to that deeper still, of the
place of Christian assembly, and capable today as in the age of
the apostles of guaranteeing to our churches that atmosphere
of interiority, of radiance, of calm and creative renewal which
comes from their paschal origin and the lasting mystery of
communion and mission for which they exist."[6]

The Domestic as Subversive

The experience of interiority, tranquility and calm Debuyst
finds in the contemplative graciousness and ("almost

gospel . . .") transparency of Japanese houses and especially in the Japanese tea ceremony.[7] Guy Dekeuleneer, author of an article in *Art d'Église* on "Art and Philosophy of the Tea Ceremony," points out that the emphasis in the tea ceremony rests on "harmony, purity, respect and calm." The quality and character of the tea ceremony, the human experience of the ritual, takes precedence over the monumentality of place. Debuyst regrets that the Western inclination is rather toward emphasis on the materiality of things, tending to stifle human spontaneity and freedom.

Burdened by the contemporary Western inclination toward materiality and monumentality, Debuyst turns to domestic spaces as a subversion of and triumph over all that overwhelms the human spirit, limits it or diminishes it by its own presence, pretense, self-consciousness. For Debuyst, the key principles of domestic architecture are their "interiority" and their hospitality.

Interiority, really a philosophical term, is related to intimacy. It deals with the experience of familiarity among a small number of persons, to the extent one knows their personalities, their needs. It deals with what Debuyst calls a "climate of unanimity"[8] that engenders openness. It is not the "style" of the house that makes a difference, but the human scale and intimacy that fosters human interrelationship.

In addition to "interiority," Debuyst sees virtue in the "transparency" of the house. No longer do houses function as massive barrier fortresses against all sorts of external threats. Instead, the outer walls of modern homes are more like movable screens, transparent and open to the outside world. Such a structure is relational, rather than introverted.

The house Debuyst describes, with interiority and transparency offering tranquility, simplicity, openness and harmony, embodies the hospitality so essential to Debuyst's understanding of the experience of church. This is a hospitality that "welcomes and protects without enclosing, which gives intimacy without cutting off from the other people present in the house, which favors the constant fusion of the community as well as the liberty of the single person."[9]

It is clear that the intimacy and hospitality Debuyst seeks is more than a middle-class coziness. It is an environment that lifts people to a spiritual level of experience, to a nobly human existence.

The alliance of the house and place of Christian assembly struck Debuyst as offering the church "a recollected atmosphere of communion and creative openness which it owes to its paschal origins and which it has for mission and function to pass on to us."[10] He recognized much opposition to the idea of the house-church as a model for Christian churches. The objection is partly because of a banality in the way many experience domestic spaces, but also because of Debuyst's observation that "the West seems to have lost sight of the fact that architecture is much less an affair of buildings and prestige than of living spaces, *human* spaces in the full sense of the word."[11]

The Human Scale of Church and Life

In addition to the more conceptual aspects of the place for Christian worship, Debuyst concerned himself with the particularities of the arrangement of the assembly and the appointments in the church.[12] Even before Vatican II was over, he saw the importance of the location of the altar in a central position in relationship to the people, with sufficient openness and space for movement of the people and for freedom for liturgical action. He pleaded for spaces and furnishings that honor human proportions.

The intimacy and transparency of which Debuyst spoke, and the profundity of total hospitality he sought in our experience of church, is a poetry that transcends the materiality of things and even place. He could describe the inner richness lying behind an unpretentious exterior in a "Eulogy of the Incognito," calling for a "being" that must go beyond the "appearing," so that simple rites of hospitality become at eucharist "a fully religious and human sharing what one has and especially what one is, in imitation of the Lord."[13]

The poetry of everyday experience formed the basis of a whole series of his articles in *Art d'Église*. A phenomenology of the walk becomes a lengthy reflection on the journey of life and the opportunities within the simplest human experiences for surprise and joy. Having entered freely and openly into the journey, one's perceptions of apparently simple and ordinary things change, so that returns become in fact new beginnings, as happened for the apostles who made that journey to Emmaus.[14]

Though articulated more than 20 years ago and reflected on during his entire tenure as editor of *Art d'Église,* Frederic Debuyst's convictions about the essentially human nature of both worship and worship spaces still are fresh, compelling and provocative. They deserve an attentive contemporary audience.

■ *Marchita Mauck*

NOTES

1. Frederic Debuyst, *Modern Architecture and Christian Celebration* (Richmond VA: John Knox Press, 1968).

2. Ibid., 10.

3. Ibid., 19.

4. Ibid., 9.

5. Frederic Debuyst, "In Praise of the Uncertain," *Art d'Église* 193 (1980), A.

6. Frederic Debuyst, "A la recherche d'une 'troisième force' III," *Art d'Église* 149 (1969), 353 ff. (English translation, A.)

7. See Guy Dekeuleneer, "Some Notes on the Art and Philosophy of the Tea Ceremony," *Art d'Église* 147 (1969/2), 289 ff. Debuyst remarks on Dekeuleneer's article in "Éloge de la fête intime," *Art d'Église* 147 (1969/2), 318–20, which was republished in English as "The Art of the Intimate Feast," *The Living Light* 6 (Summer 1969), 82–88.

8. Debuyst, *Modern Architecture and Christian Celebration,* in a chapter entitled "A Short Phenomenology of the Modern House," 34.

9. Ibid., 35.

10. Frederic Debuyst, "Towards a New House-Church," *Art d'Église* 162 (1973), B.

11. Ibid.

12. Frederic Debuyst, "Church Architecture and Christian Celebration," *Liturgical Arts* 32 (November, 1963/1), 2–9; *Modern Architecture and Christian Celebration,* 54–67.

13. Frederic Debuyst, "Éloge de l'Incognito," *Art d'Église* 150 (1970), 1–15. (English translation, C.)

14. Frederic Debuyst, "Invitation au voyage," *Art d'Église* 145 (1968), 225–45.

JOSEPH GELINEAU
Troubadour

"O PERATIONAL MODEL," Père Gelineau kept telling me in French. "You must think about the eucharistic prayer in its operational model." I wasn't sure what he meant. The year was 1978; I was in England at a Universa Laus meeting and this was the first time I had met him. Gelineau pulled out a paper napkin and drew this figure:

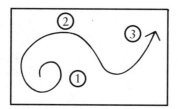

Pointing to number one on his crude drawing, he insisted, "The introductory dialogue must gather the assembly into the initial act of praise which climaxes in the Holy, Holy." The light in the room was low and Genevieve Noufflard was translating as fast as he spoke. "The prayer dives into the intensity of the institutional narrative"—he traced his pencil along the line next past number two—"and climaxes again with the assembly proclaiming the great act of assent in the Amen."

My first meeting with him was vintage Gelineau—intense, insightful and heavily laden with the idioms of his own language, almost impossible to translate fully into mine.

Joseph Gelineau was born in Anjou, France, in 1920, the son of a wine maker. He entered the Jesuits in 1941, studying theology at Lyon-Fouviere and then earning a diploma in music composition from the École Cesar Franck, Paris. His dissertation for the doctorate in theology was on the forms of psalmody in the Syriac churches during the fourth and fifth centuries.

The "Gelineau Psalms"

During his student years, he began writing a number of short articles for *La Maison Dieu* on "Popular Chant in France" (1947–1949). At that time, all liturgical music was in Latin, but Gelineau was exploring ways to sing the psalms in the French vernacular. He hit on the idea of using a "sprung" melody, in which the rhythm of the verses was based on the regular recurrence of accented (or stressed) syllables. The number of these stresses was fixed for each line (usually three), but the number of syllables between the stresses was variable. This approach was first published as *Cinquante psaumes et quatre cantiques* in 1954 by the Centre de Pastorale Liturgique.[1] In some circles, it met with almost instant success and became known worldwide as the "Gelineau psalms."

The method combines a consistent melodic formula (easy to learn) with flexible adaptability to different verses. By contrast, the psalm singing in the Gregorian chant of the day was repetitive and without reference to the text's meaning. Any words could be set to the psalm tones. Gelineau's method offered the possibility of emphasizing the meaning of the text. It also provided a way of singing the newly published "Jerusalem Bible" translation.

Two years later, an English translation of this psalm project appeared. The new "Grail" text was used; the project was led by Clifford Howell, Gregory Murray, Alexander Jones and Joseph Samson. This version adapted some of the antiphons to "fit" the English text, but some melodies that worked in French didn't translate well into English. Nevertheless, in England and the United States, the Gelineau psalms quickly spread to the seminaries and became identified as part of the liturgical movement. The importance of these compositions for promoting the liturgical movement and preparing the way for the possibility of the reforms at Vatican II cannot be overestimated.

Alongside the important historical and scholarly works that provided a justification for the liturgical movement, the popularity of these antiphons and psalm verses demonstrated that the vernacular language could be sung—with reverence, in a popular style, and with meaning. Arguments against the vernacular melted when hearing these psalms sung. And sung they were. Throughout Europe, there were successful adaptations of the "sprung melody" into diverse languages. And the "melody" worked in almost every language. There is no doubt that the Gelineau psalms spread the liturgical movement in a new and dynamic way. Gelineau went on to publish an additional 30 psalms and eventually a complete psalter,[2] but none of them reached the popularity of the first 24 psalms and four canticles.

Studies in Music and Liturgy

Gelineau joined the Centre de Pastorale Liturgique in the late 1950s and began writing a number of articles on the psalms, antiphons and the role of the music in the liturgy.[3] His initial interest was in the processional psalm chants (entrance, presentation, communion) as well as the psalm between the readings. His articles emphasized the diversity of development in our tradition.

The important pastoral music journal *Église qui Chante* (which he helped found) disseminated his thinking not only about the psalms, but about the role of music in the liturgy, including a sung eucharistic prayer. Gelineau noted that the Syriac eucharistic prayers used a number of musical interventions by the assembly and there was no reason to limit the interventions in the Roman rite to three (Holy, Memorial Acclamation and Amen).

In 1962 (the year before the convening of Vatican II), he published two important works: the first, *Le Guide du psautier de la Bible de Jerusalem,* with his good friend, the poet Didier Rimaud, and the second *Chant et musique dans le culte chrétien: Principles, lois et applications.*[4] In this second book, Gelineau developed the principles of music in the liturgy, but he drew the bold conclusion that Gregorian chant melodies could not be adapted to vernacular languages. Appearing before the discussions of Vatican II began, this was highly controverted among the musicians of his day. Some it startled, others it enraged.

Before Vatican II, European musicians had gathered at the IIIe Congres International de Musique Sacrée in Paris in July 1957; the vast majority had maintained a strict position that Gregorian chant and sacred polyphony were the supreme treasures of Catholic music and should be maintained at all costs, especially in the face of the growing interest in using vernacular languages in the liturgy. In *Chant et musique,* Gelineau took the opposite position. This created a rift in the European liturgical musical scene that exists to this day. On one side are those who support the use of the vernacular and the development of new musical forms appropriate to the demands of vernacular languages in the liturgy; on the other side stands the Consortium International Musicae Sacrae, which defends the statement in the *Constitution of the Sacred Liturgy:* "The church acknowledges Gregorian chant as distinctive of the Roman liturgy; therefore, other things being equal, it should be given pride of place in the liturgical services" (116).

Vatican II and Its Aftermath

Between 1963 and 1979, Gelineau, together with other European scholars, contributed to the basic thinking and the refinement of liturgical development that we identify as the liturgical reforms of Vatican II.

Gelineau's interest and expertise had expanded beyond the psalms to the entire liturgy. He served on the Consilium to implement Vatican II's reform. After Vatican II, there was a desire in Europe to get on with the task of developing music for the vernacular liturgies, but the existing music organizations were set against any exploration beyond chant and polyphony. Their meetings centered on whether the vernacular should be incorporated into the liturgy or not.

In 1965, Gelineau joined Helmut Hucke and Gerhardt Track from Germany, Bernard Huijbers from Holland, Gino Stefani from Italy and other European composers and musicians to form Universa Laus (UL), an international study group for liturgy and music. Its purpose was to provide a forum where ideas learned from the implementation of the new vernacular liturgy and its music could be shared from country to country.

Throughout Europe, Gelineau became more and more identified with those interested in promoting melodies that accompanied vernacular texts. Through annual meetings of UL, ideas for creative musical forms were demonstrated, debated, refined and represented for further discussion. In 1980, UL published a manifesto of its findings about the nature of music in the liturgy.

Pastoral Practice

Characteristically, Gelineau's work always has been carried out in a parish setting. He was associated for many years with St. Ignace, a community located in downtown Paris. Surprisingly, that church's facade is a retail store, though its interior retains the traditional size and shape. The community was formed as a "community of choice" (i.e., people came because they wanted to be part of what was happening) and the community was not surprised by new ritual forms or music. The musical resources of surrounding Paris were attracted and, thus, placed at Gelineau's disposal a potpourri of talent and challenge. Jacques Berthier (composer of the very popular canons and rounds of Taizé) served as organist and Genevieve Noufflard often served as flutist. Music appropriate to children was developed and sung by C. Barrenton and Eugenio Costa; liturgies for anointings, baptisms and Holy Week were explored.

More recently, Gelineau has moved to the outskirts of Paris and assumed pastoral leadership in six small parish communities, exploring the demands of limited musical resources and the challenges of forming and promoting lay leadership.

Gelineau's Ideas

Gelineau's influence as a teacher at the Centre de Pastorale Liturgique in Paris as well as a lecturer at various congresses has been immense. His ability to think on his feet, with clarity, insight and comprehensiveness, appears remarkable to anyone who encounters him.

He has developed a considerable number of insights about music and the liturgy, which can be found, in addition to a bibliography of Gelineau's own writings, in Charles Pottie's *A More Profound Alleluia*.[5] In the Universa Laus Manifesto, Gelineau maintains, for instance:

> Music . . . is not of the essence of liturgy . . . but it enters into the rite as a constitutive element of the normal and perfect form of the word in the liturgy. . . . Thus, although music is not of itself to be considered as a rite, song is in fact a "part" of the liturgy in the same way as reading or prayer; it is, moreover, a part necessary to the integrity of the rites.[6]

Our popularization of this idea is that "musical liturgy is normative."

> Gelineau also describes music as a continuing task: Music . . . is never simply "something done, once for all." It always needs to be redone, reinterpreted, re-created. It can only exist when someone makes it. Music, like the rite, is both repetition and innovation. All its evocative power rests in the fruitful interplay of these two aspects.[7]

Throughout his life, Gelineau has explored the philosophical and human aspects of music and has made a unique contribution to this thinking. He has reemphasized the important contribution and the severe limitations that a *particular* performance places on music and thus has stressed the role of culture and the musician in music-making.

In the period of experimentation and change immediately following Vatican II, he was intent on exploring the roles of change and creativity in the liturgy. He wrote:

> Even if the rite is laid down, it is like an inner model of a meaningful act whose form must constantly be reinvented or modified. Even if the rite is by nature "repetitive," it is never pure repetition. At the level of the realities of the faith, the liturgy always is newness, new covenant, paschal renewal. So shouldn't something of this newness be shown at the level of signs? New being and new appearance are inseparable.[8]

These ideas, penned during the rush of the changes after Vatican II, require a thoughtful reexamination today in the light of our current liturgical climate of "settling in," with so much emphasis on liturgy as ritual-to-be-done-repeatedly.

In an effort to validate his constant search for what changes and what remains the same in the liturgy, Gelineau developed some unique language that is quite useful today:

> What I call "the operational model" is the received capacity of reproducing an expressive and meaningful way of behaving based on a pattern and taking into account differences of time, place, people and the available abilities and resources.

The eucharistic prayer in the apostolic tradition is . . . a model; a psalm-tone is a formula-model; . . . the structure of the Liturgy of the Word . . . is a rite model. A model can be applied to separate rites or to ritual sequences. It is both fidelity in substance and the life of the forms bearing meaning.[9]

Gelineau's Influence

Gelineau's lifework began with the psalms and their music and reached out to the whole liturgy (especially the eucharistic prayer). His influences have followed these same patterns. He remains as a teacher combining these interests at the Centre de Pastorale Liturgique, Universa Laus, St. Ignace and his six small parish settings. His writings about liturgy and music have been carried through *Église qui Chante* and *Musique et liturgie* and in his 18 books and more than 100 articles. His psalm settings provided the basis for vernacular liturgy; his most recent compositions, "Psalm 104" and a requiem, integrate his current compositional ideas about religious music and performance.

Gelineau has a unique way of combining music theory with its liturgical role and then bringing all of that to pastoral practice. His liturgical scholarship and his compositional genius, combined with his pastoral practice, place him as the leading force in the liturgical movement of the twentieth century in the area of music in liturgy.

■ *Virgil C. Funk*

NOTES

1. In 1955, a second edition was published by Les Éditions du Cerf.

2. *Thirty Psalms and Two Canticles,* trans. from the Hebrew and arranged for singing to the psalmody of J. Gelineau (London: The Grail, 1958); *The Grail/Gelineau Psalter: 150 Psalms and 18 Canticles,* comp. and ed. J. Robert Carroll (Chicago: GIA Publications, 1972).

3. Cf. especially the series of nine articles, "Fonction et signification des principaux chants de la liturgie," *Église que Chante* (1959–1961), vols. 17–26.

4. *Le Guide du psautier de la Bible de Jerusalem* (Paris: Éditions du Cerf, 1962); *Chant et musique dans le culte chrétien* (Paris: Éditions Fleuris, 1962). (English translation, *Voices and Instruments in Christian Worship: Principles, Laws, Applications,* trans. Clifford Howell (London: Burns and Oates, 1964).

5. Charles S. Pottie, *A More Profound Alleluia: Gelineau and Routley on Music in Christian Worship* (Washington, D.C.: The Pastoral Press, 1964).

6. Joseph Gelineau, "Balancing Performance and Participation," *Pastoral Music* 3:5 (1979), 22. The author is indebted for a summary of these ideas to Pottie, *A More Profound Alleluia.*

7. "What No Ear Has Heard," *Music and Liturgy* 5 (1979), 89.

8. Joseph Gelineau, *The Liturgy Today and Tomorrow,* trans. Dinah Livingston (New York: Paulist Press, 1978), 90.

9. "What No Ear Has Heard," 90.

BERNARD BOTTE

He Wandered into Liturgy

ITH HOMESPUN BLUNTNESS, Bernard Botte admitted that he assimilated his vocation as a liturgical scholar from some very modest contacts with early twentieth-century liturgical pioneers: "My collaboration in the liturgical movement [just before World War I] was completely material, especially consisting in carrying chairs and washing dishes all day long."[1] He even found no trouble in claiming, "I was a biblical scholar who wandered into liturgy."[2] He lets us know elsewhere in his memoirs that his publications were written almost *malgré lui* and only on invitation from others: "When I look at my own bibliography, everything I see was requested by some publisher, magazine editor or congress organizer."[3] If we were to take him at his word, we'd be tempted to think he must have occupied at best a marginal position in the movement for liturgical renewal. That is not the case. A look at that bibliography shows 227 articles, books and book reviews that deal with the most diverse and crucial issues affecting the field of liturgy in our century.

When, then, was Bernard Botte's place among liturgical pioneers? What brought him to the contemporary phase of the quest for living liturgical practice and spirituality? At least at the beginning, he benefited from happenstance and the good fortune of being in the right spot at the right time.

Early Days

B ernard Botte began his monastic life in 1912 at the abbey of Mont César soon after the modern liturgical movement was launched by another Benedictine monk, Lambert Beauduin. With his elementary and secondary school studies behind him, marked by no particular awareness of any need for something such as liturgical renewal, as he wrote: "As innocent as could be I sang full blast along with the others: 'O Jesus you enflame me with celestial ecstasies,' or 'Fly, fly angels of prayer'",[4] young Henri Botte joined the Benedictines in their new Belgian foundation, not far from the world-famous Catholic University of Louvain. Here he came to know and assist Lambert Beauduin and to benefit from the lectures at the Liturgical Weeks organized by Beauduin. Botte found all around him the growing ferment toward better liturgical celebration and understanding or what one historian has called the "liturgical movement at Louvain."[5]

For his own field of specialization, Botte took on the study of oriental languages and gained familiarity with ancient texts that would enable him to guide students, bishops and his readers years later. This knowledge gave him access to many sources of tradition and the varied cultural trappings they carried. He saw how much evolution marked the church's pastoral use of language and, therefore, how one ought to act toward the revitalization of liturgical practice by working for reinstating the vernacular.[6] His own pastoral sensitivity grew through the contacts he made with diocesan clergy who attended the abbey's liturgical lectures,[7] through a five-year stint in the infantry during World War I and through service as a chaplain in a Belgian orphanage before the outbreak of World War II.

Contributor and Collaborator

Here is a brief look at some of his writings and his work on churchwide commissions.

Basing his research on careful attention to the ancient sources of rites, Botte often published erudite analyses of liturgical formulae. He did not let matters rest, though, with minutiae. He drew on these monographs when he eventually published a work of major importance for liturgical scholarship and practice, his critical edition of Hippolytus's *Apostolic Tradition.*

His work appeared in various German and French periodicals and series. The second book in the *Études liturgiques* series was his collaborative effort with the renowned Dutch Latinist Christine Mohrmann: *L'ordinaire de la messe: Texte critique, traduction et études.* In English-language publications, The Liturgical Press provided access to two papers of his on orders and the "collegiate character of the episcopate and priesthood" when it published *The Sacrament of Holy Orders* in 1957. *The Church at Prayer* also brought some of his writing to English-speaking liturgical audiences. He was called on to provide prefaces to the works of other eminent liturgical scholars, as with the French editions of Odo Casel's *La fête de Paques dans l'église des Pères* and of Cyrille Vogel's *Introduction aux sources de l'histoire du culte chrétien au moyen âge.*[8]

Vogel and Botte met frequently at those international study meetings that did much to prepare the way for Vatican II.[9] Botte was asked to serve on preconciliar work groups that were to draft texts on the vernacular, concelebration and the teaching of the liturgy.[10] While he did not attend Vatican II as a *peritus,* he knew well what its main tasks were regarding liturgy:

> The *Constitution on the Sacred Liturgy* had to be the liturgical movement's harvest. The direction of the reform proposed by the Council fathers was supposed to have a theological basis

and rest on authentic tradition, but at the same time keep in mind pastoral needs and adapt itself to the contemporary world—in particular to watch out for the simplicity and truthfulness of the rites.[11]

Botte was assigned to the Commission for the Implementation of the Conciliar Constitution on the Sacred Liturgy.[12] The work groups he directed devised several key changes in actual liturgical practice of the Roman church. Pierre-Marie Gy, his immediate successor director of the Paris liturgy institute, pointed to these accomplishments when Botte died in 1980:

> Thanks to him Eucharistic Prayer II stands to the Roman sacramentary next to the fourth-century Roman Canon; the ordination prayer for bishops is exactly the same as that of the *Apostolic Tradition;* and the formula for confirmation in the Roman Rite is taken from the liturgical tradition of the Greek church.[13]

Botte took satisfaction from his contribution to the reforms after Vatican II: "We will have to wait for hindsight to judge properly the value of the reform. I am convinced that the judgment of history will be favorable."[14] He also left the door open for further work by others: "The reform, although the result of the liturgical movement, is above all else a starting point. It is a plan for the future, and it would be a risky illusion to expect immediate, spectacular results from it."[15]

Innovative Mentor

Botte always was seeking avenues for instruction and dialogue. One such initiative was a four-year cycle of summer-school courses designed mainly for seminary professors of liturgy, those who would instruct future generations of presiders and preachers. From 1953 to 1967, he organized these catch-up courses for those already appointed to teach liturgy in French-speaking seminaries (many of whom lacked any background in the study of liturgy themselves).[16] At the time, liturgy often was the study of rubrics and—Botte learned this from a question-naire sent to seminaries—the seminary staff person most often assigned to be liturgy professor was the bursar.

For several years, Botte was an associate of the team that ran Paris's Centre de Pastorale Liturgique. With them, he started a graduate program in liturgy in 1956. This now is known as the Institut Supérieur de Liturgie (ISL). Here students from around the world could develop the overall vision and skills for teaching liturgical science to others.[17] Botte's direction of the ISL ceased in 1964, but the basic approach he devised has continued to produce people who have influenced contemporary liturgical studies and practice on several continents. A list of students would include Adrian Nocent (Italy), Sean Swayne (Ireland), Paul De Clerck (Belgium), Hector Muñoz (Argentina), Niels Rasmussen (Denmark), Michael Amaladoss (India), Dominique Dye (France) and many Americans: Aelred Tegels, Patrick Regan, Gerard Austin, Louis Weil, Allan Fitzgerald, John B. Ryan, this writer, Philip Sandstrom and John Gurrieri.

Botte's familiarity with the cultural milieus of the ancient patriarchates of the eastern Mediterranean earned for him the trust of some Orthodox theologians at the Russian emigré school of theology, Saint-Serge Theological Institute of Paris. They invited him to plan a Liturgical Week for 1953 that would bring them together with such leading non-Orthodox liturgical and patristic scholars as Max Thurian and Joachim Jeremias (Evangelical), F. L. Cross and C. W. Dugmore (Anglican) and the Roman Catholics Lambert Beauduin, Bernard Capelle, Olivier Rousseau, Alphonse Raes and Monsignor Khouri-Sarkis. These summer meetings continued; Botte participated actively for more than 20 years. The proceedings of the weeks still are being published.

Living with and for the Church

The mainspring of the efforts Botte made for liturgical renewal was his attachment to the church. The church housed the mystery made available by God for the salvation of humankind. Botte was willing to carry on the work as best he could, ever conscious that it primarily was God's own work in Christ under the Holy Spirit's guidance.[18] This conviction always brought him to consolation and to the confidence that it was worth striving against the inertia and the obstacles to renewal. His own words (from the closing lines of those memoirs that trace so engagingly the entire arc of the liturgical movement) would best sum up his trusting generosity:

> Nevertheless, I remain optimistic, because, above all else, I have faith in the church. . . . During the Council the Holy Spirit visibly inspired in the church the desire to purify itself and to return to its ideal. We should believe that the Spirit is still there, according to Christ's promise, and that he will complete the work he began.[19]

■ *John Sullivan*

NOTES

1. Bernard Botte, *From Silence to Participation: An Insider's View of Liturgical Renewal,* trans. John Sullivan (Washington DC: Pastoral Press, 1988), 26.

2. Ibid., 46.

3. Ibid., xi.

4. Ibid., 2.

5. Olivier Rousseau, *The Progress of the Liturgy: An Historical Sketch from the Beginning of the Nineteenth Century to the Pontificate of Pius X* (Westminster MD: Newman Press, 1951), 161–70.

6. Bernard Botte, "Vatican II et le renouveau liturgique," *Au Coeur de l'Afrique* 6 (1974), 306–8.

7. He shared the attitude of Beauduin in the following lines of *Silence to Participation,* 22: "He didn't want the magazine [*Questions liturgiques et paroissiales*] to become a technical publication reserved for specialists. He really wanted its audience to be the parish clergy, those who were in contact with the people."

8. See the English-language edition, bereft though it may be of Botte's French preface, *Medieval Liturgy: An Introduction to the Sources,* rev. and trans. William Storey and Niels Rasmussen (Washington DC: Pastoral Press, 1986).

9. See Botte, "The Movement Broadens," *From Silence to Participation,* 75–84.

10. See Botte, "Toward the Council," *From Silence to Participation,* 115–23.

11. Botte, *From Silence to Participation,* 122.

12. See Botte, "The Consilium," *From Silence to Participation,* 125–31.

13. Pierre-Marie Gy, "Dom Bernard Botte (1893–1980)," *La Maison Dieu* 141 (1980), 167–68.

14. Botte, *From Silence to Participation,* 131.

15. Ibid., 168.

16. See Botte, "Teaching the Liturgy," *From Silence to Participation,* 85–91.

17. See Botte, "The Paris Institut Supérieur de Liturgie," *From Silence to Participation,* 93–106.

18. Characteristic and very apropos are Botte's words reported for us in the homily for his funeral by his abbot, Dom Ambrosius Verheul, "Hommage à Dom Bernard Botte, OSB, 1893–1980," *Questions liturgiques* 61 (1980), 84–85:

> I still remember having let him read some new eucharistic prayers in Flemish to have his opinion of them. When he heard the prayer, "Enable us to make of this earth a new earth," he remarked with a certain amount of vigor, "What's this? Who's renewing the earth? Is it us? Or God himself?" Father Bernard had a profound sense of the primacy of God, the God of the Bible, the God of the liturgy.

19. Botte, *From Silence to Participation,* 170.

BALTHASAR FISCHER
Godfather of the
Liturgical Movement

F THERE IS ANY LIVING LITURGIST deserving of the title "Godfather" of the liturgical movement, this person would be Balthasar N. Fischer. He is one of the last of a distinguished generation of pioneers who championed the renewal that gave birth to the *Constitution on the Sacred Liturgy* at Vatican II and the subsequent liturgical reforms. The author of three books and more than 500 articles, the professor from Trier also has served as *Doktorvater* (dissertation director) for more than 32 doctoral candidates. These include such leading European liturgists as Bruno Kleinheyer, Hansjorg Auf der Maur, Reiner Kaczynski and Andreas Heinz; in this country, Aidan Kavanagh, John Gallen, Mark Searle, Lawrence Madden and John McKenna are numbered among his more noteworthy students. This writer counts among his greatest blessings the privilege to be the 22nd of the "doctor's children."

Through his visiting professorships at Notre Dame University, St. John's University in New York City and Seton Hall University, Fischer has become the "grandfather" of many American students who have been privileged to study under him. Although he lectured as early as 1950 in the Notre Dame summer liturgy program under Michael Mathis, most of these visits to America took place after his retirement from Trier in 1980; as professor emeritus he then had more time to travel abroad.

The Teacher's Teacher

Balthasar Fischer was born on September 3, 1912, in Bitburg, a city in the Eifel region north of Trier. He is the oldest of three sons born to Balthasar and Susanna Fischer. His father was an elementary school teacher in Bitburg. The name Balthasar is held in high esteem in this part of Germany because the relics of the magi are reputedly preserved in the Cologne cathedral. The faith and integrity that so mark his life are found first in his upbringing in a Christian home. Fischer attended elementary school at Bitburg and secondary schools at Bitburg and Trier. In 1931, he entered the major seminary at Trier to study for the diocesan priesthood.

From 1933 to 1936, he studied at the Canisianum of the University of Innsbruck, where he wrote a doctoral thesis under Josef A. Jungmann entitled "Minor Orders in the Letters of Gregory the Great."[1] Jungmann always regarded Fischer as his foremost disciple and favorite student. Fischer for his part credits Jungmann for opening up to him a whole new vista of the richness of the church's life or worship. For example, Fischer relates how flabbergasted he was to learn from Jungmann that it is not the reserved sacrament that sanctifies the space we call church, but rather the presence of the holy people of God.

From the shy and scholarly Jungmann, Fischer learned the method of painstaking historical research, not research for its own sake but research in the service of the church. From Jungmann came Fischer's fascination with popular piety and its relationship to liturgical spirituality. In Innsbruck, Fischer also studied patrology under Hugo Rahner. Although the talented brother of Karl Rahner did not teach liturgiology, he made the

Trier seminarian feel at home in the climate in which the liturgy developed. Patristics always has been Fischer's favorite "neighbor" discipline.

In 1940, Fischer began to prepare for his habilitation, a kind of second doctorate necessary to become a professor at a German university. At the Academy for Liturgy and Monasticism at Maria Laach, Abbot Ildefons Herwegen's spellbinding lectures on the "mystery" embodied in the Rule of St. Benedict and in ancient Christian art made a lasting impression on the young theologian. The habilitation was completed at the University of Bonn under the direction of Theodor Klauser, the foremost pupil of Franz Josef Doelger.

Fischer's thesis was entitled "The History of the Christian Interpretation of Psalms 1–20 from the New Testament to Origen." His inauguration lecture, "Die Psalmenfrommigkeit der Martyrerkirche," was translated into French for *La Maison Dieu* and into English for the very first issue of *Theology Digest*.[2]

Praying the psalms in the light of Christ has been a lifelong interest with Fischer. Christ is the one who prays the psalms as we join in his prayer to the Father as the body of Christ. At times, however, Christ also is the addressee of the psalms to whom the church prays as his bride. Indeed, the very role of Christ in liturgical prayer all together has been another one of Fischer's concerns. He rightly contends that Jungmann's classic study on *The Place of Christ in Liturgical Prayer* should have been entitled "The Place of Christ in Liturgical *Presidential* Prayer," inasmuch as the liturgy attests to the fact that Christ is the addressee of many nonpresidential prayers such as the *Kyrie eleison* and others.

Teacher, Reformer, Homilist

Balthasar Fischer was ordained to the Roman Catholic priesthood for the service of the diocese of Trier on

August 2, 1936. From 1945 to 1947, he lectured in liturgy at the major seminary in Trier and from 1947 to 1950, he was professor of liturgy at the same seminary, thus occupying the first chair for liturgy established in Germany. In 1950, the theological faculty was established in this seminary; for the next 30 years, Fischer would serve as the professor of liturgy. This was the period of his most fruitful academic activity and pastoral outreach.

In addition to guiding the dissertations of his many doctoral students, from 1965 to 1975, he also was the director of the postconciliar international study courses at the Liturgical Institute in Trier, which many American students attended. A master pedagogue in the classroom, he would punctuate his material with illustrations and stories. Perhaps this was the homiletics professor in him, for he also held this position at Trier from 1951 to 1964. He taught his students and future teachers the very art of teaching. "Always begin a lecture with the sharing of a human experience," he advised.

In 1961, Balthasar Fischer was invited to participate in the Preparatory Commission for Liturgy at Vatican II. After Vatican II began, he was the theological adviser for the Bishop of Trier. His most enduring achievements were accomplished as a consultor for the Consilium for the Implementation of the *Constitution on the Sacred Liturgy.* More specifically, from 1964 to 1970, he was the head of the *coetus* (working group) entrusted with the reform of the initiation rites, namely, the rites of Christian initiation of adults and of infant baptism. With customary humility, Fischer marveled at his selection as chair and surmises that the Consilium was looking for a German professor to head the group.

From the outset, the group wrestled with the problem of archeologism: What to do with the ancient process of becoming a Christian replete with its scrutinies and mystagogy? The group gradually came to a consensus that the catechumenate itself is a timeless pattern that has both time-bound and timeless elements. For example, pastoral experience led the group to provide for the signing of all the senses during the rite of entry into the catechumenate. On the other hand, the dialogue with Satan found that the great exorcisms of the past easily could lead to an archaic misconception of possession by Satan that would not be in keeping with the insights of contemporary theology into original and personal sin. As a result, the language was changed from an imprecatory (cursing) to a deprecatory exorcism: The Lord is bidden to liberate us from the bonds of Satan.[3]

For many years, Fischer presided at a weekly Mass with children at a parish in Trier. His students often would accompany him to observe another pastoral side of their mentor. In his collection of homilies on liturgical subjects, *Signs, Words & Gestures,* much of the material is addressed to children and treats such questions as "Why do we take holy water as we enter church?", "Why do we stand for the gospel and make the sign of the cross?" and "Why do we offer a sign of peace to one another before communion?"[4] It came as no surprise that in 1971 Fischer was named head of the Roman commission that prepared the *Directory for Masses with Children* and the three new Eucharistic Prayers for Masses with Children, all of which now are part of the sacramentary.

Balthasar Fischer has received many honors, ecclesiastical and academic. In 1961, Pope John XXIII named him a domestic prelate. Fischer served in 1982 as president of the international Societas Liturgica. Two *festschrifts* have been published to honor him: *Zeichen des Glaubens,* essays on baptism and confirmation, on the occasion of his 60th birthday;[5] and *Heute Segnen,* a study of blessings, on the occasion of his 75th birthday.[6] He has been awarded two honorary doctorates: from the theological faculty of Mainz (together with the then Archbishop of Krakow, Karol Wojtyla) in 1977 and, more recently, from The Catholic University of America in the fall of 1988. In 1989, the North American Academy of Liturgy presented Fischer with its distinguished Berakah Award.

This writer had the opportunity to meet Fischer during the fall semester of 1988 when he was the distinguished visiting professor at Immaculate Conception Seminary at Seton Hall University. Without wishing to turn this biographical sketch into a hagiographical reading, I can say that I have seen his greatness of spirit.

Balthasar Fischer enters fully into life. While with us at Seton Hall, he offered a course on the RCIA to some 80 students: laity, seminarians, religious and priests. His lectures were greeted with spontaneous applause after each session. He participated in virtually every aspect of seminary life: presiding at the liturgy, taking meals with students, attending the weekly practice of new liturgical music and giving spiritual conferences. He often would sit in on my classes and at the end would offer his own reaction, which frequently included stories about the liturgical pioneers he knew personally or events that transpired at Vatican II. He combed the seminary library discovering books of which we were unaware and surfacing titles that we should order. He availed himself of the cultural events of the university, attended a poetry reading by Stephen Sondheim and took a weekly swim at the recreation center on campus. He even went to a New York Giants football game. And there were also the side trips to Winnipeg, Washington, Notre Dame, Collegeville and nearby Brooklyn and Queens. All this at 76 years of age! A fluent linguist in Latin, French and English, his next project is to master Spanish so that he can read Teresa of Avila in the original!

How does he enter so fully into life? The reason is his enormous love of people. *Menschenfreundlich* is an adjective that could have been coined to describe his life. Everyone remembers the time that they first met him. One feels instinctively drawn toward the man. "Balti" has become a personal friend to many of his students. As Jack McKenna put it: "I went to

Trier to study liturgy; he taught me a lot more about life." He is able to relate to everyone with warmth, grace and wit. His conversation can hold a dinner party spellbound and unwilling to leave. He can talk to simple people at a parish dinner and make them feel important; he also can thoroughly charm fellow scholars. He seems to know everyone yet always is eager to make new contacts and friends. For a priest formed in an era when this was not a priority, he shows a special sensitivity to women and their important place in the church.

He is known for his empowerment of lay vocations in the church through the axiom often attributed to him as formational for ministers of the RCIA: "Not the shepherds make sheep. Sheep make sheep." His universal vision extends from his passion for ecumenism—he has been a permanent guest of the Lutheran Liturgical Congress in Germany since 1976—to his success in locating in New Jersey a Jewish chum from his childhood days in Bitburg who emigrated to the United States before the Holocaust. We also now know that he was behind the belated insertion into the schema on the *Constitution on the Liturgy* of what has become number 32, namely: no special honors to be paid to private persons or classes of persons. Actually, the wording he originally proposed was much stronger:

> In the celebration of the sacraments, at funerals and blessings, the liturgical ceremonies, vessels and vestments should without exception be the same for the rich and the poor, since they both share the dignity of the baptized, and so that it is clear in the Catholic liturgy that God is no respecter of persons.[7]

All of this information points to a very edifying spirituality that derives its life and nourishment from the wellspring of the church's worship. Fischer's goodness and compassion make him a role model for priests and other ministers. He once confided that the happiest times of his more than 50 years of priesthood were spent as an associate pastor and chaplain in a parish during the otherwise dark days of World War II. He is humble and unpretentious about all his remarkable scholarly achievements, a humility that enables him to laugh at himself and to live with a sense of holy indifference before God.

Fischer has a remarkable trust in the power of the Holy Spirit at work in the church, a grace that even our human weakness and sin is unable to frustrate. Such faith finds expression in his homily on the meaning of the sealing with the sign of the cross as enacted in the baptism of infants:

> Isn't it marvelous that we can say of a baptized child: This child will live and die as one sealed with the sign of the cross; at the end this child will take refuge in him who is stronger than death and all the powers of darkness! Parents cannot remain permanently with their children, but the Lord will be with them all days. And some day he will lead his "sealed" followers through death to the indestructible life of those who are in the Father's house with Christ for all eternity.[8]

■ *Charles W. Gusmer*

NOTES

1. Balthasar Fischer, "Der Niedere Klerus bei Gregor dem Grossen. Ein Beitrag zur Gesschichte der Ordines Minores," *Zeitschrift für katholische Theologie* 62 (1938), 37–75.

2. Balthasar Fischer, "Die Psalmenfrommigkeit der Martyrerkirche," *Theologisches Jahrbuch* (1960), 335–51; "Le Christ dans les Psaumes. La devotion auz psaumes dan l'église des martyrs," *La Maison Dieu* 27 (1951), 86–109; "Christ in the Psalms," *Theology Digest* 1 (1953), 53–57. Fortunately, all Fischer's articles about the Christian understanding of the psalms recently have been published in a collection edited by his successor to the Trier chair of liturgy, Andreas Heinz, *Die Psalmen als Stimme der Kirche* (Trier: Paulinus, 1982). For a more recent series of meditations on the psalms of morning and evening prayer, see Balthasar Fischer, *Dich will ich suchen von Tag zu Tag* (Freiburg: Herder, 1985). Finally, we are indebted to the Notre Dame Center for Pastoral Liturgy for making accessible a synopsis of his thought on this matter in Balthasar Fischer, "Praying the Psalms in the Light of Christ," *Assembly* 15/3 (1989), 434–36.

3. These insights are drawn from Fischer's response to the Berakah Award published in the *Proceedings of the Annual Meeting of the North American Academy of Liturgy*, Nashville, Tennessee, in January 1989.

4. Balthasar Fischer, *Signs, Words & Gestures* (New York: Pueblo Publishing Co., 1981); first published as *Von der Schale bis zum Kern* (Freiburg: Herder, 1979).

5. *Zeichen des Glaubens. Studien zur Taufe und Firmung. Balthasar Fischer zum 60. Geburtstag*, eds. Hansjorg Auf der Maur and Bruno Kleinheyer (Freiburg: Herder, 1972).

6. *Heute Segnen. Werkbuch zum Benedictionale*, eds. Andreas Heinz and Heinrich Rennings (Freiburg: Herder, 1987).

7. For this insight, we are grateful to Teresa Berger, "'Sacrosanctum Concilium' and 'Worship and the Oneness of Christ's Church,' Twenty-Five Years Later," *Worship* 62/4 (1988), 314.

8. Fischer, *Signs, Words & Gestures*, 2.

PIERRE-MARIE GY

Dominican, Scholar, Teacher

BECAUSE FEW OF HIS WRITINGS have been translated, the French Dominican liturgist Pierre-Marie Gy is not known to many English-speaking Christians. His name is well known, however, to academically trained liturgists and his writings and influence on the Vatican II liturgical reforms are held in high esteem.

Gy was born in 1922 in Paris. At the age of 18, he began higher studies at l'École des Chartes (the School of Palaeography and Librarianship). Two years later, he entered the Paris Province of the Dominican Order, which enjoyed a high level of respect worldwide because of its vibrant intellectual and religious life. As a student at the Dominican intellectual center outside of Paris, Le Saulchoir, he was preparing to be sent to the Dominican mission in Sweden, but in 1947, the Dominican chapter asked him to prepare himself to teach liturgy and to work with the Centre de Pastorale Liturgique in Paris.

This two-pronged request shaped his whole life as he achieved a profound scholarly understanding of the liturgy of the church and an intense sense of the pastoral dimensions of liturgy. He became a master historian of the liturgy and this very knowledge helped him make excellent pastoral applications. As the years went on, these two skills would enable him to be a bridge builder between the past and the present, between a scholarly understanding of liturgical history and the modern Roman liturgical reforms.

At the Saulchoir, Gy studied philosophy and theology. He was influenced by the brilliant faculty there, especially by Yves Congar and Hyacinth Dondaine. He acquired a great respect for and understanding of the works of Thomas Aquinas. His first degree in theology involved a thesis on the sacrament of order during the early scholastic period. His doctoral dissertation was a study of the collectary, ritual and processional manuscripts of the public libraries of France. In a sense, these two dissertations were harbingers of two major types of his future writings: theological considerations of the sacraments and scholarly investigations into the history of liturgy.

Gy the Teacher

On completing his first degree in 1949, he began a teaching career that now spans four decades and still vigorously continues. Indeed, in 1990, he not only is still teaching but also exerting great influence at the Institut Catholique de Paris in his capacity as director of the entire cycle of doctoral studies within the faculty of theology.

Gy taught first at the Saulchoir, then, in 1956, he became a professor at the Institut Supérieur de Liturgie of the Institut Catholique de Paris. He served as director of the prestigious liturgical institute from 1964 to 1986. He was influenced immensely by his predecessor there, the great liturgical scholar, Bernard Botte. During those years, students came to Paris from all over the world to study with Gy. (Between 35 and 40 students completed doctoral studies with Gy.) These students (and many more who took his courses without working on doctorates with him) now are in academic positions or are working with bishops' conferences implementing the Vatican II liturgical reforms. Thus, Gy's work has been carried to all parts of the world.

Gy's students commonly feel that he instilled in them a love of the tradition and a sensitivity to the pastoral needs of today's world. He always has given his students time and full attention and always has been extremely interested in the cultures from which they come.

Vatican II and Liturgical Reforms

From 1964 to 1988, Gy was associate director of the Centre National de Pastorale Liturgique of the French bishops, as well as adviser to the French bishops' liturgical commission.

Gy's name would be prominent among those who prepared for the *Constitution on the Sacred Liturgy* of Vatican II. This was accomplished through his writings and through his participation in important international liturgical congresses. His immediate contribution was as an expert for the preconciliar liturgical commission. Afterward, he was a consultor for the Consilium, the commission entrusted with implementing the *Constitution*. For the past 20 years, he has been active in the various reforms of the sacramental rites (penance, marriage, anointing of the sick) and served as director of the revision of the new *Book of Blessings*. Today he is a consultor for the Congregation for Divine Worship and the Discipline of the Sacraments and continues to be most influential in that role.

Gy the Writer

Gy's articles are numerous and appear in the most important journals, books and dictionaries. He has consistently contributed over the years to *La Maison Dieu* and to *Revue des sciences philosophiques et théologiques*. It is not easy to limit his contribution to a few categories, but it could be said that his general studies bear witness to his deep understanding of the various historical trends in theology; they reveal a masterful contextualization of the modern liturgical reforms in the backdrop of the liturgical tradition. His writings reveal a mastery of canon law, especially in the domain of sacraments. Another strong area of competence is the history and development of liturgical books. Finally, a number of articles show his awareness of the contributions made to liturgical and sacramental theology by Thomas Aquinas.

From 1950 to 1954, Gy served as the director of the important journal, *Revue des sciences philosophiques et théologiques*. In recent years, his contributions to the field of the scientific study of liturgy have continued through the pages of that journal. Since 1979 (except for the year 1981), he has authored annually the *Bulletin de liturgie*. By reading that bulletin each year, professors of liturgy and others interested in the scientific study of liturgy keep abreast of the major contributions to their field.

Gy the Bridge Builder

One of Gy's contributions to the modern liturgical movement is his ability to serve as a bridge between the bureaucratic element and the scholarly element within the church. His diplomatic approach often has meant the difference (the "holy compromise") between certain liturgical reforms being enacted or not. His concern for all sides, including his pastoral concern for traditionalist Catholics, as well as his desire for sound liturgical reform, has won him the confidence of bishops, curial officials and people performing pastoral work for the liturgical life of the church.

A concluding remark could well return to the title of this article about an important pioneer of the liturgical movement: "Dominican, Scholar, Teacher." There never has been a doubt in the mind of Gy's students, readers and friends that he is a

Dominican, a friar preacher. His love for the church is framed in the context of his love for the life and tradition of his own religious community. His mind and his heart have been formed in a tradition incarnated by such great thinkers as Thomas Aquinas and Yves Congar. In 1989, the Dominican Order bestowed on him their highest academic distinction by granting him the degree of "Master of Sacred Theology" in recognition of his ministry of scientific research and theological reflection.

As a scholar, Gy continues to listen, to study, to learn. His most recent articles bear the fruit of decades and disclose a crescendo of insights, especially regarding the links between liturgy and church.

Finally, he is a teacher, one who leads others to the truth. There always is a logic, a neatness to his presentations and articles, and there also is an invitation to ever-new investigations and insights.

■ *Gerard Austin*

J. D. CRICHTON
A Catalyst
for Renewal

J AMES DUNLOP CRICHTON was ordained a priest of
the archdiocese of Birmingham, England, in 1932.
He served as pastor in Pershore, Worcestershire,
from 1955 to 1977 and is now retired there. From
1952 to 1972, he was editor of Great Britain's principal liturgical journal (known by various titles through the
years). A self-taught scholar as well as a pastorally oriented
priest, Crichton used his skills of language and insight within
Great Britain and beyond its boundaries to assist his reading
audience in understanding and practicing the liturgical reforms
of Vatican II.

At the time of Crichton's birth in Birmingham (1902), the
Roman Catholic Church was seeking to establish itself within
the post-Victorian era. It had become an enclave, preoccupied
with remaining uncontaminated by the secular and religious
culture that surrounded it. The two wars and the reconstruc-
tions that followed would force English people to stand
together in suffering and in common effort.

Crichton's earliest convictions about the liturgy were built on
secure foundations that were later endorsed in the *Constitution
on the Sacred Liturgy*. During his seminary years at Cotton College, North Staffordshire, and Oscott College, Warwickshire, his

curiosity sought satisfaction in reading Leo the Great and Thomas Aquinas. The writings of Odo Casel, Columba Marmion and Jacques Maritain led him to perceive the church as the Mystical Body of Christ with the people of God as a vital and indispensable part of that Body. Thus, from the beginning of his formation, the full and active participation by all the people was the goal of his liturgical efforts.

The Society of St. Gregory

Crichton's work with F. H. Drinkwater and C. C. Martindale ushered him into a world of biblical and liturgical catechesis. He quickly became known for his ability to articulate issues through the written word. From 1935 to 1944, the in-house magazine of the Society of the Magnificat provided an outlet for his skill. To a great extent, however, Crichton's work in the liturgical apostolate found its basis in the Society of St. Gregory (SSG). Bernard McElligott of Ampleforth Abbey founded the SSG in 1929. Its primary focus was the restoration of plainsong to the people. In the early 1940s, Crichton directed his attention to the SSG's journal, *Music and Liturgy.* He was convinced that the base of the Society's concerns had to be broadened; liturgy included more than musical concerns.

By 1944, *Music and Liturgy* was renamed *Liturgy* and in 1952, Crichton became its editor. His first editorial made his priorities explicit: He would not cater to back-bench Catholics nor liturgical specialists; he set out to provide practical information for clergy and laity concerned with the pastoral dimensions of liturgical practice. He alerted his readers to continental liturgical centers, institutes and congresses. As an adept editor who knew the juridical mind-sets of his readers, Crichton often incorporated quotations from *Mystici Corporis* (1943) and *Mediator Dei* (1947) in order to demonstrate the pastoral implications of papal encyclicals.

Even in these early years, Crichton did not wear a rigid juridical or institutional mind-set nor did a classicist notion of religious culture—in which the church is perceived as permanent and changeless—control him. A dynamic sense of religious culture freed him to understand the church as historically conditioned and always changing. Thus he rejected an imperial tone, which lingered in English liturgical style, and preoccupations with aesthetics that tended to caricature liturgy as static and liturgists as precious. In Crichton's view, the liturgy had to be more than polyphony, plainsong and procession if it were to be anything more than a museum piece.

Although liturgical congresses throughout the 1950s helped to escalate the momentum of the liturgical movement among specialists, tensions percolated on the continent among those who were not specialists, and resistance also was felt in England. English Catholics remained unmoved. Crichton held that "in this, as in other matters, the English Channel proved to be an all-too-effective Water Curtain" (*English Catholic Worship* [London: Chapman, 1979], 73). Crichton gave careful attention to national and international liturgical meetings on the pages of the SSG's journal, hoping that this would fuel the imminent liturgical reform.

Catechesis for the Reforms

Crichton was convinced that preliminary spadework had to be done as reforms were issued, and he took on this responsibility as a pastoral duty to the Roman Catholic community in England. At the end of Vatican II's first session in December 1962, it was clear that something of significance was taking place in Rome and that it would have extensive consequences at all levels of ecclesial life. The mood of England was divided; spirited enthusiasm was mixed with suspicion and fear. The very center of the world seemed on the verge of being dislodged for some, while for others fresh air was blowing through the dusty corridors of the Roman church.

A month before the September 1963 opening of the Council's second session, Crichton visited the United States. At the invitation of Gerard Sloyan, he taught a course at The Catholic University of America on the scriptural dimension of liturgy. He also participated in the Liturgical Week in Philadelphia, which had the renewal of scriptural, catechetical and liturgical education as its theme. His contacts in the United States made it possible for him to publish several articles in various American journals during the 1960s.

In the April 1964 issue of *Liturgy,* Crichton began a catechesis on the *Constitution on the Sacred Liturgy;* it had been approved overwhelmingly by the bishops the previous December. He attended to the delicate connection between the advised reforms and the spirit of renewal. With a look back to *Mediator Dei* and with a vision of the pastoral possibilities latent in conciliar ecclesiology and expressed in the new liturgical document, Crichton called on laypeople and priests to promote the liturgical movement now endorsed by the church in council. If the reform of the liturgy was to bring about the desired renewal of Christian life, a change of heart was needed, not simply a change of rubrics. In the July 1964 issue of *Liturgy,* Crichton informed his readers of various publications on the liturgy constitution, including his own commentary, *The Church's Worship,* published by Geoffrey Chapman of London (with an American edition released later in that year by Sheed and Ward of New York).

Throughout the 1960s, Crichton discussed the conciliar liturgical reform in the pages of the SSG's quarterly and through articles in various journals and newspapers. At the same time, he worked on larger projects. In September 1964, the first General Instruction on the liturgy was published. By January 1965, Crichton's commentary was available under the title *Changes in the Liturgy* (London: Chapman; Staten Island: Alba House, 1965). He wanted to highlight the pastoral implications of the text and to prod pastors toward active response and renewal. In January 1966, he published *The Liturgy and the Future*. This book presented the teaching of the liturgy constitution for the general Catholic population.

Crichton rallied enthusiastic people to stimulate reform and renewal on various levels of English ecclesial life. English Catholics who aligned themselves with the spirit of the Council found mutual support and stimulation in sectors of the SSG's membership and in the priests' Conference for Practical Liturgy. In England, a profound secrecy often hovered over the publication of official instructions and revised rites, but a friend in Rome regularly informed Crichton about the promulgation of various documents. In frustration with official silence, he pointed out to the English hierarchy the progress made in other countries.

Crichton resigned as editor of SSG's magazine in 1972 (at that time it was entitled *Life and Worship*). This freed him for more concentrated effort in extending the reform. He was occupied in liturgical catechesis and ecumenical affairs throughout Great Britain, put together popular pamphlets, published practical articles in various magazines and newspapers and wrote letters to their editors, compiled a handbook for lectors and a small book for the pastoral care of the sick and contributed articles to theological dictionaries.

Liturgical Commentary Continues

During this time, Crichton also continued his longer commentaries on the reform. *Christian Celebration: The Mass* (London: Chapman, 1971) is a study of the new order of Mass and the documents that followed it. In 1973, *Christian Celebration: The Sacraments* was published, a study of the revised rites—baptism, confirmation, matrimony, order, the anointing of the sick, the burial of the dead. (At the time of its writing, the new order of penance had not been issued. It was promulgated in 1973 and Crichton's commentary, *The Ministry of Reconciliation* (London: Chapman), followed in May 1974.) In 1976, the third and final volume of his project, *Christian Celebration: The Prayer of the Church,* was completed. In 1981, Chapman published the three volumes under one cover.

During the first year of his retirement from full-time pastoral ministry in 1977, the Veritas company in Dublin published Crichton's *The Once and the Future Liturgy.* The following year, his "A Theology of Worship" keynoted *The Study of Liturgy* (London: S.P.C.K., 1978). The distinguished editorial board for that book invited him to write the article and accepted it without alterations. The golden jubilee of the SSG in 1979 occasioned a collection of essays entitled *English Catholic Worship* (London: Chapman) edited by Crichton, H. E. Winstone and J. R. Ainslie. Brian Newns reviewed the collection and concluded with a tribute to this outstanding pioneer of liturgical reform in England: "I cannot conclude without expressing my particular pleasure in reading Father Crichton's contributions on the years he knows so well, expressed with the insight, lucidity and charity we have long known and valued. For many of us he embodies the liturgical renewal—a scholar and pastor."

Crichton's liturgical commentary continued in the 1980s. *The Living Christ* (London: Collins, 1988) focuses on one of his earliest interests, paschal life within the liturgical year. *Worship in a Hidden Church* (Dublin: Columba Press, 1988) tells of the worship of the recusant English Catholics from the sixteenth to the early nineteenth centuries. *Servants of the Lord* (London: St. Paul's Publications, 1989) reflects upon the work of the pastoral priest and *The Story of a Parish* (1989) chronicles the life of his beloved Holy Redeemer parish in Pershore. In the midst of untiring productivity, his articles still appear in the SSG's journal, *Music and Liturgy.*

As a catalyst in preconciliar preparation and postconciliar renewal, Crichton affected change on various levels of English ecclesial life. He has encouraged and motivated young people in the field to pursue necessary training in order to secure competence and credibility. His writings broadened the horizons of many readers in England and beyond. In his three decades of involvement in the liturgical apostolate before Vatican II and the almost three transitional decades following it, James Dunlop Crichton will indeed remain a significant figure in the pastoral liturgical reform and renewal movement in England and throughout the English-speaking world.

■ *Daniel P. Grigassy*

THE

AMERICAN
LEADERS

VIRGIL MICHEL

Founder of the
American Liturgical Movement

 OM VIRGIL MICHEL (1888–1938) has been called
the bridge that brought the liturgical movement
from its European roots to the fresh soil of America.[1] What distinguished Michel from his predecessors in Europe—Guéranger, Casel, Herwegen and
Beauduin—is a characteristically American pragmatism and a
conviction that liturgy is not the preserve of monks and nuns
but the lifeblood of the entire church. Like these others, Michel
was a monk, but a monk of a different type. The monasteries
of Belgium and Germany fostered what may be called a classical Benedictine life, marked by enclosure and dedicated almost
exclusively to contemplation. St. John's Abbey in Collegeville,
Minnesota, Michel's religious home, however, was a missionary community, established in 1856 to serve the needs of the
German immigrants in Minnesota.[2] Among these immigrants
was Michel's father.

Perhaps it was the elder Michel striving for success in the
New World that gave Dom Virgil Michel his intensity and tire-
less commitment to work, a dedication that led eventually to a
breakdown and perhaps contributed to his early death. Paul
Marx, his biographer and confrere, writes that "Michel at
times gave the impression of being too busy to have time for

students and sometimes even for his brother religious. To know him was to work."[3]

Virgil Michel sought to show how work is intimately linked to prayer. He campaigned to unite liturgy and life, ritual and social justice. In this, he sought to capture an aspect of the motto of the Benedictines, *Ora et Labora:* Pray and Work. Michel knew that Christian work and worship give birth to one another. This is the lesson he has to teach the contemporary church.

Education of a Pioneer

Michel, the founder and first editor of *Worship* magazine (for its first decades titled *Orate Fratres*), never studied liturgy at a university. His doctoral work at Catholic University was in philosophy, which remained his great interest and dreamed-of field of study throughout his life. Michel never was to see that dream fulfilled; other interests that developed while he studied at Catholic University were to occupy him. The first and most captivating was the study and renewal of the liturgy.

Michel began further philosophy studies at Sant' Anselmo, the international Benedictine College in Rome, in 1924. He was greatly disappointed by his mentor in philosophy but was delighted by another faculty member, Dom Lambert Beauduin, the famous liturgist and monk of Mont César. Beauduin gave Michel not only further instruction in liturgical studies but also introduced him to the doctrine of the Mystical Body of Christ. This was a controversial perspective in those days and would be made respectable only in 1943 with Pius XII's encyclical, *Mystici Corporis.* Yet Michel accepted the concept with enthusiasm and used it as the key idea in his subsequent work. As he wrote:

> There is only one answer I know of to the problem of the balanced harmony between the individual and the social: *The Mystical Body of Christ.*[4]

Michel returned from Europe in 1925, zealous for the liturgy and for bringing to the church's consciousness its identity as the Mystical Body of Christ. His methodological mind devised a practical scheme for bringing this about. His plan had three parts: first, to publish English translations of the great European works that had so enlightened him; second, to sponsor the writing and printing of American pastoral liturgical works, a project he called "The Popular Liturgical Library"; and finally, to issue an American liturgical periodical that he dubbed *Orate Fratres*. He named the publishing house The Liturgical Press. Sixty years later, it is still one of the foremost American sources of liturgical, theological and pastoral literature, and continues to publish *Worship*, the principal journal of liturgical scholarship in this country.

An Unwanted Work

Michel planned that, once it was well established, he would hand the Press over to managers and would take up full-time work in the study and teaching of philosophy. Abbot Alcuin Deutsch decided instead that Michel himself would direct the Press. Michel accepted the decision with regret. Except for a brief period (1930–1933) when he was sent away from the abbey to recover from a physical and nervous breakdown and to work among native Americans, he never left the position of editor in chief.

Although it was not a work he sought, it was one in which he excelled. Under his leadership, St. John's published works on the nature of the liturgical life, laypeople's guides to using the missal and Prime and Compline booklets (predecessors of Collegeville's exceedingly popular *A Short Breviary*, 1941). To stay current on the development of the liturgical revival in the United States, Hellriegel, Busch, Ellard, Lavanoux and Michel formed a kind of network through the mail. In Michel's responses to the "avalanche of letters"[5] that came his way, he encouraged the progress of the American liturgical movement and placed his mark forever on it.

The Movement in America

Thanks to Virgil Michel, the liturgical movement throughout the United States was concerned more with the spirit of the liturgy than its rubrics. At the heart of this uniquely American approach was a concern for social justice, a component of what in those days was called "Catholic Action." This focus grew even stronger after Michel's sojourn with the Indians.[6]

The church's understanding of "Catholic Action," a term that once signified the mission of the laity, has changed significantly since Virgil Michel supported it. "Catholic Action" was seen in the 1930s as the participation of the laity in a mission that belonged to the hierarchy. By contrast, Vatican II's *Dogmatic Constitution on the Church* (1964) sees the lay apostolate as "a participation in the saving mission of the church itself,"[7] of the entire church and not just the hierarchy. Virgil Michel taught that this apostolate of the church is both revealed and expressed most fully in the liturgy:

> Through the liturgy rightly understood and lived . . . all our life is centered in Christ and the Christ-life radiates out into every action of the day.[8]

This linking of liturgical renewal, understanding through education and social action was such a refrain in Michel's teaching that he created a shorthand way to sum it up: the three C's—cult, creed and code.

Cult: How We Worship

Looking back from our vantage point, we might suppose that Virgil Michel envisioned the liturgical reforms that have come to pass since the Council or even that he encouraged them. Actually, he seems not to have been very much concerned with radical ritual revision. In Michel's time, critics supposed that he and his colleagues would settle for nothing short of the "dialogue Mass," the reciting of all the chants and responses by the assembly. It was an extreme charge to make in the 1930s. Michel countered that:

> Active and intelligent participation does not necessarily mean this more complete form. It means above all an understanding of the true nature of the Mass as the making present of the sacrifice of Christ for our sake and some understanding of what our part should be in the action of the Mass. It means above all that the faithful knowingly and willingly assist at the Mass and do not perform other foreign devotions while present at Mass.[9]

He was not absolutely indifferent to the reform of the rites, however, and by the late 1930s, he broke his cautious silence to praise the regulated use of the vernacular in some parts of the Mass. He also supported evening Masses as a sensible accommodation to modern conditions.

In all of this, Michel showed himself as a liturgical renewer but not as a revolutionary one. His hope for the cult was intelligent participation of all members of the church in the words and gestures of the liturgy, even when they were said and done only by a few.

Creed: How We Teach the Faith

Michel saw poor methods in religious education as one of the greatest contributing factors to the laity's lack of liturgical understanding. He also attributed to ill-devised catechisms the inability of most Catholics to see any connection among the three C's. In collaboration with two Dominican sisters from Grand Rapids, Michel edited religion texts to remedy the mistakes. First came a tentative series of "laboratory manuals" and the eight-volume (mimeographed) Christ-Life Series soon followed. The aim of these books was to shift religious education away from the memorizing of dogmatic formulas toward the integration of belief, worship and daily activity.

> It is, moreover, necessary to teach children to center all the efforts of their lives in the altar of God. . . . In other words, to coordinate and integrate all their daily efforts, especially their religious endeavors, with the action of Christ unto continued growth in the divine life.[10]

The series was a complete one, offering books from grade school to college. Unfortunately, it met with little success. As one colleague of Michel remarked, Dom Virgil was proposing in these books a kind of thinking to which Catholics were not accustomed and one which they also found impossible to teach.[11] Still, the method bore a great insight: that human beings are emotional and physical, not just intellectual, and that religious education must be rooted in the liturgy because liturgy touches people in each of these facets of their lives.

Code: How We Live the Gospel

Virgil Michel lived between the two World Wars when cultures were in turmoil and theories of the ideal society abounded. Michel had his own theory of a Christian society born of the liturgy. "We cannot give ourselves to God in God's own way, i.e., through Christ in his liturgical life," Michel wrote, "without also becoming ardent apostles of social action."[12] In this Christian social action, he saw a remedy for both capitalistic individualism and Marxist collectivism and the source of a just society.

With great foresight, Michel commented at length on the role of women in society. He saw the liturgy as the model of a society where women would have "wide scope in the important professions of public life."[13] His only fear was that women would abandon the Christian ideal as they sought to overcome their oppression and would follow instead the demons of individualism and greed. Michel was unaware of some of the subtleties of the oppression of women that recent thinkers have brought to consciousness. Still, his concern for women and his insight into their social rights—even mentioning the early church's office of deaconess as a model—is remarkable. It is but one timely example of the many manifestations of Virgil Michel's concern for justice.

Years of Remembrance and Revival

In July 1988, a national symposium on the life and work of Michel was sponsored by St. John's Abbey and The Liturgical Press. The Press also published a new book on Michel,[14] while *Worship* marked the occasion with a commemorative issue. This scholarship and these discussions testify to the place Michel holds in the memory of American Catholicism. But Virgil Michel is more than an interesting marker along the way to our postconciliar church and our increasingly post-Christian world. The challenges Michel's discerning eye saw in their infancy have grown to full stature. Perhaps the solutions he foresaw also have reached their time.

Recent authors suggest that they have. Franklin and Spaeth claim that their book was worth writing only because "idea after idea, essay after essay, project after project issuing from Virgil Michel speak across the years to today's Christians."[15] In their book, they examine in particular the problem of individualism. In the commemorative issue of *Worship*, Kenneth Himes wrote on eucharist and justice, Joseph Chinici on affective prayer and David Beaudoin on catechetics—all issues of concern for the church today and key issues in the work of Virgil Michel. Michel saw to the heart of things, to the issues that are perennial to Christianity well lived. His insights not only have survived changes and fads in the church and world, but are increasingly recognized as key issues in the church's work and worship. Michel's solution—an organic view of the world and of the church, a belief in the Mystical Body—also may have weathered the passing of time.

Perhaps it is time that Virgil Michel be invited to step off the pages of history so that his solutions can be tried again. Just as the impact that Michel had in his brief years continues to be felt today, so also he may provide the future agenda for the "ora et labora" of the American church.

■ *Patrick Malloy*

NOTES

1. Paul B. Marx, OSB, *Virgil Michel and the Liturgical Movement* (Collegeville: The Liturgical Press, 1957), 42.

2. Colman J. Barry, *Worship and Work: Saint John's Abbey and University, 1856–1980* (Collegeville: The Liturgical Press, 1980). Barry gives an extensive history with numerous illustrative photographs.

3. Marx, *Virgil Michel*, 386.

4. Ibid., quoted by Marx, 186. See also Cecilia Himebaugh, OSB, "Virgil Michel's Design for an Integral World Order and Twenty Years Afterwards," *Benedictine Review* 13 (1958), 8 ff.

5. Ibid., Marx, 127. See also Chapter 6, "Diffusing the Movement," 137–75. In this chapter, Marx shows in detail how Michel shaped the liturgical renewal throughout the English-speaking world through his letter writing: "Letters, letters, letters poured out to priests, religious, and laypeople" (137).

6. Kenneth R. Himes, "Eucharist and Justice: Assessing the Legacy of Virgil Michel," *Worship* 62:3 (1988). Himes believes that "Michel's great contribution to liturgical renewal was his effort at linking liturgy to social justice" (224).

7. *Lumen Gentium, #33.*

8. Unpublished manuscript, "The Liturgy and Catholic Life" (1937), 20.

9. Ibid., 18.

10. Unpublished manuscript, 114.

11. Himebaugh, "Virgil Michel's Design," 7.

12. Unpublished manuscript, 134.

13. Ibid., 94.

14. Franklin and Spaeth, *Virgil Michel: American Catholic.*

15. Ibid., 8.

MICHAEL MATHIS
Magnificent Latecomer

THE FIRST LOVE of Michael Ambrose Mathis (1885–1960) was the foreign missions. From the time of his ordination as a Holy Cross priest, he preferred pastoral missionary work to academic study and teaching, despite his obvious gifts for these occupations. For more than 25 years, he vigorously involved himself in the mission apostolate of his religious order, working in a wide variety of ways to support missionary efforts in the United States and abroad.[1] Despite pioneering work in this field of ministry, however, Mathis now is remembered for missionary work of a very different kind.

With great delight Michael Mathis often told the story of his conversion to the liturgy. It happened in 1936 when he received a gift: the first volume of Pius Parsch's *The Church's Year of Grace*. Until then he considered himself an enemy of the liturgy "or what I thought was liturgy at the time."[2] But his own doctoral work in scripture and his appreciation of serious scholarship enabled him to discover in Parsch's rich biblical and patristic commentaries on the liturgical year "the real stuff."[3] He immediately ordered the remaining volumes and began his own regime of reading scripture, early church writings, liturgy, architecture and history in several languages. This conversion launched him—at the age of 51—on a whole new career. His personal study served as the foundation and model for all he would contribute to the liturgical movement in America.

The Zeal of a Convert

Mathis's first efforts on behalf of liturgy combined his long involvement with the missions and his newfound liturgical studies. In 1937, he was asked to organize something for the missions on the Notre Dame campus. He gathered groups of students who met daily for the study of the missal and for a *Missa recitata,* a Mass in which all present joined in the responses ordinarily made only by the server. While this might have seemed a strange sort of missionary endeavor, Mathis believed that adequate spiritual formation was necessary for raising mission consciousness. He called the missal "the best primer for the understanding of Christian teaching on the missions."[4] Through this daily meditation on the texts of the Mass and Divine Office, the groups sought to develop their spiritual and practical lives based on the liturgy.

After several years of this approach, Mathis decided the actual celebration of the liturgy would be a better school for prayer. He chose the church's office of Matins as his vehicle. His pastoral and liturgical concern is clear in this explanation:

> My object, first, is to make available to a greater number of the faithful the rich and varied prayer forms which the church has given us to praise God, to deepen our understanding and appreciation of divine revelation, and to seek, especially in the Mass of the Faithful, special graces whereby we may be helped to translate into action the lessons taught. Secondly, I wish to show how the church has selected from sacred scripture and tradition and hagiography appropriate passages to illustrate the lessons she teaches on each of these feasts and the motherly exhortation she gives to put these into practice.[5]

Mathis had two key concerns regarding the use of this "vigil service," as he called it. First, there was the catechetical mission of bringing the scriptures to the faithful so that they would be formed more fully according to God's revelation. To this end, he published volumes of these services for subscribers, wrote bits of commentary and rubric throughout the text and offered long, hearty homilies as part of the service. Like Parsch, his inspiration, Mathis sought to open the storehouse of scripture and early church writings for the nourishment of the partici-pants and the whole church.

His second concern was that the church's liturgy would be sung so that it could be most pastorally effective. Mathis moved from a recited to a sung office of Matins because song created "the right atmosphere" for hearing God's word and allowing it to work; in fact, that allowance for God's activity was "the whole reason for song in the liturgy."[6] The best for-mation in liturgy, he felt, was the celebration of the rites themselves, but they must be celebrated with understanding.

School of Liturgy

The concern to celebrate liturgy with understanding led Mathis to propose a school for liturgy at Notre Dame. It is difficult to trace the genesis of this idea. From 1940 on, he was urging the Congregation of the Holy Cross to found a gradu-ate school of the missions and the liturgy school may have been an offshoot of that idea. Or it may have been the increas-ing interest in liturgy on campus and around the country that encouraged him to seek a place for such a school in the univer-sity's academic program. After persistent negotiation with congregational and university administrators, an undergradu-ate program in liturgy was opened in the summer of 1947.

From the beginning, Mathis was involved in all aspects of the program: planning courses, securing professors and funding, advertising, corresponding with prospective and already-enrolled students and preparing his own lectures and homilies. Despite the success of the first summer, however, the university seemed reluctant to continue the venture or to invest responsibility for it in Mathis alone. But Mathis had indomitable persistence and great energy. He won approval for a graduate program in 1948 with a permanent place in the university's academic program.[7]

Finding qualified faculty was a difficult matter, requiring multiple contacts, endless correspondence, even visits to Europe. Nevertheless, Mathis found the best and the listing of professors over the years of Mathis's directorship reads like a "who's who" of the liturgical movement in both Europe and the United States: Josef Jungmann, Jean Danielou, Louis Bouyer, Balthasar Fischer, Pierre-Marie Gy, Donald Atwater, Johannes Hofinger, Christine Mohrmann, Godfrey Diekmann, Martin Hellriegel, H. A. Reinhold and many others.

Mathis knew that liturgical scholarship was an absolute necessity. He developed a cycle of courses that included the major periods in the history of the liturgy, the scriptural and patristic sources for the interpretation of the liturgical texts and the integration of chant into all study and celebration.[8] Recognizing the contributions that his professors were making to liturgical studies, Mathis undertook the translation and editing of their lectures for publication. Ultimately, nine volumes appeared in the Liturgical Studies series published by the University of Notre Dame Press. These include classics such as Louis Bouyer's *Liturgical Piety* and Joseph Jungmann's *The Early Liturgy.* They are still in valuable use.

Related Projects

Despite increasingly fragile health, Mathis's involvement in all the details of the summer school enhanced his creativity rather than exhausted it. For example, he outlined a preparatory program in "Christian Latinity and Liturgy" in the firm belief that it would aid the understanding of the liturgical texts and would be the soundest approach to "the vernacular problem." This was a disappointment: Only two students registered and the program was canceled. More successful were seminars for architects and artists held annually for six years, summer workshops for priests and seminarians and a conference held in 1956 at the request of the Liturgical Conference on the restored rites of Holy Week. The implementation of this Holy Week conference is typical of Mathis's inexhaustible energy. The announcement of the restoration of the Holy Week liturgies came from Rome on November 16, 1955. The request by the Liturgical Conference was made to Mathis in early January 1956. He then scheduled speakers and advertised the program in time to hold the seminar on February 7–9, 1956, and by the end of that same month he had the proceedings available in printed booklet form!

Mathis also was involved in the translation of the *Collectio Rituum* into English.[9] The move to provide a vernacular ritual for the American church had begun at the 1946 National Liturgical Week and gained momentum as France, Germany and Great Britain received permission from Rome for similar books. After Gerald Ellard resigned from the drafting committee for reasons of ill health, Mathis was appointed chairperson to complete the work for the American bishops. This involvement in the cause of vernacular liturgy seems out of character for Mathis who so staunchly insisted on a fully sung Latin Mass and Office. His concern that the rites be celebrated with understanding, however, caused him to favor the pastoral and catechetical benefit of a ritual in English.

When the project was completed and approved by Rome, Mathis began to write catechetical commentary on the ritual as a resource for busy pastors and all teachers of religion.[10] Unfortunately, despite its valuable purpose and Mathis's negotiations with two publishers, the commentary never was published.

Michael Mathis was involved in many other projects too numerous to mention here. More important is consideration of his principles. First, he sought to bring the liturgy of the church as it was in his time to its fullest potential and vibrancy, to demonstrate that the liturgy could be celebrated well and fruitfully as it was. Second, liturgy always was for him an art as well as a science. Practice and theory had to be integrated because liturgy was above all an expression of the faith and right spirit of the people. Third, following from this second principle, the faithful were to be brought to full participation in the liturgy by increasing the understanding of their role in the liturgy. And finally, he understood that what he was about was an apostolate, a pastoral service meant to build up the body of Christ.

These principles combined in Mathis to produce a unique force in the American liturgical scene, especially in his providing scholarly background for the celebration of the liturgy. The establishment of the liturgy program at Notre Dame is significant not only because of the hundreds of students formed by its curriculum, but also because it gave the movement in America an academic center and a vision that wedded theory and practice. Bringing the best scholars in Europe and America to teach in the program and making their seminal research available in book form gave the program respectability and produced in English a unique body of liturgical resources that remains beneficial to students and researchers today. The English translation of the ritual aided in the pastoral care of the faithful and their participation with understanding; it paved the way for greater use of the vernacular in the liturgy.

Michael Mathis died on March 10, 1960, aware that a church council had been called to respond to the signs of the times, but unaware of the contribution he had made to its teaching on the liturgy. His legacy is the scholarship he brought to the American liturgical movement in its understanding of the liturgical rites, the vision of a fully participatory sung liturgy, the role of the assembly in the liturgical act and the hospitable pastoral care that motivated all he did.

■ *Robert J. Kennedy*

NOTES

1. For a fuller treatment of Mathis's early years and missionary work, see my "American Essays in Liturgy," *Michael Mathis: American Liturgical Pioneer* (Washington DC: The Pastoral Press, 1987).

2. Letter of Michael Mathis to Joseph McGlinn, April 9, 1988, Michael A. Mathis Collection, Archives of the University of Notre Dame (UNDA).

3. "The Real Stuff," *Apostolic Perspectives: A Quarterly Devoted to the Apostolate of the Church* 3 (1958). This is a publication from Notre Dame. No author is cited. The article seems to be the summary of an interview.

4. Ibid.

5. Michael Mathis, *A Vigil Preparation for the Masses of Six Feasts, with a Brief Commentary* (Privately published: 1946), 4.

6. Michael Mathis, "The Vigil Service," *Education and the Liturgy: 18th North American Liturgical Week, 1957* (Elsberry MO: The Liturgical Conference, 1958), 158.

7. George E. Schidel, "Never Too Much: In Memoriam: Rev. Michael A. Mathis, CSC (1885–1960)," *Yearbook of Liturgical Studies* 3 (1962), 22.

8. Michael Mathis, "Special Lecture," transcript, 6 August 1948, Michael A. Mathis Collection, UNDA.

9. Edwin O'Hara, "The New American Ritual," *The New Ritual/Liturgy and Social Order, 16th National Liturgical Week, 1955* (Elsberry MO: The Liturgical Conference, 1956), 4. See also Edwin O'Hara, "Memorandum of Progress on the Revision of the *Collectio Rituum*," June 18, 1953, Michael A. Mathis Collection, UNDA.

10. Manuscript, "Teaching with the Church: A Commentary on the American Ritual, by the Notre Dame Liturgical Committee" (n.d.), Michael A. Mathis Collection, UNDA.

GERALD ELLARD

He Wrote the Book

WHEN ONE CONSIDERS an influential life, one of the first questions is "How did it all get started?" This is especially true of Gerald Ellard who seems to have studied and lived the liturgy all his life. In an interview given in the early 1940s, however, he hinted at how it began. When his older brother Augustine took his vows as a Jesuit, he gave his younger brother Gerald, then a novice, his copy of the *Roman Missal* and the *Manual for Clerics.* That was in 1912—long before the missal gained any popularity and 16 years before the liturgical movement took any visible shape in the United States. But in these two secondhand gifts, the seed had been planted.

John Ernest Fitzgerald Ellard was born in Commonwealth, Wisconsin, in 1894, the second of four children. During his childhood, he came to be known simply as Gerald, a shortened form of his mother's name. After studying at what now is Regis College in Denver, he entered the Society of Jesus in 1912. In 1919, he received his master's degree in philosophy from Gonzaga University in Spokane, Washington, and returned to Regis to teach history and English to high school and college students.

When Ellard began his theological studies at the Missouri Province theologate in St. Louis in 1923, the seed planted over a decade before found nourishment. He heard about the European liturgical movement from his fellow Jesuits who were returning from study and travel there; and from his own studies, he began to learn of the nineteenth-century renewal of the theology of the Mystical Body of Christ. These two combined in Ellard to produce an energetic scholarly interest in the liturgy.

"Opening Up the Liturgy"

These factors also produced a challenging letter to the editor of *America* (April 25, 1925). The young theologian spoke of "the liturgical renaissance we seem to be approaching" and lamented that "the liturgy is a whole world that to the ordinary Catholic has been singularly unexplored." He then challenged his readers to "open up the liturgy":

> The matter must be put before the faithful by the priest in the pulpit, and secondarily by the teacher in the classroom and the editor in the newspaper. Why not a series of sermons and classroom lectures? Why not an *American Journal of Liturgical Studies?* Why not special efforts until one generation has been fully initiated into, penetrated with, the hidden beauties of the throne room of God-with-us?

The letter caught the eye of Martin Hellriegel, who had begun his work of pastoral renewal of the liturgy in O'Fallon, Missouri. Hellriegel invited Ellard to O'Fallon for conversation and to see for himself that the work of opening up the liturgy had begun.

It was on such a visit on Christmas Eve in 1925 that Ellard met Virgil Michel, who recently had returned from his studies and his tour of all the European liturgical centers. On that night, these three—Michel, Hellriegel and Ellard—planned a liturgical journal for the United States to be published at St.

John's Abbey, Collegeville, Minnesota. After much discussion and just before they were to celebrate the Christmas Mass at midnight, they agreed on a name: *Orate Fratres*. When the first issue appeared in 1926, Ellard's name was listed as an associate editor; he remained such until his death 37 years later.

Michel and Hellriegel also provided strong encouragement and solid guidance for Ellard's graduate studies in Europe, which he began in 1927, the year after he was ordained a priest. He studied under Joseph Kramp at the University of Munich, and although his doctorate was not in liturgy per se, Ellard concentrated on learning the techniques necessary for historical research of the liturgy. In addition to his academic work, he traveled to all the centers of the liturgical movement in Europe and experienced firsthand the research and pastoral experimentation being conducted there. He became acquainted with Josef Jungmann, Ildefons Herwegen of Maria Laach, Pius Parsch of Klosterneuberg and many others.

Teacher and Writer

From all this experience, he learned how much progress had been made on the European scene and also how important the need was for solid organization to spread the word of liturgical renewal. When he returned to the United States in 1931, he was the first American academically trained in liturgy and he resolved to bring his scholarly experience and ability to bear on the opening up of the liturgical experience for all the faithful.

In 1932, Ellard was assigned to teach liturgy and church history in the Jesuit theologate at St. Mary's, Kansas. This provided him with a perfect platform to make his contribution to the liturgical movement. Not only would he be able to teach seminarians, he also would be able to research and to write. His biographer, John Leo Klein, has said that:

His first major contribution to the American liturgical movement was typical of so much of his later popularization based on solid scholarship, serving the pastoral need of American Catholics.

The popularization Ellard did came in the form of the written word. His initial teaching experience at high-school, college and graduate levels already had alerted him to the need for a theology textbook that would "open up the liturgy" and initiate a generation into the integral unity of liturgy and life. In 1933, Ellard wrote such a text, *Christian Life and Worship,* which provided an understanding of the communal nature of Christian life and its expression through liturgical participation. Like most of the liturgical pioneers, Ellard understood that the unity of the baptized with Christ is the foundational and integrating principle for Christian life and worship. He wrote elsewhere, "I look for success in the liturgy movement itself, and in its ultimate consequences, only insofar as this basic notion of corporate worship is popularized." The book was very well received; by the time of Ellard's death, an incredible 63,000 copies of its several editions were in print.

In 1940, Ellard published *Men at Work at Worship: America Joins the Liturgical Movement* to introduce the main currents of both the European and American liturgical movements to a wider audience, to place them in historical perspective and to demonstrate how the corporate piety of the liturgy is the best expression of Christian life. In the book, he introduced all the key themes of the movement: the theology of the Mystical Body of Christ, the priesthood of the faithful, active participation in the dialogue Mass and congregational singing. The possibility of evening Mass and the liturgy in the vernacular—two highly controversial topics at the time—were gently proposed.

Two years later, Ellard produced another volume, *The Dialogue Mass: A Book for Priests and Teachers of Religion.* Not only was this another effort to help pastoral ministers promote the liturgy, but it also provided both the remote and recent history of the dialogue Mass. It should not be considered a faddish innovation, Ellard noted, but a restoration from the earliest days of the church of the much-needed and much-desired active participation of the faithful in the liturgy.

The next book appeared in 1948: *The Mass of the Future.* Actually, its title was a bit misleading because the book included sections on the Mass of the past and of the present as well. In the third section, on the future, however, Ellard began to call more loudly for a thorough reform of the liturgy: the celebration of afternoon and evening Mass, the increased use of the vernacular in the liturgy, the simplification of the rubrics, the revision of the liturgical calendar and lectionary, the planning of new churches and the renovation of old ones to enable the active participation of all, the use of the offertory procession and of congregational singing. The present reader may find in these proposals only what one would expect. In 1948, however, the book caused a storm of controversy; the archbishop of Milwaukee gave the book only a conditional *imprimatur.*

Advocacy for liturgical change would characterize the next decade of the liturgical movement. Ellard's book was most helpful in that cause, but such change was clearly an idea whose time had not yet come. When the assistant to the Jesuit Father General in Rome thanked Ellard for the complimentary copy that had been sent, he wrote: *"The Mass of the Future* is an idea that does not bear very close analysis, if indeed it is intended to do more than attract curiosity."

Despite such opposition, which accompanied Ellard and all the liturgical pioneers, his was a faithful commitment to the work of the liturgical apostolate. In addition to the four books already mentioned and four others, Ellard authored nearly 200 articles over the course of his 30-year service to the cause: 54 of these appeared in *Orate Fratres* (later *Worship*). In all his writing, Ellard balanced scholarly and pastoral concerns. In articles meant to foster popular piety, he supported his discussions with solid historical and theological research; in his scholarly work, he kept the pastoral renewal of the liturgy as his context. And in all his efforts, the spiritual welfare of God's faithful people was foremost in his mind.

Contributions to Pastoral Liturgy

Ellard's scholarship and writing skills were put to use on several important pastoral projects. In the early 1940s, he developed an English translation of the Ordinary of the Mass for uniform use by publishers of hand missals, so that diversity would be avoided and unity promoted. In 1948, he produced a popular edition of Pope Pius XII's encyclical *Mediator Dei,* which included a brief commentary and sets of discussion questions for study groups. In the 1950s, he wrote several booklets explaining the rubrics and meaning of the restored rites of Holy Week and collaborated on a series of high-school religion textbooks.

At the invitation of Archbishop Edwin O'Hara in 1952, Ellard chaired the committee that would provide the American Catholic church with a *Rituale Romanum* in English. Most of the work on this pastoral project was completed when Ellard suffered a cerebral hemorrhage in 1953; the work was finished by Michael Mathis and Mary Perkins Ryan.

Ellard's pen was not the only way he contributed to the liturgical movement of the United States. He was a frequent lecturer in parishes and at colleges across the country and a regular speaker at the national Liturgical Weeks. He often gave priests' retreats that introduced them to a communal, liturgical spirituality. By all accounts, he was a lively, engaging speaker, blessed with a "mischievous, elfin humor." His influence through the Sodality movement cannot be measured, but from its earliest days he spoke of the liturgy as the source of the true Christian spirit and celebrated the dialogue Mass regularly in the Sodality's Summer School of Catholic Action. One can assume that many of that generation had been "initiated into the hidden beauties" of the liturgy by Ellard, just as he desired in his 1925 letter.

Gerald Ellard died on April 1, 1963, in Boston; it was eight months before the affirmation of his life's work in the promulgation of the *Constitution on the Sacred Liturgy* by Vatican II. He personified the various stages of the movement prior to the *Constitution:* laying the theological groundwork, developing popular support and advocating the liturgical reform needed for the spiritual welfare of God's faithful. His best epitaph is from the lips of Thomas Carroll, who preached at Ellard's *evening* funeral Mass in Cambridge, Massachusetts:

> [He was] blest by God in his early grasp of the full import of the apostolate, of the true meaning of the liturgy, of the depth and riches of its scripturally-based spirituality . . . blest with the qualities of scholarship and a great capacity to bring the fruits of scholarship to the ordinary person.

■ *Robert J. Kennedy*

NOTES

The only full-length study of Gerald Ellard and his work is the unpublished doctoral dissertation of John Leo Klein, *The Role of Gerald Ellard (1894–1963) in the Development of the Contemporary American Catholic Liturgical Movement* (Bronx: Fordham University, 1971). This article has relied heavily on that work and the various tributes to Ellard published shortly after his death. Complete bibliographies of Ellard's own work appear at the end of Klein's dissertation (251–63) and in Everett Diederich's tribute in *Yearbook of Liturgical Studies,* Vol. 4, ed. John H. Miller (Notre Dame: Fides Publishers, 1963), 3–21.

H. A. REINHOLD

The Timely Tract
to the American Church

ANS ANSGAR REINHOLD (known later to everyone as H.A.R.) was born in Hamburg, Germany, on September 9, 1897. His father, Bernhard, was a prominent citizen in the shipping and brokerage business. Reinhold would later describe his father as a committed Catholic "who did not hold any romantic notions about religion."[1] He knelt only during the consecration, bowed his head when he entered the church rather than genuflecting and sang loudly all of the hymns. He was ecumenically minded and took the young H.A.R. to visit Protestant churches after attending Mass on Sunday.

His mother also was a person of deep faith. Like her husband, she was "opposed to all sentimental religious expression and emotional mysticism." She loved the baroque architecture of southern Germany and the music of Bach and Handel. She taught H.A.R. and his sister the social graces, insisting that they learn the manners of polite society.

Schools and Teachers

In the fourth grade, Reinhold's parents transferred him to a public school that was predominantly Lutheran in its orientation. He was grouped with the Jews and learned firsthand what it was like to be treated as a minority. Undoubtedly, this experience contributed to his advocacy of ecumenical exchange and cooperation.

At the age of 15, Reinhold went to confession and communion once a week. He also went through periods of depression and melancholy, an affliction that would last his lifetime. He became convinced that Catholicism had a "solid rational foundation, and that it was an intellectually tenable religion."[2] He was developing in these years an avid interest in languages and history, in art and architecture. At this time, too, he gave his first serious thoughts to becoming a priest. In 1914, however, he joined the German army, persuaded by government propaganda that Germany had been attacked.

During his time in the army, Reinhold was wounded in the throat, suffered amnesia and broke his leg. He worked with army intelligence as a translator of French- and English-language codes. After the war, he studied for a year at the University of Freiburg, where he became acquainted with Heidegger and Husserl. During this time, he also discovered Romano Guardini's *The Spirit of the Liturgy*. That book was a turning point in his life:

> The legalistic body of restrictions and commandments which I used to have in my mind and which I used to defend in fierce and dull despair, had vanished before the vision of Christ's Mystical Body and the incredible beauty of his mystical life among us through his sacraments and mysteries.[3]

This vision of the Mystical Body and the *mysterium-sacramentum* would become the twofold focus of much of his future writings.

In 1920, he entered the Jesuit seminary at Innsbruck. There he was exposed to a school with an international student body and high standards of scholarship and spiritual formation. He especially enjoyed his studies with Father Hatyer, who taught the historical development of the liturgy and introduced Reinhold to the possibility of its reform.

In 1922, Reinhold spent a year at the famous Benedictine monastery, Maria Laach, where he came under the influence of its abbot, Ildefons Herwegen, and the scholar-monk, Odo Casel. At Maria Laach, he experienced for the first time the "dialogue Mass" in which the congregation made the appropriate responses. He also witnessed the pastoral value of celebrating Mass facing the people as well as the importance of having an offertory procession.

This new approach to the eucharist opened his eyes to the weaknesses of the parochial celebrations of his day:

> This form flowed quite naturally from the real meaning of the Mass; it was almost suggested by its ceremonies and texts. The amazing thing was only this—why on earth had we never thought of it before?[4]

Spreading this good news was to become his lifelong task.

The following year, Reinhold enrolled in the University of Münster, where he studied scripture and dogmatic and moral theology and where he was exposed to the philosophies of Kierkegaard, Hegel and Voltaire. Johannes Quasten, who later became famous for his studies in patrology, was a classmate. Reinhold's thesis was directed by Franz Josef Doelger, "The Christian and Pagan Habits of Burial in the First Centuries after Christ."

On December 19, 1925, he was ordained a priest of the diocese of Osnabruech. Soon after his ordination, he celebrated his first dialogue Mass with a Benedictine community of sisters at Herstelle, a community where Odo Casel also served. Many times he rode his bicycle to visit friends at their farm, where he would stay overnight and say Mass the next morning on a kitchen table facing the family. In 1928, the bishop sent him to the Pontifical Institute of Archaeology in Rome, where he developed his interests in liturgical spirituality and the influence of the environment on worship.

Liturgy and Justice

In 1929, Reinhold returned to Germany and became the bishop's secretary to the seaman's apostolate. This work helped solidify his convictions about the necessary connection between liturgy and social justice. "For him, social concern was implied in a living out of the mysteries of Christ."[5] For how could one be the body of Christ at Mass without also being concerned with the body of Christ in the world?

In 1930, Reinhold was among the national and local directors who founded the International Council of the Apostolate of the Sea in England. Fortunately for Reinhold, this involvement with the seaman's apostolate provided him with the type of background that enabled him to find work when he was forced to flee to the United States.

Ever since his exposure to the dialogue Mass at Maria Laach, Reinhold had sought to implement the type of liturgical reforms that would make the liturgy more intelligible to the people. For years, many liturgists had bemoaned the fact that the Easter Vigil, which originally had been a night vigil, was celebrated on the morning of Holy Saturday. In 1935, he celebrated the Easter Vigil at a Hamburg parish one and a half hours before sunrise on Easter morning, timing it so that "the Benedictus coincided with the rise of the sun."[6]

Because of Reinhold's outspoken criticisms of Hitler, he was forced to flee the German Gestapo in 1935. He escaped over the border to Holland and eventually made his way to England with nothing but "a fountain pen and a toothbrush."[7] On August 20, 1936, he sought refuge in the United States and began working with the Catholic section of the Protestant Refugee Committee in New York.

H.A.R. *in the United States*

Ironically, the archbishop of New York became suspicious of Reinhold for being an anti-Nazi agitator. Reinhold left the city to live in Long Island and to commute to Columbia University, where he began working on a doctorate in history. Eventually, he dropped out of the university to accept a teaching post at Portsmouth Priory in Rhode Island in 1937.

In October 1938, he accepted the invitation of the Bishop of Seattle, Washington, to serve as port chaplain of that coastal city. He soon founded the Seaman's Club of Seattle, working with the seaman's apostolate much as he had done in Niendorf. In time, he moved to a parish in Yakima, Washington, where he came under investigation for his German background. One who fled Germany because of his anti-Nazi rhetoric was investigated by the Federal Bureau of Investigation and the enemy-alien control board as a possible Nazi sympathizer. In fact, his movement was restricted for a time to the five-mile radius of Yakima. Eventually, his status was clarified and in 1944 he became an American citizen. On achieving his citizenship, Reinhold was appointed the pastor of St. Joseph's church in Sunnyside, Washington, by Bishop Shaughnessy.

The Years in Pittsburgh

In 1951, the Seattle diocese was divided with Sunnyside becoming part of the new Yakima diocese under Bishop Joseph Dougherty. After five years of a strained relationship with his bishop, Reinhold offered to resign the parish. At this same time, he learned that he had contracted cystitis and needed medical treatment. On May 1, 1956, he left the diocese, thinking he had the bishop's permission for a leave of absence. The bishop accused him of deserting his parish and demanded that he return. Again Reinhold offered to resign his parish and again the bishop refused to accept his resignation. Finally, Bishop John Wright of Pittsburgh agreed to accept Reinhold into his diocese.

Bishop Wright was especially kind to Reinhold in his final years. Wright found him almost penniless, living in a Cistercian abbey in Pittsburgh. He gave him a rectory to live in and provided for his medical care. He allowed him to continue his writings and speeches uninhibited. Medical problems, however, grew worse with the first symptoms of Parkinson's disease being diagnosed in the summer of 1957.

The bizarre conditions under which Reinhold left the Yakima diocese continued to haunt him. The bishop of St. Cloud convinced Godfrey Diekmann, the editor of *Orate Fratres* magazine, to cease publishing H.A.R.'s column, because his irregular canonical status would reflect poorly on *Worship*. And so, in December of 1957, H.A.R. wrote his last article for *Worship*. He then turned his talents to writing books: *The American Parish and the Roman Liturgy* (1958), *Bringing the Mass to the People* (1960), *The Dynamics of the Liturgy* (1961), *Liturgy and Art* (1966) and *H.A.R., The Autobiography of Father Reinhold* (1968).

In 1961, Bishop Wright appointed Reinhold to the diocesan liturgical commission. It appeared that his position in the diocese had stabilized and he was able to take a more active role as a liturgist. In 1966, his physical condition worsened and he was forced to give up writing. On January 26, 1968, he died.

Because a great deal of his life was devoted to writing, it is interesting to read what H.A.R. intended to be his last words to us. They are recorded in his autobiography, which was published posthumously, although it was written some years before he died. He spoke of his long career, of the small numbers who began the liturgical movement, of the renewal finally taking root:

When I had first ventured out the road was narrow and the wayfarers were few; with the help of others and despite my falterings, I have reached this resting place. The road is wider now, and the goal is closer to sight. To those now traveling that road, I wish good luck and godspeed.[8]

Because of his many gifts, his clarity of insight and his willingness to suffer for his ideals, the road, indeed, has widened and the travelers seeking liturgical renewal are many.

Liturgical and Social Ideas

What were some of the ideas and ideals to which Reinhold devoted his life? Many of them are recorded in the pages of his column, "Timely Tracts," which he wrote for *Orate Fratres* (later *Worship*) from February 1938 until December 1954. "Timely Tracts" provided a sounding board for educating the American church in the best insights of the European liturgical movement. Strongly influenced by Odo Casel and his *mysterium-sacramentum* theory and as a pupil of Beauduin and an admirer of Parsch, Reinhold wanted to close the gap that found America 20 years behind Europe in liturgical renewal.

Reinhold emphasized the parochial celebration of Mass, the liturgical year, church art and architecture. He wanted to move people away from an allegorical interpretation of the eucharist and beyond any preoccupation with adoration of the host in the tabernacle. He wanted people to recapture the original understanding of eucharist as an action of the whole church, an activity requiring full and active participation by all.

In 1940, he urged a return to the "essentials of a Catholic life."[9] In his writings, he describes these essentials as

simple symbols like bread, wine, altar, table; unmistakable words of Christ, like body and blood; the separation of both in his words of institution with its allusion to his own sacrifice and death; and the fresh gestures of blessing, breaking, and offering to the Father. These were the primary things of liturgy, of the mystery of eucharistic worship.[10]

Like other liturgical leaders, Reinhold emphasized the ecclesial dimension of the liturgical celebration. He writes:

> We are the body of Christ. We offer the body of Christ. We share the body of Christ. It is in, and as, and with the body of Christ that we celebrate our redemption, regularly renew our pledge of discipleship, and our "yes" to God's covenant.[11]

He warned against overemphasizing the sacrificial nature of the Mass to the detriment of the meal aspects. In many ways, his theology of eucharist anticipated the advances made after Vatican II.

The Ideal Mass

His most prophetic essay, "My Dream Mass," was written for the April 1940 issue of *Orate Fratres*. In it, he dreams of a small parish church built of good, local, inexpensive material in no particular historical style, but with one obvious purpose: to serve the liturgy. It would be quadrangular in shape, have a freestanding altar facing the people, who would be gathered around it as close as possible in a fan formation. There would be no pews, but low stools with no backs.

The sacristy of this parish church would be located near the foyer. A father of a family carries the processional cross into church, followed by one server carrying the missal and another carrying the gospel book. Also in the entrance procession would be a small schola to sing the full entrance psalm. The people will make all the responses. There will be no collection at the offertory, but people would drop their offerings in baskets at the door of the church as they entered. The Mass would be in English, with only the offertory prayers and the Canon in Latin.[12]

Reinhold advocated liturgical reforms long before it was fashionable to do so. He favored the dialogue Mass (1922), evening Masses (1934), vernacular in the liturgy (1940), daily homily (1945), breviary reform (1948), three-year cycle of readings (1952), communion from the cup (1952) and con-celebration (1953). He strongly advocated the dialogue Mass as a way to correct two extremes in liturgical celebration: total dominance by the choir in Europe and total silence of the con-gregation in the United States.

On architecture, Reinhold emphasized the two principal foci of the building: the altar and the baptistry. They should be on an axis with the baptistry placed at the door of the church in the foyer. Confessionals are located near the baptistry. Shrines with altars or devotions such as Stations of the Cross belong in separate chapels apart from the main worship space. He described the parish church of the future as having the marks of a "rapidly rising tent,"[13] manifesting a temporary, inexpen-sive character in contrast to the monumental structures of the past. He decried the use of tasteless, cheap, commercial "art" work in so many of our churches.[14]

In his "Timely Tracts," Reinhold frequently addressed the need for a new social order (noting the abuses of the American economic system, the exploitation of property and the immoral practices of capitalism). Liturgy must be related to life and translated into social action. People must be active both inside the church during the liturgy and outside the church, carrying on the work of Christ. We need to renew our appre-ciation of the way baptism deputizes all Christians to complete Christ's mission in the world.

H.A.R.'s story is amazing, moving, inspiring, yet also tragic. He was a prophet, an exemplary pastor, a pastoral theologian, a Renaissance man with an unquenchable thirst for beauty and knowledge. When he came to the United States, he was shocked by the low state of liturgical practice that he found. He dedicated the rest of his life to help Americans come to a fuller understanding of the mysteries of liturgical prayer that he had known in Europe.

His writings stirred controversy and he often was misunderstood by people. Always a gentleman, he never attacked. His enemies were ignorance, mediocrity and complacency. While he was not afraid to ask embarrassing questions, his concern was only for the truth. He was first, last and always a churchman, who remained faithful to his calling both in good times and in bad. Happily, he lived long enough to see many of his ideas vindicated at Vatican II.

■ *Robert L. Tuzik*

NOTES

1. H. A. Reinhold, *H.A.R., the Autobiography of Father Reinhold* (New York: Herder & Herder, 1968), 11.

2. Ibid., 17.

3. H. A. Reinhold, "Cloister and Society," *Commonweal* 28 (May 20, 1938), 98.

4. Ibid.

5. Joel Patrick Garner, *The Vision of a Liturgical Reformer: Hans Ansgar Reinhold, American Catholic Educator* (Ann Arbor: University Microfilms, 1973), 23.

6. Reinhold, *H.A.R., the Autobiography,* 74.

7. Ibid., 90.

8. Ibid., 150.

9. H. A. Reinhold, "Anglican," *Orate Fratres* 14 (1940), 221.

10. Garner, *The Vision,* 51.

11. H. A. Reinhold, "The Eucharistic Bread," *Sunday Morning Crisis,* ed. Robert Hovda (Baltimore: Helicon, 1963), 93.

12. H. A. Reinhold, "My Dream Mass," *Orate Fratres* 14 (1940), 265–70.

13. H. A. Reinhold, "Liturgy, Architecture, and the Arts," *Irish Ecclesiastical Record* 95 (May 1961), 302.

14. H. A. Reinhold, *Liturgy and Art* (New York: Harper & Row, 1966), 80 ff.

MARTIN HELLRIEGEL

Pastor

S OMEONE ASKED MARTIN B. HELLRIEGEL late in his life how he came to be so deeply interested in the liturgy. He answered: "By the grace of God, the example of a good mother, and the inspiration of a holy priest." All of these were in Heppenheim, Germany, where Martin Hellriegel was born in 1891 and where he grew up as the eldest of four children. When he had finished school, he accompanied Reverend George Hoehn to the United States, where he thought that he was going to "convert the Indians." Instead, he spent three years in a parish in Starkenburg, Missouri. Hoehn was the pastor and Hellriegel lived in the rectory and assisted in parish duties.

At age 19, he began his studies for the priesthood at St. Meinrad's Seminary in Indiana. He then pursued his theological studies at Kenrick Seminary in St. Louis, Missouri. His ordination was delayed for six months so he could reach the required age of 24. World War I broke out and Hellriegel was unable to celebrate the ordination with his family. As he put it: "Man proposes, but God disposes, and the Kaiser opposes." Only when the young man became 32 was he able to celebrate with his family in his native Heppenheim—18 months after his father had died.

During the early years of his priesthood, Hellriegel's vision of the church's liturgy became clearer. He had experienced at St. Meinrad's the vitality and the mystery within the celebration of the eucharist and the Divine Office. Several early works of Romano Guardini, in the original German, as well as Karl Adam's *The Spirit of Catholicism,* had a profound influence on him. He said that these books made him recognize that rubrics are a fence that protects the sacred liturgy, a garden rich in flower and fruit.

Abbot Ildefons Herwegen and Odo Casel, both of Maria Laach monastery in Germany, also made a deep and lasting impression on him. He clearly grasped Casel's controversial mystery-theology and delved into the reality that the mysteries of salvation become truly present in the church's celebration of the liturgy. This insight made a radical difference in his awareness and in his attitude whenever he celebrated the sacraments or the Liturgy of the Hours.

His first assignment was as assistant to Reverend F. X. Wilmes at St. Peter Parish in St. Charles, Missouri. He was there only three years.

His next 22 years as chaplain for the Sisters of the Most Precious Blood in O'Fallon, Missouri, must have been the best of times and the worst of times for the young priest. His zeal for and deep understanding of the liturgy met with not a few obstacles and he learned the truth of the words of his former pastor: "With the appointment goes the grace."

When he introduced the dialogue Mass at the convent and insisted that no other devotions were to be carried on during its celebration, the superior remonstrated with him, telling him that it always had been their custom to pray the Precious Blood Litany during Mass. He assured the sister that the tradition he was reviving dated much further back than hers did. As he prepared the sisters to celebrate fully the solemn seasons of the church year, he quoted over and over again the words of

Pius X: "Active participation in the sacred liturgy and the solemn prayer of the church is the primary and indispensable source of the true Christian spirit." His efforts were directed not toward new devotions but toward enhancing the liturgical celebrations. Processions at the entrance, offertory, communion and closing of the Mass were directed to this goal, as was his enthusiastic use of sacramentals, such as water, ashes and palms.

With what he characterized as "the cooperation of the maternal, energetic Mother Wilhemine," particular emphasis was placed on making the daily holy sacrifice, especially the Sunday high Mass, the greatest experience of all. The day hours of the Roman breviary were chanted at their proper times and replaced other community devotions.

Hellriegel's work also attracted attention outside of the O'Fallon community and other persons in the early liturgical movement were frequent visitors to the convent. We read the following in *A Time to Sow* (a history of the convent):

> In the holy night of Christmas 1925, half an hour before Midnight Mass, Father Virgil Michel, OSB, Gerald Ellard, and our chaplain [Hellriegel] made the final decision concerning the title of the liturgical review to be published November 28, 1926, by St. John's Abbey of Collegeville, Minnesota. Its name: *Orate Fratres*. Father Hellriegel became one of its associate editors.[1]

Hellriegel was to be a frequent contributor to this magazine, which received a good deal of criticism and even ridicule in its early days.

What he was promoting seemed so new. John Joseph Glennon, archbishop of St. Louis, was on his side, however, while the vicar general and chancellor opposed him. A letter to Hellriegel, dated October 14, 1925, said in part: "Your work is not an innovation. It is a restoration, and especially I am pleased to see your endeavor to associate more closely, indeed incorporate, the Catholic laity in this liturgy."[2]

Hellriegel helped the community of sisters to see itself in the light of the church's tradition. The postulants and novices were carefully trained to find their spiritual life grounded in the sacred liturgy. Each week a particular examen was chosen from the readings or chants of the Sunday celebration, then placed on the altar at offertory and lived out during the week that followed. The life of the religious was seen to be the flowering of the baptismal life and its growth always was in keeping with the life of the church.

"Proceed with Tender Tenacity"

When Monsignor Hellriegel was transferred to Holy Cross Parish in St. Louis in June of 1940, he proceeded to prove wrong those detractors who maintained that he never could do in a parish what had been accomplished in a community of religious women in O'Fallon. Holy Cross was a well-established parish whose members were largely of German ancestry. Hellriegel had many opportunities to live out the maxim of his friend, Pius Parsch: "Proceed with tender tenacity."

He began during his first year to lead the parishioners into the mystery of the liturgical year. Advent became for them a time to celebrate the coming Christ in glory as well as a time for active spiritual preparation for the coming of Christ. Christmas and Epiphany became full celebrations and the people resonated with the unspeakable mystery contained therein. Priests and people celebrated the Easter season with even greater involvement. Lent with its call to conversion led the entire parish to enter as fully as possible into the Triduum. Hellriegel worked long and hard for the restoration of the Easter Vigil. When this jewel was returned, he "was overjoyed to do what he had hoped for so long, and his enthusiasm was communicated to the people."[3] The single most important factor leading to his ultimate success was the consistency with which he kept on living the mysteries of the church year, undaunted by setbacks and apparent indifference.

Part of his consistency was the close congruence between what he claimed to be important and the efforts he made to put his convictions into practice. He said that singing was important, so he started a children's choir and supported the adult choir as well as congregational singing. He claimed that reverence was due every action around the altar, so he trained two groups of altar boys, the younger ones as well as the St. Pius X senior servers. He maintained that the liturgy was the fountain of catechesis, so he saw to it that the children were schooled adequately in the celebration of the sacraments and in living the liturgy in their daily lives.

Liturgy is not the only parish activity, but it is the natural support for all the actions of the Mystical Body of Christ. Hellriegel stood up for the family as the most important unit in the parish. Furthermore, the parish maintained at least 25 active groups, from Scouts and athletic teams to the Catholic Youth Council and the Archdiocesan Council of Men and Women.

During his years as pastor of Holy Cross, he was much in demand as a lecturer, retreat master, preacher and writer. Numerous prominent liturgists from the United States and abroad visited him at the parish. Among the names in the guest book are Godfrey Diekmann, Jean Danielou, Clifford Howell, Bishop Bush of St. Cloud and Bishop W. Cobben of Finland. He was active in the Liturgical Conference, serving on its board of directors and for one year as its vice president. He also made outstanding contributions to the Liturgical Weeks.

Instaurare Omnia in Christo

To incorporate everyone and everything into Christ" seems really to have been Hellriegel's motivating force. For him, the church's liturgy was infinitely more than a cause to be championed; it was a life to be lived.

Here is just one example that illustrates this. As postulants and novices (I was in the novitiate in the 1930s), we were well schooled by him in the meaning of the liturgical *memorial*. When he presided at Mass in the convent, the great eucharistic prayer never was ordinary or routine. Praise and thanks rang out from his lips. After the words of consecration, we stood up as we entered into the anamnesis. There we were: *nos servi tui* (presider) and *plebs tua sancta* (the rest of the congregation) as the blessed passion, resurrection and glorious ascension of Christ became present before us and within us. Yes, *really!* I still can see our offerings being taken to the throne of God—that very bread that would be our sacramental food. *Ex hac altare participatione.* These words prompted Hellriegel's great concern, even in the 1930s, that we should receive in communion hosts that were consecrated at that Mass. We looked forward to growing more deeply into the Mystical Body of Christ by partaking in that meal. The great doxology chanted by him with marvelous enthusiasm evoked from us a soul-stirring "Amen!"

Hellriegel had ample share in that essential ingredient of the paschal mystery: suffering. Long absences from family and friends along with the premature death of his father came early in his life. There were the ambiguities of his pioneering work in liturgy, along with the suspicion and ridicule of fellow clergy. In later years, he endured the diminishments that came with advancing years; the most grievous suffering of all was the loss of his eyesight. He said with an effort of good humor: "God is taking me piece by piece." Finally, he retired to the infirmary of the sisters in O'Fallon, still the gentleman he always had been. James Rutkowski, who assisted Hellriegel at daily Mass after he became blind, said: "Monsignor Hellriegel was able to be with rich and poor alike and everyone was enriched. It was never a burden to serve him for he always lifted me up." On March 16, 1981, he made his final journey through the paschal mystery to be himself incorporated fully into Christ.

■ *Mary Pierre Ellebracht*

NOTES

1. Jean Thomas Lake, *A Time to Sow: A History of the Sisters of the Adoration of the Most Precious Blood of O'Fallon, Missouri* (1972), 123.

2. Transcript, Rt. Rev. John J. Glennon to Rev. Martin R. Hellriegel, October 14, 1925 (O'Fallon Archives: X.A. 18, Box 1).

3. Anne Huneke, "Monsignor Martin Hellriegel and the Church Year," Part 2, *The Priest* (February 1983) 31–32.

REYNOLD HILLENBRAND

The Movements in Chicago

R EYNOLD HILLENBRAND WAS A PRIEST of the archdiocese of Chicago; rector of St. Mary of the Lake Seminary; national chaplain of the Christian Family Movement, the Young Christian Students and the Young Christian Workers (known collectively as the Specialized Lay Apostolate); a founder of the Vernacular Society; a consultant to the Vatican II commission that produced the *Decree on the Laity;* a founding member of the Chicago archdiocesan liturgical commission; and pastor of Sacred Heart Church in Hubbard Woods, Illinois.

Hillenbrand was born in Chicago in 1904 and grew up in the German parish of St. Michael on the near north side of the city. St. Michael's was known for active participation in the liturgy and for a commitment to social justice. Hillenbrand studied at Quigley Preparatory Seminary in downtown Chicago and at St. Mary of the Lake Seminary. Cardinal Mundelein sent Hillenbrand to Rome to study at the Gregorian University for a year (1931–1932). During that year, Pius XI issued his famous encyclical, *Quadragesimo Anno,* which advocated a restoration of the social order based on an organic conception of society as the Body of Christ. The encyclical had a lasting influence on Hillenbrand.

While studying in Europe, Hillenbrand visited several liturgical centers: Maria Laach in Germany, Mont César in Belgium and Klosterneuberg in Austria. He became familiar with the thinking of Joseph Cardijn, a Belgian priest who founded the Young Christian Workers in 1912. He wanted to train young workers to become lay apostles by ministering to their peers. It was an effort to solve the problems of laborers and to bring the church closer to the people. Hillenbrand returned to the United States filled with zeal and enthusiasm for the ideals of the liturgical and social-action movements.

Teacher, Rector, National Leader

In 1932, Hillenbrand was assigned to teach Latin and English literature at Quigley Preparatory Seminary. He had the good fortune to live at Holy Name Cathedral, where he came under the influence of the rector, Joseph Morrison, a strong advocate of liturgical renewal and Catholic Action. In addition, the Chicago archdiocese was becoming known as a place where social-justice activities were given strong public support by archdiocesan clergy.

The 1930s was a decade during which the social conscience of American Catholics was increasingly challenged by activists such as Dorothy Day, Peter Maurin, Maisie Ward, Frank Sheed, Catherine de Hueck Doherty and others. The poor working conditions of many laborers and the suffering of so many unemployed people created a new openness to examining the social teachings of the church. Both liturgists and social activists found the solution to society's problems in the organic conception of society as a Mystical Body. In 1943, the papal encyclical *Mystici Corporis* gave strong expression to these directions.

In 1936, Cardinal Mundelein named Hillenbrand, who then was 31, the new rector of St. Mary of the Lake Seminary. In one of his early talks as rector, Hillenbrand challenged the seminarians

> to see beyond their comfortable parishes and beyond their own comfortable lives—to see the suffering in the world, to have a heart for the unemployed, not to shy away from misery, but to feel the injustice of inadequate wages . . . to have some of the vision that Day and Maurin and priests have who are coping with social problems.[1]

In his liturgy course at the seminary, Hillenbrand taught the students the best insights of the European and American liturgical and social-action movements. He also conducted classes for the seminarians and faculty on the social encyclicals.

As the liturgical leader at the seminary, Hillenbrand introduced the practice of the dialogue Mass and encouraged priests to celebrate the Mass of the day, rather than the frequent requiem Masses. He expected presiders to preach a daily homily based on the scriptures, the particular feast or the liturgical season. He also required all the seminarians to learn to sing plainchant, so the psalms could be sung instead of recited at Matins and Vespers.

His emphasis on corporate worship, his explanation of the eucharist as the "effective presentation of the Mystical Body" and the liturgical year as "the reproduction of the life of the Head in the lives of the members of the Mystical Body"[2] sounded quite radical to the Jesuit faculty of the seminary. Even more radical were the ideas of some of the visiting lecturers that Hillenbrand invited, among them William Boyd, Dorothy Day, Gerald Ellard, Catherine de Hueck Doherty, Francis Haas, Martin Hellriegel, John LaFarge, Maurice Lavanoux, Robert Lucey, Virgil Michel and H. A. Reinhold.

The first Chicago Summer School of Social Action for priests took place at the seminary under Hillenbrand's leadership from July 18 to August 12, 1938. This summer school introduced Hillenbrand to the ideas of Donald Kanaly, a priest from Ponca City, Oklahoma, who recently had returned from studying in

Europe and was interested in bringing the ideals of the Young Christian Workers to the United States. During 1939 and 1940, additional Summer Schools of Social Action were held at the seminary, always with a segment of the program devoted to liturgy. These summer schools served as important preludes to Hillenbrand's involvement with the Liturgical Conference.

Liturgical Weeks, Summer Schools, Catholic Action

In 1940, under the influence of Father Louis Putz of Notre Dame, Hillenbrand established a Young Christian Students group at Senn High School in Chicago.[3] He also experimented with "liturgical missions" similar to those recommended by H. A. Reinhold in Everett, Washington. His greatest challenge came, however, when the Benedictine Liturgical Conference asked him and Joseph Morrison to cochair the first National Liturgical Week to be held in Chicago at Holy Name Cathedral in 1940.[4] The theme of this Week was "The Living Parish: Active and Intelligent Participation of the Laity in the Liturgy of the Catholic Church."

Hillenbrand gave the keynote address on the history and ideals of the liturgical movement.[5] The Week brought together 1,260 people from across the country and achieved the much-needed goal of obtaining an episcopal sponsor from a prominent archdiocese. This experience led Hillenbrand to organize the first national Summer School of Liturgy, held at Mundelein from July 14 to August 1, 1941.

Hillenbrand was active in the Liturgical Conference from the beginning. He served on the first Board of Directors, becoming treasurer in 1944 and vice-president from 1949 to 1955. In addition, he served as a member, sometimes as the chairman, of the Program Committee, which was responsible for deciding on the speakers, obtaining episcopal sponsors and publishing the proceedings of these weeks.

While his involvement in liturgical renewal was increasing, Hillenbrand also spoke at numerous Catholic Action gatherings. In fact, a month after the founding of the first Catholic Action "cell" (or group) in Chicago, Hillenbrand was invited to speak to them about the theology of the Mystical Body. One of the founders of this group, Patrick Crowley, helped Hillenbrand organize a men's group at Sacred Heart Church. This group was the basis for the Christian Family Movement.[6]

Hillenbrand's social and liturgical activism came under attack by pastors and seminary faculty. They criticized him for "liberal" ideas—supporting the rights of laborers to organize unions and to bargain collectively, recommending social reconstruction as a necessary complement to liturgical participation, advocating that the laity take more leadership in the work of the church.[7]

On July 15, 1944, Archbishop Stritch notified Hillenbrand that he was being promoted to the pastorate. While Hillenbrand never mentioned to anyone the exact reasons for his dismissal, few people saw his change in assignment as a promotion.[8] His eight years of leadership at the seminary produced many strong, liturgical-minded, socially oriented priests who went on to provide local and national leadership.

Pastor and National Chaplain

As pastor at Sacred Heart Parish in Hubbard Woods, Hillenbrand could pursue his liturgical and social action interests with greater freedom. He even was vindicated in his social activism when Cardinal Stritch appointed him the Coordinator of Catholic Action cells in the archdiocese in 1945.[9] As a result of this new mandate, Hillenbrand became associated ever more closely with the expansion of Young Christian Students (YCS), Young Christian Workers (YCW) and eventually

the Christian Family Movement (CFM). In 1947, Hillenbrand
became the national chaplain of YCW and national chaplain of
YCS and CFM in 1949.

Eventually, a four-year training program evolved for the
training of lay apostles. The topics included marriage and family life, economic life, political life, international life, parochial
life, leisure time and the racial problem. The spirituality of
these programs was based on the liturgy. In addition, these
training programs emphasized the laity's participation in the
priesthood of Christ by virtue of their baptism and confirmation. To think that all the leadership, initiative and responsibility
for the apostolate could be clerical was "to have a deficient
sense of church as a living, organic oneness of all its members."[10]

In 1945, Hillenbrand introduced the dialogue Mass and
formed a boy's choir at Sacred Heart Parish. In his preaching,
he explained the rationale for these changes and the importance of the sung Mass. He also established study clubs on the
Mass as well as Catholic Action cells. He sponsored the first
Cana Conference for married couples[11] and the first Pre-Cana
Conference for engaged couples. In 1948, he obtained the services of the renowned chant expert, Ermin Vitry, to begin a
music program that would become a national model of active
participation in the liturgy.[12]

Sacred Heart Parish was one of two parishes in the archdiocese to receive the cardinal's permission to celebrate the
experimental rite of the Easter Vigil in 1952. Hillenbrand
began the Vigil at 10:30 PM and baptized five children, all from
one family. In his report to Cardinal Stritch, he evaluated his
experience in these words:

> The people gathered—in a way not hitherto possible—three
> profound impressions: the transition from darkness to light,
> from death to life; the tremendous meaning of baptism; the
> joyful impact of the first Easter Mass.[13]

The experiment was typical of Hillenbrand's approach to liturgical change. As soon as a certain change was allowed, he would explain it to the parish and then implement it.

Throughout the 1940s, Hillenbrand grew in stature as a national leader of the liturgical and social action apostolates. In the 1950s and into the mid-1960s, Hillenbrand was such a popular speaker that his lectures always were scheduled in a prominent spot (often, the keynote address) at national conventions of CFM, YCS or YCW. He was often the presider at the convention eucharist, modeling the type of leadership needed for the active participation of the assembly. When the *Constitution on the Sacred Liturgy* was promulgated in 1963, the people of the Specialized Lay Apostolate were ready to accept its understanding of liturgy, thanks in part to Hillenbrand's efforts to prepare them.

While Hillenbrand continued as a national figure until the late 1960s, his effectiveness was hindered in later years by a number of medical problems. He was in a car accident in 1949 that severely damaged his right leg. Repeated operations could not remove the pain and stiffness. In addition, he was plagued by chronic migraine headaches.

Hillenbrand had become so identified with the Specialized Lay Apostolate that Bishop Ernest Primeau, a member of the conciliar commission preparing the *Decree on the Laity,* sought Hillenbrand's critique of the document. Some of his recommendations were incorporated in the final draft (e.g., mention of the principle of "like ministering to like," the importance of Catholic Action groups and the necessity of apostolic training).

His Place among the Liturgical Pioneers

Hillenbrand retired as pastor of Sacred Heart Parish in 1974. His last five years were filled with much suffering and he was frequently in and out of the hospital. He died on May 22, 1979.

Many of Hillenbrand's convictions triumphed at Vatican II —the use of the vernacular in the liturgy, full and active participation in the liturgy, lay ministry training, the priesthood of the laity, the necessary connection between liturgy and social justice and the parish as a ministerial training center. He had a permanent influence on thousands of priests and laity in their vision of church and liturgy.

Godfrey Diekmann evaluated Hillenbrand's achievements in these words:

> In any historical overview of the Catholic church in the United States in this century, Monsignor Hillenbrand would certainly have to be numbered among the top dozen who influenced its apostolic developments. In fact, I cannot think of more than three or four others who could rank with him in this respect. He inspired generations of priests and laity with his vision of the social gospel rooted in the community-formative dynamic of the Mass.[14]

Hillenbrand was a popularizer, a sensitive intellectual, someone who did his homework and couldn't be dismissed lightly, willing to suffer for what he believed in, a man who loved and lived the liturgy:

> It isn't enough to seek Christ's history. We have to sense Christ in the world today and realize that we are one with him. He does his work through us and he won't get his work done without us. We get that in the liturgy.[15]

■ *Robert L. Tuzik*

NOTES

1. Hillenbrand, "Seminary Social Thoughts, 1936," University of Notre Dame Archives (UNDA), Msgr. Reynold Hillenbrand Collection (CMRH) 3/25. The University of Notre Dame Archives has the most complete collection of Hillenbrand's papers.

2. Hillenbrand, "Liturgy Course Notes," UNDA, CMRH 5/21.

3. See Martin Quigley, Jr., and Edward Connors, "Youth Apostolate," *Catholic Action in Practice* (New York: Random House, Inc., 1963), 91–99.

4. The National Liturgical Weeks were to bring together people interested in a better understanding of and participation in the liturgy, thus accomplishing in the United States what the Belgian *Semaines Liturgiques* (Liturgical Weeks), held annually from 1910 to 1939, had accomplished in Europe.

5. October 21, 1940, National Liturgical Week, Chicago, Illinois. In *National Liturgical Week 1940* (Newark: Benedictine Liturgical Conference, 1941) 5–13. In all, Hillenbrand spoke at ten National Liturgical Weeks: 1940, 1941, 1943, 1945, 1946, 1947, 1948, 1951, 1955 and 1956.

6. Quigley and Connors, *Catholic Action in Practice*, 149–50. See Rose Marciano Lucey, *Roots and Wings, Dreamers and Doers of the Christian Family Movement* (San Jose: Resource Publications, 1987).

7. See Edward R. Kantowicz, *Corporation Sole, Cardinal Mundelein and Chicago Catholicism* (Notre Dame: University of Notre Dame Press, 1983), 123–27.

8. See Andrew Greeley, "The Chicago Experience," *The Catholic Experience, An Interpretation of the History of American Catholicism* (New York: Doubleday and Company, 1967), esp. 249–53; see also Dennis Geaney, "The Chicago Story," *Chicago Studies* 2 (1963), 287–300.

9. Cardinal Stritch to Hillenbrand, April 6, 1945, UNDA, CMRH 7: Cardinal's Letters re: Movements and Catholic Action.

10. Hillenbrand, "Prayer and Sacrifice," April 1, 1948, lecture, UNDA, CMRH 18/26, YCW Priests' Study Weeks, 1948–1956.

11. See Leo R. Ward, *Catholic Life, U.S.A., Contemporary Lay Movement* (St. Louis: B. Herder, 1959), chapter 4: The Cana Movement, 53–74.

12. See Bob Senser, "How a Parish Came to Sing," *Worship* 26 (1952), 257–59.

13. Hillenbrand to Cardinal Stritch, April 18, 1952, UNDA, CMRH 35.

14. Godfrey Diekmann, "Msgr. Reynold Hillenbrand," *Liturgy 70* 10 (1979), 2.

15. Hillenbrand, "Catholic Action," June 17, 1947, lecture. UNDA, CMRH 8/36.

WILLIAM BUSCH

Educator

ILLIAM BUSCH'S TEACHING and writing sowed the seeds of the liturgical movement in the United States far beyond his own native Minnesota. Although perhaps not so well known as others in his circle, Busch, through his lectures and articles on a great variety of topics, gave an invaluable clarity and impetus to the growing "liturgical apostolate" in the 1920s through the 1940s.

Busch viewed his vocation as a teacher in an expansive light, articulating the views and objectives of the liturgical movement to seminarians, laity and clergy alike.

Biographical material on Busch is quite scarce. Enough exists, however, to provide a brief sketch.[1] William Busch was born in Redwing, Minnesota, on October 6, 1882. He studied classics at the college of St. Thomas in St. Paul, went on to study philosophy and theology at St. Paul Seminary and was ordained a priest on June 12, 1907. During that year, Busch also was a student at the Apostolic Mission House in Washington, D.C. He returned to Minnesota to serve as a parish priest first at Excelsior and then at St. Luke's in St. Paul. Sometime after July 1911, Busch went to Louvain to study church history;

he returned from Europe in September 1913 to a teaching position in church history at St. Paul Seminary, a post he occupied for more than 50 years.

Busch served as an associate editor and frequent contributor to *Orate Fratres* from its inception in 1926 until the late 1950s. In addition to his duties at the seminary and at *Orate Fratres,* Busch served the parish of St. Mary of the Lake, White Bear Lake, until 1940. In 1957, Busch was made a monsignor. He retired from seminary teaching in 1970 at the age of 88 and died in St. Paul on February 5, 1971.

Discovering the Liturgical Movement

Busch was "slowly converted" to the cause of the liturgical movement. He tells his own story in a 1951 article:

> How does one awaken to [the liturgical movement's] meaning and to the great need of it? Some have told me of their experience as of a sudden reorientation, a flash of insight. In my case it was a gradual growth—like the turning of successive pages of a book—although I reckon the year 1919 as the page where the plot became clear to me. My first contact with the liturgy was of course in baptism in infancy. After that there was the influence of parents and home, of pastor and parish church and school, and of contacts and studies in my seminarian years. In Louvain in the years 1911–1913 I learned something of what was being done in the abbeys of Mont César and Maredsous, but, while this served me well later on, it appeared at the time as something beautiful and proper to monastic life—I did not yet recognize a liturgical movement destined for every member of the church.[2]

"The plot became clear" while Busch was teaching a course on the Mass at the College of St. Catherine in St. Paul; there he "came to see the need of a general liturgical movement."[3] He discovered what was being done in Europe and in 1920 read Guardini's classic *The Spirit of the Liturgy.*

Busch campaigned in his diocesan newspaper for a liturgical renewal and received encouragement from Athanasius Meyer of St. John's Abbey to begin the liturgical movement at St. Paul Seminary.[4] Busch wrote letters to *America* and *Commonweal* concerning a need for a "return to the liturgy."[5] In the summer of 1925, Busch gave a speech on "The Liturgical Movement" to the National Catholic Education Association meeting in Pittsburgh. He remarked, "The liturgical movement is of immense importance, and I am tempted to say of supreme importance in the life of the church in our country and particularly in seminary life."[6] Abbot Alcuin Deutsch already had informed Busch that Virgil Michel had proposed the establishment of *Orate Fratres*.[7] In the summer of 1925, Michel invited Busch to join the staff of his new journal as one of its eight associate editors. Michel called Busch his "chief worker and counselor."[8] The first issue of *Orate Fratres* appeared in December (Advent) of 1926 and Busch became a regular contributor.

Writing for *Orate Fratres*, 1926–1951

Busch's literary output on behalf of the movement in America consisted largely of apologetic writing; a bibliography in the December 1951 issue of *Worship* enumerates 39 articles between 1926 and 1951.[9] He clearly wished that the entire American church would embrace a movement that he saw as far-reaching: "The fundamental purposes of the liturgical apostolate lie at the very root of all Catholic life and extend to every part of it."[10] It is not surprising to discover, therefore, that Busch touches on many topics in his articles. Nevertheless, certain themes recur: the church as the Mystical Body of Christ; the social dimension of the liturgy; the importance of education about liturgy; the participation of the laity. Busch was a conservative in matters of liturgical revision, a characteristic he shared with others in the movement both in Europe and in the United States.

Busch insisted on understanding the doctrine of the Mystical Body before anything else: "The church is not merely an organization, it is a vital organism, the one body of the mystical Christ."[11] Although Pius XII promulgated the encyclical *Mystici Corporis* in 1943, the proponents of the liturgical movement had made the theology of the Mystical Body the cornerstone of their work long before that time. For Busch, the liturgical movement was nothing less than a recovery of a "traditional doctrine of the Christian teachers and writers of ancient and medieval times"[12]: the salvific incorporation of believers into Christ's body where they share Christ's priesthood, uniting their self-offering with Christ's through their active participation in the liturgy.

Busch defines the "inner nature" of the liturgical movement as a "revival of Christian social consciousness and a determination to restore the worship of God to its rightful place in social life."[13] In "The Liturgy: A School of Catholic Action," Busch deals directly with the social dimension of liturgy: "It is necessary . . . that our redemption in Christ be understood in its social as well as its individual aspect."[14] Catholic Action springs from the *actio* of the Mass.[15] Busch apparently believed (along with others of his time) that Western civilization was coming to an end and that the times in which he lived were the beginnings of a period of time marked by decline. Busch saw the loss of the doctrine of the Mystical Body as the reason behind social deterioration. The moral evils of the time manifested themselves even in the liturgy: "Can we hope to cure the selfishness in our modern economic life while we allow it to continue in our spiritual life?"[16] The Mystical Body extends far beyond the doors of the church.

Education and Participation

For Busch, the liturgical movement was above all a set of principles. He believed strongly that the people must understand these principles before renewal could take place. Busch the professor argued for the spread of the tenets of the liturgical movement through education:

> There is need for a large amount of instruction in regard to the Mass and the entire liturgy. Besides what must be done in our schools, the subject needs to be set forth in sermons and courses of instruction in our churches, on popular missions, in retreats and study clubs. Moreover, instructors must go beyond the texts and rites of the liturgy and must explain the entire nature of our corporate life in Christ and the progressive process of the redemption and transfiguration of humanity in him.[17]

Busch also contributed a series of articles to *Orate Fratres* extolling the virtues of the Christ-Life Series, primary school texts for religious instruction centered on the liturgy.[18] He also was interested in the formation of clergy "discussion clubs" and in the state of liturgical education in the seminaries. Busch's thoughts on liturgical education are striking in their inclusiveness; it is clear that he did not believe in liturgical knowledge as an arcane discipline. Liturgical knowledge is "popular" in the best sense: It is meant for all the people.

Busch saw a vital relationship between education and participation, remarking in 1930, "If you study the liturgy without taking an active part in it, you are only doing half of what you ought to do."[19] He pushed for the use of the missal by the laity and called for a "return to the corporate celebration of the Mass through study of the missal."[20] Busch used education as a vehicle for more active participation in the liturgy. In January of 1936, he called for the beginning of a campaign for the use of the breviary by laity,[21] arguing that the use of the missal led naturally to the use of the breviary because the hour prayers of the breviary were an extension of the sacrifice of the Mass. In February of that year, Busch produced plans for the establishment of the American League of the Divine Office.[22] The League was modeled on the Society of the Magnificat, founded in Great Britain in 1927.

While Busch clearly desired that all Catholics be as knowledgeable as possible about the liturgy and their role in it, his attitude toward liturgical revision is more ambiguous. In his article "On Liturgical Reforms," Busch objected "in a general way to all undue haste in proposals for liturgical reform."[23] He warned against the manipulation of the liturgical movement and asked the question: "If modern life finds the liturgy difficult, is it the liturgy that should be changed?"[24] Busch held up Pius Parsch as the model reformer, "at once progressive and conservative."[25] He feared that an "individualistic piety" would try to modify the liturgy, the objective nature of which it does not understand. Perhaps Busch's attitude is best illustrated by his belief that the laity who used English translations of the breviary eventually would return to the Latin text, for "people are drawn to the official language of the church."[26]

William Busch above all was a teacher. He emphasized the essential, radical role of education in the process of liturgical renewal. He was a teacher whose own work and vision were shaped profoundly by the theology of the Mystical Body and the participation in that Body effected by the liturgy.

Many of Busch's ideas foreshadow postconciliar efforts toward popularizing liturgical renewal and solid liturgical theology. Since Busch's time, however, the term "popular" has acquired a pejorative flavor in some circles. William Busch's work reminds and challenges powerfully all who are engaged in the work of liturgical renewal. Still vivid for today is his insistence that, at its best, all liturgical education—from the university to the church school—is a popular endeavor, part of the work of God's people, Christ's body.

■ *Grant Sperry-White*

NOTES

1. Compiled from a telephone conversation with the chancery office of the archdiocese of St. Paul-Minneapolis, September 10, 1987, and from Godfrey Diekmann, "In Memoriam: Msgr. William Busch," *Worship* 45 (1971), 179.

2. William Busch, "Past, Present and Future," *Orate Fratres* 25 (1951), 481–82.

3. Ibid.

4. Paul B. Marx, OSB, *Virgil Michel and the Liturgical Movement* (Collegeville: The Liturgical Press, 1957), 47, note 44.

5. Ibid., 108.

6. Ibid.

7. Busch, "Past, Present and Future," 482.

8. Ibid., 481.

9. Diekmann in Busch's obituary mentions 42 articles as of 1971. I have been unable to locate the additional articles.

10. Busch, "The Liturgical Apostolate," *Orate Fratres* 5 (1930), 99.

11. Busch, "The Mass: The Community Drama of the Christ-Life," *Orate Fratres* 4 (1930), 356.

12. Ibid., 355.

13. Busch, "Christ in the Church," *Orate Fratres* 8 (1933), 62.

14. Busch, "The Liturgy: A School of Catholic Action," *Orate Fratres* 7 (1932), 11.

15. Ibid.

16. Busch, "Christ in the Church," 65.

17. Busch, "The Liturgy: A School of Catholic Action," 11.

18. *Orate Fratres* 8 (1934), 216–21; 8 (1934), 253–60; 8 (1934), 302–9.

19. Busch, "The Liturgical Apostolate," 101.

20. Busch, "Missal and the Breviary," *Orate Fratres* 3 (1929), 344.

21. Busch, "The Breviary for the Laity," *Orate Fratres* 10 (1936), 103.

22. See Gerald Ellard, *Men at Work at Worship* (New York: Longmanns, Green and Co., 1940), 258–72.

23. Busch, "On Liturgical Reforms," *Orate Fratres* 11 (1937), 353.

24. Ibid.

25. Ibid., 355.

26. Busch, "The Breviary for the Laity," 104.

MAURICE LAVANOUX
Tenacious Commentator

**T**HE EARLY PIONEERS of the American Roman Catholic liturgical movement, imbued with a Thomistic sense of the cohesiveness of human experience, were convinced that renewal of the liturgy must involve all aspects of Christian life—politics, social welfare, family and community life, the arts, ecclesiology and piety. Although it is not surprising that the environment for Christian worship also should come under scrutiny, the creation of a climate within which artists and architects, liturgists and theologians could reach some agreement on the shape of reform for liturgical space can be largely credited to one man: Maurice Emile Lavanoux. For nearly 50 years, through the work of the Liturgical Arts Society and in the pages of its quarterly magazine *Liturgical Arts,* Lavanoux did battle against all that was vain and tasteless and false in church building and furnishing. To trace the work of Maurice Lavanoux is, in many ways, to trace the role of art and architecture in the modern liturgical movement.

In September 1927, a small group of Roman Catholic laymen, fledgling architects and draftsmen from Boston and New York gathered for a retreat at Portsmouth Priory in Rhode Island. They were drawn together by a common concern over what they saw as the debilitated state of Roman Catholic church architecture and by a deep desire to participate in its renewal. Among those present was 34-year-old Maurice Lavanoux, then a draftsman at the prestigious Boston architectural firm of Maginnis and Walsh. Having come into contact with the work of Prosper Guéranger and Lambert Beauduin while a student in Paris, Lavanoux had been a careful observer of the progress of liturgical renewal in the United States for several years. His interest in church architecture had led him to understand that the architectural setting of the liturgy could serve as either a barrier or an aid to a vital liturgical life.

The Liturgical Arts Society

Out of this Portsmouth retreat and others that followed, Lavanoux discovered that many of his companions believed that the way to improve the liturgical environment was to establish a semimonastic guild of artists, architects and craftspersons who would work and pray together. But Lavanoux resisted this inclination, favoring a more "worldly" enterprise, and so the Liturgical Arts Society was born in 1928 to "increase the interest of its members in the spiritual value of the liturgical arts and to coordinate the efforts of those concerned with its development." Lavanoux was elected its first (and, as it would turn out, only) secretary.

He originally was cautious in his approach to the Society's program, always seeking to temper the extravagant (and often misguided) enthusiasm of his companions. Although he believed that plans for publication of a journal were premature, other opinions prevailed and in October 1931, the Society began publication of *Liturgical Arts* magazine. Within a few years, Lavanoux left Boston to take over full operation of the Society and the editorship of the magazine in New York.

His energy seemed limitless. Although he lived on a pittance in a tiny flat in Queens, Lavanoux traveled widely—visiting architects and artists and their works, gathering material for the magazine, lecturing and raising money for the Society. He often boasted that he had seen 75 percent of all the buildings that were illustrated in *Liturgical Arts* and that he had met nearly all of the individuals whose works were highlighted. Eventually, with the help of wealthy benefactors, he was able to travel throughout the world, opening the eyes of his readers to the very best of church art and architecture. As the years went by, the life of the Liturgical Arts Society, of *Liturgical Arts* and of Maurice Lavanoux became virtually indistinguishable.

Lavanoux was convinced that the church could be served best by a liturgical environment that was shaped in response to the liturgy itself and *Liturgical Arts* was organized to provide a platform for that point of view. In articles, book reviews and photographs, the quarterly monitored the process and the product of liturgical reform and translated it into principles of design for ecclesiastical space and furnishings. As editor, Lavanoux was able to foster the establishment of an agenda for liturgical art and architecture that fully embodied the reform agenda of the American Roman Catholic liturgical movement.

The Arts and the Movement

Lavanoux was committed to the idea that the liturgy itself was the starting place for any discussion of the appropriate design for churches and furnishings. Moving from this conviction, the Society and *Liturgical Arts* were especially sensitive to the direction that liturgical reform was taking. As the reform agenda of the American liturgical movement evolved, every change was mirrored by changes in the Liturgical Arts Society's recommendations for the reform of ecclesiastical design.

The movement's call for more careful attention to rubrics led to the Society's advocation of rubrical correctness in the design of altars, tabernacles and altarware. Focus on the spirit of the liturgy led the Society to demand that churches proclaim the public nature of Christian worship. Growing emphasis on the full participation of the faithful resulted in the call for free-standing altars and a more hospitable sacred space. Insistence on a return to the dignity of a liturgy freed from accretions was mirrored in the Society's plea for honesty of materials and simplicity of design.

On a few major issues, Maurice Lavanoux and *Liturgical Arts* broke company with certain of the liturgical pioneers. The magazine's constant demand for a living, modern art for the church, for example, met with a fair amount of opposition from those who viewed the Middle Ages as the "golden age" of both the church's liturgy and its arts. The Society continued to insist that a modern church must find its religious expression in contemporary art forms.

Because Lavanoux staunchly refused to compromise the quality of *Liturgical Arts,* the production of each and every issue was a financial struggle. Many times the funds came only at the eleventh hour. But there came a day when the Society's cries for help went unanswered and, quite suddenly, in the fall of 1972, *Liturgical Arts* ceased publication and the Society disbanded. During the previous year, the magazine had marked a phenomenal 40 years of publication, an occasion for celebrating, as Lavanoux put it, "the reality of dreams." Now, it seemed, the reality had become harsh and the dreams insubstantial.

Lavanoux had hoped that both the Society and the magazine would be resurrected by popular demand, but as the months went by his hopes began to fade. Although there were kind words in abundance from friends and supporters, kind words alone were not enough to rescue *Liturgical Arts* and Maurice Lavanoux gathered up the 45 years' worth of files and notes and offered them to the University of Notre Dame Archives. "I feel a bit sad and empty," he wrote to a friend after the moving van had left.

But his despair was short-lived and the 78-year-old Lavanoux moved on to other pursuits. He was named editor of the periodical *Stained Glass,* wrote a monthly "Visual Arts" column for *Liturgy* (the journal of The Liturgical Conference), wrote his autobiography and served as president of the Society for the Renewal of Christian Art (the heir to the Liturgical Arts Society). He planned and raised funds for a Gallery of Christian Arts in New York City.

Many people tried to tell Lavanoux during this period that it was time for a well-deserved rest, that his work was over, with the *Constitution of the Liturgy* as its seal of approval. But for Lavanoux, the *Constitution* was just the beginning, a Magna Charta that would liberate artists and architects to perform their work more fully. On the presumption that *Liturgical Arts* would be revived, he continued to seek material on religious art from all over the world, referring to himself as an "editor without venue." "It is hard to accept the fact," he wrote, "that I am now without the means to make known the work of talented architects and of the many artists who can be found in all parts of this land."

At the end of his life came bitter disappointment. Although Lavanoux had long suffered from the indifference of those in the church who had the power to advance the goals of the Liturgical Arts Society, in 1974 that indifference reached a climax. Papal representatives came to the United States in search of American religious art to be placed in a proposed Vatican museum of modern art. Instead of contacting Lavanoux, the Vatican delegates visited New York art galleries and employed an artists' agent (a non–Roman Catholic) to identify and purchase examples of modern American religious art. Lavanoux felt utterly betrayed. "Why are those of us who have worked and slaved for decades for a modern and living religious art, the work of gifted and talented artists, so crudely bypassed? What cruel irony!" he wrote in his diary.

This final insult after years of official neglect seems to have consumed the last of Lavanoux's seemingly boundless energy. On October 21, 1974, he was entertaining a visitor in the apartment in Queens where he had lived and worked for half a century. "Sorry I don't have all my old pep," he said to his companion and died quietly in his armchair.

His Legacy

This is the end of a beautiful adventure!" Maurice Lavanoux wrote to a friend just before his death. During his 80 years, Lavanoux-as-adventurer had traveled through the establishment of a liturgical renewal movement and through the changes it produced in the church. He had navigated the twists and turns of ecclesiastical politics and the publishing world and had witnessed the gradual acceptance of contemporary art as a valid form of religious expression. Most amazingly, perhaps, throughout all his journeys he had managed to retain integrity and wit and faith.

It has been suggested that in the tumultuous world of the early 1970s, the passing of *Liturgical Arts,* of Maurice Lavanoux and of the Liturgical Arts Society was hardly noticeable. Be that as it may, they left behind a very real vacuum. Four times a year, *Liturgical Arts* would arrive. Four times a year, pastors and architects and students and church leaders would have in their hands a manual of visual theology, a source of inspiration for what the church, at its best, could be. Four times a year, Maurice Lavanoux would come into our homes and our schools and our parishes, arguing with intelligence and insight for a creative dialogue between the arts of the church and the needs of the church at prayer. He sought to create in the American church a climate within which the arts could flourish and grow. And perhaps to the extent that that climate is with us today, we can claim it as the legacy of Maurice Lavanoux.

■ *Susan J. White*

BERNARD LAUKEMPER

A Chicago Pastor

ERNARD LAUKEMPER WAS BORN in 1888 in Germany, came to the United States in 1910 and was ordained in 1916 by Cardinal Mundelein of Chicago. In 1932, he became pastor of a German-American parish, St. Aloysius (later to be predominately Polish and, by the late 1980s, a thriving Hispanic parish), on the northwest side of the city. Until his death in 1949, this was Laukemper's ground for his passion to restore all things in Christ.

How St. Aloysius Parish Taught the Country

In 1936, Laukemper sponsored a "liturgical week" at his parish (four years before the North American Liturgical Weeks would begin). He brought to Chicago speakers such as Abbot Columban Thuis, Martin Hellriegel, Michael Ducey and Virgil Michel. From this experience, Laukemper went on to plan the national weeks with Joseph Morrissey, Reynold Hillenbrand and others. When the Liturgical Conference was created, he served in various offices and was himself a frequent speaker at the weeks.

At these and other presentations, Laukemper often witnessed to the liturgical life of his parish where he was implementing the writings of Pius Parsch and other European liturgists. He wanted to prove that the insights of the European liturgical movement could take root in the burgeoning American church of immigrants and their children, Catholics much given to building churches and schools and convents and rectories. Here amidst American pragmatism and efficiency Laukemper brought the riches of European liturgical scholarship and put it to work.

In addresses to the Liturgical Weeks and in articles in *Orate Fratres,* he presented a liturgical tapestry of insights and ideas:

> To introduce the dialogue Mass in English, it is first of all necessary to acquaint the people with the missal. The price is very low: 20 cents. We have a supply of 500 missals at the door of the church for the convenience of those parishioners who have not yet invested in a copy of their own. A practical instruction in the use of the missal is essential, but this can be done progressively from Sunday to Sunday. . . . When the Mass begins another priest is ready in the sanctuary to lead the congregation in their parts. . . . The practice has changed bystanders to partakers who worship with attention and devotion. The man in the pew says that the Mass seems to him very short and very interesting when he can participate in its celebration. Certain it is that this dialogue Mass is always crowded and that people from other parishes come to it. (*Orate Fratres,* 1938)

Laukemper was at home with the rich biblical and historical imagery of the church. He told the 1940 Liturgical Week participants: "The ecclesiastical year may be considered as the holy ring and wreath which has been given to the church as a sign of espousal by her divine Bridegroom Jesus Christ. . . . The great cycle is the joining of the Christian with Christ in baptism and the expectation of the return of Christ." He then went on to speak of practical ways to make this cycle come to life in the parish.

Laukemper looked for an expanded use of the scriptures, but he tried to make the most of what was already present in the liturgy. At that same Liturgical Week he said: "If we return to a more extensive use of the Bible, it must be a return to the prayerful use of it. Here the liturgy is our leader. The Masses of the entire year acquaint us with many psalm verses. An explanation of the introit and gradual, of offertory and communion verses, would hasten the return of the people to the prayer book composed under the inspiration of the Holy Spirit. I believe we have too many prayers composed by humans."

He saw also how the Sunday liturgy had to be caught up with the domestic liturgy: "We need family worship. Would it be very difficult to induce our people to read the epistle and gospel of the Mass of the day after dinner in the evening when the whole family should be together? The daily missal can be used outside of Mass as a book of spiritual reading." The liturgy was the whole environment of Christian life, as Laukemper saw it.

Teaching in the Parish

Each week in *The Aloysian*, the parish bulletin, Laukemper used illustrations appropriate to the liturgy of the Sunday and wrote a feature article often based on the breviary and other sources. The heading announcing baptisms proclaimed: "Divine Life in the Parish. Reborn in Holy Baptism into divine life, and became our fellow in the Mystical Body of Christ . . ." The readings, the time for Sunday Vespers and for Benediction and whatever was in season were well marked.

The school was of great importance. He knew each student by name and they remember him well, telling of how, during Holy Week, they would spend more time in church than they did in school during other weeks. Attendance was taken at Sunday Vespers as it was at school.

Laukemper was not without crisis. When he cleared the statues and vigil lights from the church, some parishioners left and others complained to the cardinal. Laukemper was called in and admonished to introduce changes gradually. He reportedly told the cardinal that his aunt in Germany "cut the dog's tail just a little each year. Wouldn't it have been better for the dog if she cut it all and only once?" Like many pastors of his day, Laukemper knew little of collaboration.

On another occasion, when he had placed the Christmas crib outside, not in church, a parishioner wrote to the Catholic diocesan paper: "Jesus Christ came to St. Aloysius at Christmas and there was no room for him in his own house."

Life at St. Aloysius anticipated many of the changes of Vatican II. On special occasions, Mass was celebrated facing the people. There were entrance and offertory processions and choirs singing from the front of the church. The building was remodeled and the baptistry placed in front to be a focus for Laukemper's strong theology of baptism.

When Laukemper died in 1949, the Office of the Dead was sung by his vested boys' choir. Monsignor Martin Hellriegel, his lifelong friend, presided. Like Hellriegel, Laukemper was a pastor who knew the scholarship and knew the sources and who had a love for the way all of this could be lived in a parish.

■ *Dennis Geaney*

JOSEPH STEDMAN
My Sunday Missal

I N 1925, A STILL BOYISH-LOOKING priest, clutching under his arm a statue of Mary, arrived at the Monastery of the Precious Blood in Brooklyn to begin his ministry as chaplain to the sisters there. No one would have thought that he would spend the rest of his life in this monastery and from it touch the lives and hearts of millions of people on three continents. This man, ordained only four years, was Joseph Francis Stedman, who (in his own words) "took the Big Book off the altar and put it into the hands of Catholics in the pew"[1] as *My Sunday Missal.*

Editing *My Sunday Missal* and getting it into the hands—and languages—of people around the world would have been work enough for one lifetime; it was not enough for Stedman's zeal and drive. He carried out numerous other projects so ably that on hearing of his death a fellow priest exclaimed, "Not just one priest had died. A thousand priests have died in him."[2] Godfrey Diekmann said of Stedman, "He was the Pius Parsch of our country." Seemingly unbounded energy and enthusiasm characterized Stedman and so did joy, compassion, deep prayerfulness and reverence, gratitude for his priesthood and genuine love of God and neighbor.

Joseph Stedman's early life seemed fairly ordinary. He was born in Brooklyn on March 11, 1896, the first of Joseph and Eleanor Dunlea Stedman's five children, and was educated in Brooklyn Catholic schools. Edwin Stedman, a priest of Brooklyn and Joseph's youngest brother, tells that times were hard when Joseph was ready to enter college. Their father was a baker and had a modest income. Realizing the drain a college education would be on the family finances, Joseph offered to work a few years before continuing his education. His parents refused the offer.

There is no record that in his seminary days he met any outstanding influence either among his professors or in his reading. His contact with the works of Abbot Marmion and Gerald Ellard would come later. These were years of prayer and study that simply deepened the faith that had been a hallmark of the Stedman family for generations, a faith that recognized and trusted the hand of God in all the events of life.

Joseph Stedman was ordained for the diocese of Brooklyn on May 21, 1921, and his first assignment was to Holy Child Jesus parish. The four years he spent there appear to have been as ordinary as the first 25 years of his life except for one event. He fell seriously ill with pneumonia and, because antibiotics were then unknown, he lay for days near death. Marie Rita, Stedman's only sister, so valued his priesthood and ministry that she made an offering of her life to God that her brother might be spared. It seemed that God took her at her word for Stedman recovered and when Marie was 21, she developed encephalitis and suffered for 19 years until her death in 1940. The spirituality of victimhood, which influenced so many of that era, had entered Joseph Stedman's life and would not only be at the heart of his life's work but also, some believed, woven into his own final surrender to God in death.

In 1890, the Sisters Adorers of the Precious Blood had brought to their Brooklyn monastery the Confraternity of the Precious Blood. The ministry of all Confraternity members is twofold: to comfort those who are suffering and to atone for the world's sins. Stedman entered into this little-known apostolate when he crossed the threshold of the monastery on that eve of the feast of the Most Precious Blood; in it his whole life found its focus and goal.

His deep friendship with Jesus, his devotion to the Mass, his organizational skills, his creativity and business acumen, his ability to speak and to convince and, above all, his *joie de vivre* and sincere love for people—all were energized by and given completely to this apostolate. Providentially, it was this Confraternity that provided the strong financial backing that made it possible for so many millions of books to be sold for so little (often for less than 25 cents) or to be given outright. Stedman realized this and he refused to make a profit or to take any royalties for himself. All was sent back into the Confraternity or to support the sisters. He lived on his chaplain's meager salary and, at the time of his death, had only $168.

When Stedman began his work as director of the Confraternity, its mailing list was small. In slightly more than a year, he had increased the number of active members to 25,000. The number reached several hundred thousand by the time of his death. At first, his friends took care of the records and mail that went with this work. Eventually, people were hired for this, but Stedman never disturbed the cloistered sisters' lives of prayer and penance.

He did involve the sisters, however, in the retreat apostolate. He believed that it was necessary for women to have other women with whom they could speak in confidence, women with whom they could pray. At first he gave all the retreat conferences, then enlisted the help of the Passionist Fathers because their spirituality also focused on the suffering Christ. Moved by Stedman's conferences, many young people entered convents and seminaries. It was said that he was responsible for more vocations to religious life and priesthood on the East Coast than any other single person. When pressed to say what it was about the man or his conferences that evoked such a generous response, one now elderly sister said, "He preached well, told stories, made his point, but most of all, he was so much like Jesus."

My Sunday Missal and Other Books

Not long after his arrival at the monastery, Stedman's realization of the bond between the Precious Blood and the Mass convinced him that these sisters more than anyone else should be responding to the appeal of Pius X to "*Pray the Mass.*" From his own salary, he bought a *St. Andrew's Daily Missal* for each of the 50 members of the community and taught them how to use it.

The gratitude and enthusiasm of the sisters intensified Stedman's belief that the laity, too, hungered to pray the Mass, to break through the barriers posed by Latin and the complications of existing missals and to enter into the prayer itself. Zeal ignited genius and the book that a colleague called the "Stedman-you-can't-get-lost missal" was born.

Joseph Stedman did something that seemed so obvious that he, along with many others, wondered why no one had thought of it before. He devised a system of guiding people through the missal with numbers and pictures. Following the numbers, which were accompanied by a brief explanation, users easily could make their way from the ordinary to the proper parts of the Mass and back again. Simple and clear pictures were created by Adé Bethune, *Catholic Worker* artist.

The missal was printed in type clear enough "to be read even without eyeglasses" yet was small enough to fit into a pocket or purse. The introduction explained the Mass and its various parts, as well as the church year. It gave reasons for "praying with the church" and was supplemented by short reflections on the feast or the gospel of the Sunday. Users were urged to read these reflections before, not during, Mass. Concise yet complete catechesis marked Stedman as *the* adult educator of his day. The first missals rolled off the press in 1932, but its vocabulary, theology and tone are amazingly similar to those of Vatican II. The book could be purchased for 25 cents and quickly came to be the *vade mecum* of Catholics all over the world. Thirty million copies were in use before Stedman's death.

The appearance of *My Sunday Missal* in so many countries was due in large part to United States military personnel who carried the missals wherever they went. Hundreds of touching stories about the missal came back from troops and chaplains alike. One copy battered in the attack on Pearl Harbor was sent by its owner to Stedman along with the message, "This didn't survive as well as I did. Can you send me a new one?" A chaplain said these missals were in such demand that he could not keep a supply for any length of time and told of seeing them in shirt pockets or protruding from pants pockets as the men made their way into tanks or foxholes. Pictures came of men using them at Mass on the edge of a battlefield or on board ship.

Requests were made—and were granted—for translations of the missal into Polish, Italian, French, Spanish, Chinese, one of the American Indian languages, Dutch, German, Japanese and Portuguese.[3] At home, this missal was no less popular. Dorothy Day wrote in *Catholic Worker*, "During a trip to our Seattle House, I saw a Pullman car porter reading the day's Mass in Fr. Stedman's little Sunday missal. In our backyard at Mott Street I saw a man on the breadline reading one of his New Testaments."[4]

This latter book, *Daily Readings from the New Testament*, resulted from Stedman's conviction that scripture itself provides the best way to acquire a genuine knowledge of Jesus. Omitting repetitions, he unified the four gospels into one continuous narrative. He divided this gospel narrative, the Acts of the Apostles, the epistles and Revelation into sections that could be read in three to four minutes. Following the calendar provided, one easily could read this new testament in one year.

The *Missal* and the *New Testament,* a lenten daily missal and the manual of prayers for Confraternity members were at the heart of Stedman's publications, but he arranged and combined them in various ways to meet changing needs. *My Requiem Missal* contained the funeral liturgy and texts to be used for anniversary Masses. *My Military Missal* was watch-pocket size but contained prayers, a good catechetical section and, of course, a simplified missal. On the back cover, a rosary was embossed. This edition contained a special arrangement for soldiers to follow the Mass in the absence of a chaplain, a practice valued and widely adopted at home by the sick and others who could not get to Mass.

Stedman provided priests with an ordo that included *daily* sermon helps and a brief "thought for the day." *The Chalice,* a booklet of inspiration and instruction, was sent to Confraternity members four times a year. All these publications were printed by the Confraternity and distributed from Brooklyn.

Helping People Understand, Love and Pray the Mass

Stedman once said of himself, "I'm a one-book man, and my book is the missal."[5] To help people understand, love and enter into the Mass was really at the heart of everything he did, not just of everything he published. For example, after much study, he introduced the dialogue Mass to the sisters whom he served.

Over a period of years and in consultation with the sisters, Stedman led the renovation of the public chapel of the monastery so that it might more dramatically teach in marble, stained glass, murals and symbols the meaning of the Mass and its significance for people's lives.

Stedman arranged for the National Liturgical Week to be held in New York in 1944. He then was vice-president of the Liturgical Conference. The following year, he was elected president but did not live to preside at the annual meeting.

To seek relief from the cold of New York and its effect on his asthma, Stedman regularly stayed with friends in Florida during January and February. He always took with him a trunk of books and materials for the projects he was working on. In February of 1945 he wrote to the sisters:

> I have been constantly aware of your prayers for my protection and inspiration. The mornings and nights have seen me at the privileged work of writing a commentary on the psalter, not only for insertion in the Latin-English breviary [which he was preparing] but for publication and illustration of the new translation for use by laity and religious as a meditation and prayer book. May the Divine Author allow us to bring it out this year.
>
> Normal life for me seems to have disappeared. The bulk of my time is given to others. It's almost impossible to count one consecutive hour on my own destiny, outside of holy Mass and the breviary. . . . But through your prayers, the liturgy, the New Testament, and now the breviary, all written in the Precious Blood, have come to be better known and loved, I hope. As for myself—a mere natural thought, however— I feel sad, because in giving me the big things of life, this has taken away the precious little things. Sometimes I feel like sitting down for a good cry because my "old life" is gone. Some confessions, eh![6]

A year after writing this, Stedman collapsed with a malignant brain tumor. On March 23, 1946, as the noon Angelus was ringing, he died.

During the four days of his wake at the monastery, 25,000 people came to thank this apostle of the Mass, to kiss his vestments, to touch their rosary to his hands. Three public requiem Masses were offered in an effort to accommodate all who wanted to attend his funeral. Major newspapers and periodicals carried tributes to this apostle who gave all he had that the Mass and scripture might be known and loved by as many as possible. Letters of appreciation flooded in from across the country. Then a strange silence fell about this man who had sought only God's glory. The Latin-English breviary that would have been ready in a few months never was published.

Stedman was a pastor, not a theologian. The Mass and the scriptures had captured his mind and his heart. They formed his thinking and directed his action. He addressed the multitude. He did not seek to be erudite, but rather to be clear and convincing, to draw people to what was essential. His genuinely universal love poured itself out as he used his many-faceted genius to hand on the gift he had received in a way that was understandable, attractive and available to even the simplest and poorest of the church. He truly had discovered what Vatican II would teach: The liturgy is the source and summit of all the life and activity of the church.

■ *Frances Krumpelman*

NOTES

Much of the content for this article was provided by conversations with Father Edwin Stedman, Sister Mary Berchmans and Sister Mary Mediatrix.

1. "Monsignor Joseph F. Stedman: R.I.P.," *The Catholic Choirmaster* 32 (June, 1946), 59.

2. Sister Helen Therese, "Fr. Stedman Remembered," *The Tablet* (August 3, 1978).

3. "Msgr. Stedman Is Buried," *The Tablet* (March 30, 1946), 1.

4. *The Catholic Worker* 13 (April 5, 1946), 2.

5. Sister Helen Therese, unpublished manuscript, 26.

6. Letter of Joseph Stedman to the Sisters of the Monastery of the Precious Blood, February 22, 1945.

JUSTINE WARD
The Gift of Chant

**F**OR TWO GENERATIONS of parochial school children and their teachers, the name Justine Ward was synonymous with school music. Each day, beginning in the first grade, the Ward chart on its large wooden frame was brought to the front of the classroom. This was supplemented with a book when children were old enough to manage it.

Children were taught to "place" their tones by singing the syllable "nu" and to sing increasingly complicated melodies, using the notes of the scale (do, re, mi, etc.) to which numbers one through eight had been assigned. Children were introduced to the four-line staff of Gregorian chant, learned the name of and how to execute the various neumes (notes) and to feel the undulating rhythms by doing the chironomy (directing), waving their right arm gracefully in the arsis (ascending) and thesis (descending) pattern used at Solesmes.

The entire chant was kept light and flowing by asking the singers to imagine a silken scarf gently being tossed into the air and then floating downward and repeating this motion over and over. Rising on the toes for the arses and lowering the heels back to the floor for the theses helped the whole body feel the undulation. Eventually, the five-line staff and modern notation were introduced and then harmony, often polyphony.

The goal of the Ward Method was to bring about the restoration of Gregorian chant called for by Pius X in his 1903 *motu proprio,* "On Restoration of All Things in Christ." There was no doubt about its success. The more simple chant melodies were learned quickly and the natural facility children have for language enabled them to sing the Latin—and Greek of the "Kyrie"—with ease. Fidelity to the method gave children in the upper elementary grades a repertory of three or four Gregorian Masses and a few hymns with Gregorian melodies.

Justine Ward placed high value on the prayerfulness of the singing and no less on its musical perfection. Teachers were trained to work for excellence in tone quality and rhythm, in blending of voices and skillful breath control that made the melodies flow in unbroken, undulating patterns.

The Love for Christ

That Justine Ward should seek a career in music was not surprising; that she should make her whole life into "a response to the call of Pius X"[1] was. She had been born in 1879 into the wealthy Cutting family and named Justine Bayard. The family's appreciation of culture and the arts was well known. Her father, William Bayard Cutting, was one of the founders and patrons of the New York Metropolitan Opera Company and his children were educated in the arts. By the time Justine Ward reached the close of her teen years, her musical education included piano, harmony, musical form and orchestration.

Ward was introduced to Gregorian chant by John B. Young, SJ, choir director of St. Francis Xavier Church in New York City. He was the pioneer of chant in the United States and the priest who prepared Ward for reception into the Roman Catholic church in 1904, three years after her marriage to George

Cabot Ward. In 1928, the 25th anniversary of Pius X's *motu proprio*, Ward said, "I was not a Catholic yet but this papal document made a profound impression on me and I promised myself that when I was received into the Catholic church, I would work for this good cause."[2]

Until 1910, Ward carried out this resolution by writing articles for Catholic periodicals. In these she encouraged the use of liturgical music: chant and polyphony. Her own musical education had convinced her that "music does not leave one indifferent and that its effect on one's spiritual development is important because music acts directly on intelligence, will and sensitivity."[3] She termed the music in vogue in Catholic churches as "musiquette" and strove to convince others of its artistic mediocrity and inferiority to Gregorian chant.

Ward's opportunity to be involved in teaching Gregorian chant to a broad audience came when meeting Father Thomas Shields, an educator. With him, she developed the practical method of teaching music to children that came to be called the "Ward Method." Her first courses were taught at The Catholic University of America. With Mother Georgia Stevens, RSCJ, in 1916, she founded the Pius X Institute of Liturgical Music at Manhattanville College of the Sacred Heart. Its goal was preparing teachers to give to children the training in Gregorian chant that would enable them to participate actively in the liturgy.

Solesmes and America

The Pius X Institute flourished and in 1920, Ward, with the collaboration of Mother Stevens and others, organized the International Congress of Gregorian Chant. Dom Mocquereau, choirmaster of Solesmes, was invited to direct the singing at the Congress. Mocquereau was continuing the research in the manuscripts of chant that had been begun by Dom Pothier. Mocquereau's work culminated in the official versions of the Gregorian melodies, based on the most ancient and authentic manuscripts. These are the versions that came into universal use in the church. To the Congress Mocquereau brought those rhythmic patterns that he had researched so painstakingly and learned to express with such artistic skill.

The 1920 Congress was held in New York at St. Patrick's Cathedral and drew leaders of the Gregorian movement in the United States and Canada. Children (3,500 of them) from New York's Catholic schools sang the ordinary of the Mass on the opening day. A group of seminarians sang the propers each day, while a choir made up of priests, religious and college students sang the ordinary. These two choirs alternated for the singing of Vespers. The resolutions of the Congress gave Gregorian chant a prominent place in the American church for at least the next four decades.

At the close of the Congress, Mocquereau told Justine Ward that she knew nothing at all of Gregorian chant. Her response, "Will you teach me?", led to the first of her many visits to Quarr Abbey, where the Benedictine monks were living in exile, and then to Solesmes, their home. Participating in the liturgy of the monastery was a profound spiritual experience for Ward. There she sank her spiritual roots. With Mocquereau as her spiritual director, she made vows as a Benedictine oblate on March 21, 1923. Ward wrote:

> I doubt that anyone with the slightest artistic sense could possibly stay for awhile at Quarr Abbey without being converted to the method of the monks of Solesmes. There is great art, art at its summit, but something else which surpasses art itself. It is something so holy that one is overwhelmed with fear, with faith and with adoration. If such a beauty could be spread out and invade our churches, all sin would dissipate like germs under the rays of the sun.[4]

And at another time:

> The sense of that Invisible Presence animated each note, each phrase, each movement, while clouds of incense rose in spiral

design and, mixing themselves with the sunbeams, entwining their mutual rhythms, executed an aerial dance that flooded the church with rays of perfume and patterns of light.[5]

So important to her was the experience described here that for many years Ward donated the incense used at Solesmes.

Summer sessions at the Pius X Institute flourished. When 5,000 teachers had been prepared there, Ward exclaimed, "And they are teaching more than a million children!" She went to Rome to secure permission for the semicloistered Mother Stevens to also teach the men who attended the Institute. From her own funds, she financed the building of a new hall to house the growing number of students.

Disappointments and Sadness

Ward worked to have a Benedictine monastery founded on the grounds of The Catholic University in Washington. She envisioned this monastery as the nucleus of a national school of chant. Political changes in France, however, enabled the Solesmes monks to return to their own monastery and this dream never became a reality.

Exhausted by this failure and the death of Mocquereau, Ward centered her attention once again on the very successful Pius X Institute, but even here she found no peace. Disagreements arose between Ward and Mother Stevens. Part of this involved some materials Mother Stevens had published. Ward accused her of plagiarism. In an effort to placate Ward, Mother Stevens recalled and destroyed the materials. In 1931, the situation reached a climax. Ward resigned from the faculties of both the Pius X Institute and the College of the Sacred Heart and withdrew her financial support of the Institute. The consequences were serious: Wealthy friends stopped funding the Institute; Ward arranged that no monk from Solesmes would be allowed to teach at Pius X for almost 30 years.[6]

The Ward Method won wide acceptance in Europe as well as in America. In 1927, teachers trained at Pius X took the method to Holland. The classes Ward's protegés had begun in Italy in 1925 were highly acclaimed: By 1930, a group of Italian children sang chant for Pius XI. Dr. Maria Montessori was at this audience and, in the presence of the pope, proposed collaboration between Ward and herself, but Montessori did not live to see this initiated. In 1936, the Ward Method made its way to France. Its success resulted in the establishment of the Gregorian Institute in Paris in 1949 and the Dom Mocquereau Foundation the following year. The amazing success in France led to the teaching of classes in Switzerland and, by 1969, there were Ward Centers in England, Ireland and Portugal. Such centers still may be found in Switzerland, France, Portugal and Holland. In 1969, the International Center of the Ward Method was set up in Washington, D.C., at The Catholic University of America.

With the liturgical changes initiated by Vatican II, especially with the introduction of the vernacular, Gregorian chant quickly fell into disuse in this country. Ward's world collapsed. In her anguish she wrote:

> They want to lower the prayer of the church to mud level in order to attract the most ignorant people. We ask for ourselves your prayers while remaining always united with the beautiful prayer of Solesmes which will always last, despite the "progressives" in all countries. Give us more liturgical treasures. It is the only chant we have here. Only Solesmes has mercy for people who have taste.[7]

Until her death in 1975, she offered the sufferings of her declining years to hasten the return of the chant. Her life spanned almost a century of dramatic liturgical change.

The Justine Ward archives are in the Center for Ward Method Studies at The Catholic University of America's school of music. At Solesmes, a choir stall bears a plaque with her name. Each year, on Ward's anniversary, an obituary notice is read in the refectory of Solesmes in appreciation of her support of the cause of Gregorian chant. On that day also, her name is read aloud in the prayers of the faithful during the monastic liturgy that had been the inspiration and challenge of her early years, the only strength and consolation of her final ones.

Justine Ward was one of the few women to stand along with the monks and priests as leaders of the liturgical movement. Virgil Michel chose her to be one of the associate editors of *Orate Fratres* from its foundation in 1926. She was one of the two lay members of this group. In conjunction with Mother Stevens, Ward made a unique contribution to the liturgical renewal in this country and in Europe, a contribution that enabled adults as well as children to pray the Mass in the gentle beauty of chant. It was largely through her untiring work that the restoration of chant called for by Pius X became a reality in the United States.

■ *Frances Krumpelman*

NOTES

1. Dom Pierre Combe, *Justine Ward and Solesmes* (Washington DC: The Catholic University of America Press, 1987), 3.

2. Ibid, 1.

3. Ibid, 1.

4. Ibid, 9.

5. Ibid, 370.

6. Catherine A. Carroll, *A History of St. Pius X School of Liturgical Music: 1916–1969* (St. Louis: Society of the Sacred Heart, 1989), 38.

7. Combe, *Justine Ward*, 134.

ADÉ BETHUNE
Image Maker

ADÉLAIDE BETHUNE, BORN IN BELGIUM in 1914, is rightly called a matriarch of the liturgical movement. She was nurtured for that role within her family. In the mid-nineteenth century, her great-grandmother Terlinden was a daily communicant. Her grandparents built a brick church in which the family worshiped. They founded a parish and established a school because the digging of a canal had made it difficult for the people of the tiny hamlet to get to Mass. Adé remembers the plainchant sung in that church and she heard tales of the liturgical instruction that her grandmother had given a generation earlier to the young pastor fresh from the seminary.

During the school year, Grandfather Terlinden attended daily Mass at the parish church in Brussels. Adé went with him. Soon she outgrew her child's prayer book and began to carry a school textbook to study. When her mother saw her come back from Mass with her large fifth-grade geography book, she went to the religious goods store and bought her a missal:

> I was ten years old, and this year, 1924, proved to be the beginning of my love for sacred scripture. I was fascinated by the little tidbits from the Bible in the epistles and gospels.

They were solid food, much more nourishing than the pious prayers in my children's prayer book.

Adé treasures the story of how the missal had come into her family through her mother's mother. Probably under the influence of Dom Prosper Guéranger, the publishing firm of Mame in Tours had produced a four-volume French/Latin layfolk's missal. Adé's grandmother immediately had sent to Tours to procure a set of this treasure. She died two years before Adé was born, but she had passed on her knowledge and love of the liturgy to Adé's mother.

Adé was a teenage boarder at the Institute of the Holy Family, where her mother had studied as a child, and where her own liturgical formation was deepened. Emphasis in the religion class was Christological and liturgical. The bibliography included: Dom Gaspar Lefebvre's *Daily Missal* and writings by Columba Marmion, Cardinal Mercier and Lambert Beauduin.

The Bethune family emigrated from Brussels in 1928. Adé describes their disappointment with the New York City parish:

> There was no plainchant and no celebration of the liturgy involving the people. The priest did his job at the altar; the people did whatever they wanted to do in the pews, and that was that. There was no communication between the two. We were just part of a human herd in the pews. Because I had my missal, I was way ahead of the game; I knew what was happening.

The Catholic Worker Movement

In New York, Bethune met a kindred spirit, another missal lover, Dorothy Day. During their first encounter in the Catholic Worker storefront in 1934, Day sat the young artist down on a pile of newspapers, brought out her missal and commissioned pictures of Catherine of Siena and Don Bosco for the April issue of the *Catholic Worker* paper. Then Day told Bethune that they would use her pictures of St. Joseph and the works of mercy in the March 1934 issue. So began her regular contribution to the *Worker*.

When conducting research and drawing her pictures, Bethune came to realize that the spiritual and corporal works of mercy were what the lives of the saints were all about. As a Catholic Worker, her love of liturgy was grounded in acts of merciful love for her neighbor. She announced the good news in simple pictures of people past and present caring for one another with love and tenderness. The poignancy and power of the images were related directly to experience; she recorded concrete daily acts of love that she saw and in which she participated.

Bethune's pictures were received enthusiastically as nourishment; religious images of the 1930s were tawdry and steeped in sentimentality. Her characters, drawn in modern dress, helped people find themselves in the pages of the *Catholic Worker;* believer and unbeliever were confronted by a profound reality.

She soon realized that the pocket New Testament in French that she had received as a school prize in Belgium was not enough. She bought a book of psalms like the one she had found in Charles J. Connick's stained-glass studio library in Boston. Then she ordered a complete Bible from the religious goods store even if it cost all of three dollars. Her love for the Bible grew through the years. (In 1989, she was faithfully studying the Sunday texts during a Hebrew and Greek lesson each Saturday.)

Drawing on Books and Churches

In 1934, Jesuit Father Daniel Lord gave Dorothy Day some scholarships to his Summer School of Catholic Action at St. Xavier's Academy in New York. Day gave one to Bethune and advised her to take a course in liturgy. For two unforgettable weeks, she studied the sacramental life of the Mystical Body. Her teacher was Father Gerald Ellard. Bethune kept in

THE
EUROPEAN
LEADERS

1. Prosper Guéranger

2. Lambert Beauduin

3. Pius Parsch

4. Romano Guardini *(From* Romano Guardini *by Hanna-Barbara Gerl)*

5. Abbey of Mont César *(Courtesy of John Sullivan)*

6. Odo Casel

7. Josef Jungmann

8. Balthasar Fischer, preaching at 1981 Eucharistic Congress in Lourdes.

9. Pierre-Marie Gy *(Courtesy of Gerard Austin)*

10. Joseph Gelineau, with Genevieve Noufflard. *(Courtesy of GIA Publications)*

THE
AMERICAN
LEADERS

11. First cover of *Orate Fratres*, drawn under the direction of Eric Gill

12. Virgil Michel *(Courtesy of William Leonard)*

13. Gerald Ellard *(Sketch by Gerard Rooney, courtesy of William Leonard)*

14. H. A. Reinhold *(Courtesy of Adé Bethune)*

15. Martin Hellriegel *(Courtesy of Mary Pierre Ellebracht)*

16. William Busch *(Sketch by Gerard Rooney, courtesy of William Leonard)*

17. Michael Mathis

18. Reynold Hillenbrand *(Sketch by Gerard Rooney, courtesy of William Leonard)*

19. Maurice Lavanoux, second from left, receives the Beni-Morante Award from Cardinal Spellman in 1950. Also pictured are John LaFarge and Anna Lavanoux.

20. Joseph Stedman *(Courtesy of Frances Krumpelman)*

21. Adé Bethune *(Courtesy of Judith Stoughton)*

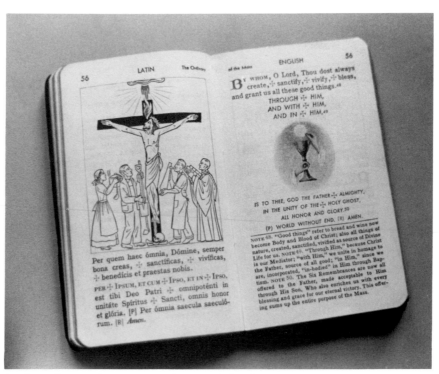

22. Pages from Stedman's *My Sunday Missal*; the illustration at left is by Adé Bethune. *(Photo by Ken Davies, courtesy of Frances Krumpelman)*

23. Godfrey Diekmann *(Photo by Rohn Engh, reprinted with permission; courtesy of Kathleen Hughes)*

24. Frederick McManus is welcomed to the 1962 Liturgical Week in Seattle. *(Photo by Heis, Seattle; courtesy of The Liturgical Conference)*

25. Members of the board of directors of The Liturgical Conference, 1961. From left to right: John Mannion, Frederick McManus, Johannes Quasten, Godfrey Diekmann. *(Courtesy of The Liturgical Conference)*

26. Robert Hovda

27. Gerard Sloyan *(Courtesy of The Liturgical Conference)*

28. Franz and Therese Mueller and family

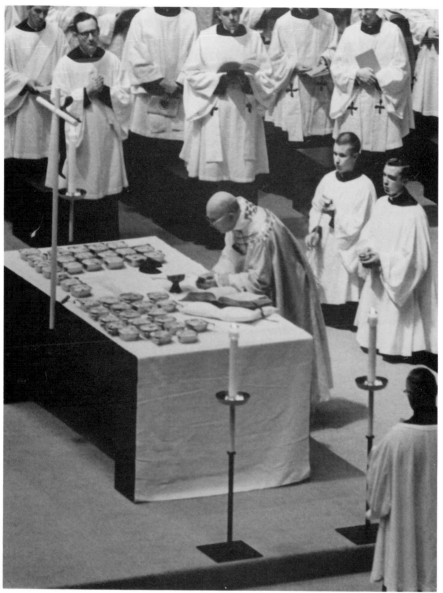

29. Martin Hellriegel celebrates Mass at the 1964 Liturgical Week. For the first time at this Mass, English was used for some parts of the liturgy. *(Photo by Westrich Photography, courtesy of The Liturgical Conference)*

30. Theophane Hytrek at the 1987 premiere of her "Fantasy for Five," commissioned for the Centenary Celebration of Alverno College. *(Courtesy of Charles Conley)*

31. The assembly at the 1964 Liturgical Week. *(Courtesy of The Liturgical Conference)*

32. Alexander Schmemann (*Courtesy of Paul Meyendorff*)

33. Shawn Sheehan (*Photo by Fabian Bachrach, courtesy of William Leonard*)

34. Experts from The Liturgical Conference conducted a study day for Philadelphia priests prior to the 1963 Liturgical Week. Shown here with Archbishop Krol from left to right are: William Leonard, Joseph Connolly, John Miller, Shawn Sheehan and Eugene Walsh. (*Photo by Charles F. Sibre, courtesy of The Liturgical Conference*)

35. Clarence Rivers *(Photo by Walt Weidenbacker, courtesy of The Liturgical Conference)*

36. Frank Kacmarcik *(Courtesy of St. John's Abbey Archives)*

37. Exhibit at the 1965 Liturgical Week in Chicago. *(Courtesy of The Liturgical Conference)*

38. Alexander Peloquin *(Courtesy of The Liturgical Conference)*

39. Omer Westendorf *(Courtesy of J. S. Paluch, Inc.)*

40. Sisters singing at the 1965 Liturgical Week. *(Courtesy of The Liturgical Conference)*

41. Archbishop Cody addressing the assembly at the 1965 Liturgical Week. *(Courtesy of The Liturgical Conference)*

touch with Ellard; in 1937, he invited her to illustrate a new edition of his book, *Christian Life and Worship* (the book would become a classic text in colleges and seminaries for a generation).

For consultation about the book, she went to St. Louis where Ellard arranged for her to be a guest in the home of Emil Frei, the stained-glass artist. The Freis introduced her to liturgical leaders in the St. Louis area: Monsignor Martin Hellriegel, the sisters of the Precious Blood at O'Fallon and their chaplain, Dom Ermin Vitry. Through the Catholic Worker movement, Bethune already was in contact with other liturgical leaders: Virgil Michel, Godfrey Diekmann, Damasus Winzen, Mary Perkins Ryan, John Julian Ryan, Mary Reed Newland, John LaFarge, Paul Bussard and H. A. Reinhold.

When Father Joseph Lonergan contacted the Catholic Worker artist for help with his church of St. Paulinus in Clairton, Pennsylvania, Bethune responded with enthusiasm. Jobless parishioners had built their own beautiful stone church and stood ready to help her adorn the interior. Together they painted 22 larger-than-life figures on sanctuary panels: nine male saints on one side, facing nine female saints on the other. This iconographic scheme, planned by the pastor, is linked with the ancient traditions of visual theology, faithfully kept by the Eastern Orthodox churches. Bethune knew little of that tradition at the time. She simply stood on common ground with the earlier icon painters as she delineated the sacred images, guided by her great love of sacred scripture and the liturgy. As her work expanded, she gained a deep respect for Orthodox Christians as faithful guardians of primitive Christian traditions and, in particular, as builders of coherent traditions of sacred images.

In 1937, Father Joseph F. Stedman contacted the 23-year-old artist to illustrate *My Sunday Missal*. Millions of copies were sold. A few years later, Stedman sought her cooperation on *My Lenten Missal*. For each day's Mass texts, Stedman wrote a short explanation and asked Bethune to make wood-engraved initial letters for them. The small engravings bring to life the biblical characters: They are tender, sometimes witty, always convincing. The viewer soon does not forget the biblical stories, nor their contemporary and personal application. *My Lenten Missal,* a small graphic treasure, was widely translated and Adé Bethune's wood engravings published in German, Spanish, French and Polish editions.

St. Leo Shop

John Howard Benson, master calligrapher and stonecutter, and Arthur Graham Carey, silversmith, writer and architect, also had sought out Bethune soon after her pictures were first published. On their initial visit in New York, they introduced her to Maurice Lavanoux, the editor of *Liturgical Arts* magazine. The four became good friends and collaborators in the Liturgical Arts Society and the Catholic Art Association.

In 1938, Bethune moved into the second-floor space of the John Stevens Shop in Newport, Rhode Island, where she lived and worked with apprentices for several years and eventually became a John Stevens partner with Benson and Carey.

At nearby Portsmouth Priory Chapel, she loved to join the Benedictine community for Sunday liturgy. There she found once again the familiar plainchant of her Belgian childhood. One of the monks gave her a French/Latin copy of the Day Hours, thus initiating her into the liturgy of the Divine Office.

On great occasions, Bethune and her apprentices started out at 5:00 AM to walk the eight miles to Mass at the priory. And Holy Week was their spiritual retreat time when they celebrated the climactic events of the Sacred Triduum with the monastic community.

St. Leo Shop grew out of Dorothy Day's love for Bethune's *Catholic Worker* pictures, which she had printed on cards for thank-you notes. The demand for these cards grew and she tried to answer whatever needs people presented to her for art-work worthy of Christian themes: liturgical calendars and banners, baptismal robes, icons, crib sets and even simple wooden coffins.

In 1961, after writing for *Liturgical Arts,* editing the *Catholic Art Quarterly* and publishing the *St. Leo Bulletin,* Bethune initiated a new quarterly called *Sacred Signs.* Only 15 issues were published, but they contribute important thematic studies to a developing theology of sacred images.

Since 1965, by designing hundreds of religious artifacts in metal, Bethune has applied her knowledge of Christian iconography and her exacting standards to the mass market. As art director of Terra Sancta Guild, she continues to draw the sacred signs that put her in contact with people all over the world.

The Need for Beauty

In addition to being called to perform direct corporal works of mercy, Catholic Workers were invited to a continual clarification of thought, leading to a reform of societal structures. Bethune's significant contributions to liturgical renewal are part of her way of living out this call.

She was a member of the Liturgical Conference and for some years St. Leo Shop had an exhibition booth at Liturgical Weeks, where she met hundreds of enthusiastic people who made up the lively liturgical movement of the 1940s and 1950s.

As a Catholic Art Association board member, she was influential in scheduling its annual convention just before the Liturgical Week in the same city.

For decades, Bethune has been in demand as liturgical consultant for new and renovated churches. Her particular genius is in the simple clarity and common sense with which she champions the needs of the gathered people. Church buildings and furnishings start there, not on the drawing board.

For many years, Bethune served on the liturgy commission for her own diocese of Providence. She presently is an adviser for the Providence Office of Worship. In 1977, the New England Liturgical Committee bestowed on her the Maurice Lavanoux Medal for "her singular contribution to liturgical renewal in the cultic arts."

Fortunately for us, Bethune's abundant liturgical legacy includes the written word. Her writings on sacred architecture and furnishings have secured her position as a liturgical consultant with a wide and deep range of expertise. In the ferment of liturgical change, Bethune's corpus of writings about the environment of worship stand as prophetic and eminently practical.

No account of Bethune's role as liturgical pioneer would be complete without calling attention to her work for children. She has patience neither with pompous "learned" language nor with words brought "down" to the level of children.

In 1962, she was invited by editor Dorothy Andrews to write for and illustrate *Our Little Messenger,* published by Pflaum for the primary grades. Her facility in drawing figures with expressive gestures makes her a marvelous graphic storyteller for little ones and, through the *Teacher's Edition,* she passed on a wealth of background information.

Love of work is the key to Adé Bethune's life and she has long understood that *the* greatest public work of the people of God is liturgy. She continues to work as liturgical artist, writer, consultant and lecturer, hoping to restore the use of worthy liturgical images in sacred spaces.

■ *Judith Stoughton*

NOTES

Much of the information in this article is taken from Judith Stoughton, *Proud Donkey of Schaerbeek: Adé Bethune, Catholic Worker Artist* (St. Cloud MN: North Star Press, 1988).

FRANZ AND THERESE MUELLER
The Domestic Church

IFE IN THE CATHOLIC YOUTH MOVEMENTS of
Germany in the 1920s and early 1930s stimulated
intellectual, liturgical, social and spiritual growth. In
that world, Franz and Therese Mueller, with fresh
doctorates in economics and sociology from the
University of Cologne, gave birth to their first three children,
daughters Mechthild, Hildegard and Gertrud. These gifted parents laid a solid foundation for their family on the rocks of the
domestic church, the parish church, the universal church,
human society at large, the whole created world and the reign
of God. But exuberance turned to struggle. In the mid-1930s,
they made a Nazi-enforced move from Germany to St. Louis,
Missouri, where Franz became professor of sociology at St.
Louis University.

Embracing Their New World

Helping give birth to a liturgical movement in the United
States proved a prolonged task. Gone were the open and

invigorating student social movements. Far away were the theological and liturgical giants: Guardini, Herwegen, Parsch and Casel. But familiar values and resonances of a possible church rushed in from new giants (Huelsmann, Hellriegel, Reinhold, Ellard, Day, Maurin, Bethune, Vitry, Michel and Diekmann) and new places (Holy Family parish and school, St. Louis, staffed by the liturgically aware sisters of the Most Precious Blood from nearby O'Fallon).

During the Muellers' first St. Louis years, it was the local Catholic Worker people who "made us feel that we had something to give." Later, Dorothy Day and Peter Maurin were houseguests of the Muellers whenever their paths crossed. One of the things Therese Mueller came "to give" was the baptismal garment. For even in these early years in the United States, through lectures, articles and example, she worked to bring the baptismal garment to the American church.

In mid-November 1938, William Huelsmann, pastor of Holy Family, invited Franz, Therese and their daughters to meet Virgil Michel. Michel's *Orate Fratres* and other liturgical, educational, philosophical and social projects needed no introduction for Franz and Therese. Michel told Therese that the *Orate Fratres* staff in Collegeville considered her writings a real "find." When Michel hurried off to board a train, the family quickly knelt down on the sidewalk for his blessing. A few days later, Michel died. With their newborn son Reinhold, the Muellers moved to Minnesota not long after.

Franz Mueller took a position in the department of economics at the College of St. Thomas in St. Paul. He taught, wrote and published, served for two decades as a chairperson and gave generous leadership for almost 30 years. Mueller's articles, monographs, pamphlets and letters to editors cover topics such as the future of the local church, the parish in an industrial society, a comparison of the social philosophies of individualism and socialism, the principle of subsidiarity, married saints, the theological use of sociology, liturgy and sociology, person and society according to Thomas Aquinas, beauty and sentimentality in Christian art and the social teachings of Vatican II.

The six Muellers increased to seven in St. Paul when son Francis was born. Each daughter attended the school for liturgy and spirituality run by the Ladies of the Grail, Loveland, Ohio, and each daughter lectures on liturgy and the home. Mechthild Ellis designs and crafts liturgical vestments. Hildegard Kerney is a member of her diocesan liturgical commission and works with Hospice. Gertrud Mueller Nelson lectures on education, art and Jungian psychology. She has published liturgical clip-art volumes and the book, *To Dance with God: Family Ritual and Community Celebration.* Reinhold teaches history at the University of Venice, Italy, and Francis practices family medicine and serves as a medical director for Hospice.

The Fullness of Catholic Life

When the children were young, despite a long-standing commitment *not* to become a two-income family, requests for Therese's insight and words on liturgy and family came from all sides. Godfrey Diekmann asked her for many articles for *Orate Fratres/Worship* for more than two decades. Church bulletins sought her recipes related to religious customs, patterns for baptismal garments, words and ideas. Both the College of St. Catherine and the College of St. Thomas employed her for part-time teaching. Parishioners of the Church of the Nativity, the Muellers' home parish in the St. Paul years, know her as a eucharistic minister, resource person on Christian home life, dedicated friend and faithful community builder. She served for several years on the archdiocesan speakers bureau, giving presentations on the liturgical seasons. Since the early 1970s, Therese has served as a staff member of the archdiocesan ministry for engaged couples. She is known as a kind and wise teacher of young people preparing for marriage.

In 1941, Therese delivered a paper, "The Christian Family and the Liturgy," at the second National Liturgical Week. After the paper, a respondent said: "We are thankful to Mrs. Mueller for her estimation of the sacramental dignity and the mystical beauty of the Christian family."

Therese has authored three books: *Family Life in Christ, Our Children's Year of Grace* and *The Christian Home and Art*. Forty-plus years ago, in *The Christian Home and Art* (Kansas City MO: Designs for Christian Living, 1950), she did more than lament the secularization of Christmas. She met it head-on:

> We are sliding into Christmas too early, I am afraid, and this certainly is not according to the mind of the church. The church keeps us in the attitude of expectation and preparation up to the very last day before Christmas when it will announce to us in a joy that breaks through even the purple vestments: "Today you shall know and tomorrow you shall see." How much anticipation gets lost by our customary predating of Christmas, by early gift exchanges and Christmas parties when we should be deep in Advent; how much of the real climax we level off by creating little climaxes that only distract. . . .
>
> We like to have our tree "hover" over the crib, so that the crib is the centerpiece and the tree the background. However, since it is a symbol of brightness and abundance, there is no limit to the tree's decoration. Good things to eat like apples, oranges, nuts, cookies or chains of popcorn and cranberries are traditional ornaments. Glass baubles eventually took the place of shiny apples. We like our glass balls clear, and we decorate them with enamel, using as designs the alpha and omega, the three crowns of Epiphany, the star of Bethlehem above the manger and the three gifts of the magi.

In her books, talks, classes and articles, Therese Mueller brought the Advent wreath to the American home. (See, for example, her 1941 paper for the National Liturgical Week or her presentation in *Our Children's Year of Grace* [St. Louis MO: Pio Decimo Press, 1943].)

She introduced families to the *Exsultet* of the great paschal Vigil: "One *Exsultet* 20 years ago in my home parish has never been excelled. To me it was the very 'discovery' of this great hymn; and this experience rings through each *Exsultet* I have heard since—and perhaps, if God wills, through the one I want to pray at my life's end."

She acquainted people with customs appropriate to Sunday observance, including dress, decorum and dinner. She opened families to the domestic meaning of the feasts and the seasons of the church year (the incarnational focus of exchanging gifts at Christmas, for example, the "most admirable exchange"). She offered ideas to celebrate more actively the sacramental life (the yearly anniversary letter from baptismal and confirmational godparents to their goddaughters and godsons, for example). She endorsed a healthy veneration of saints (including a "saint-of-the-month study club at home").

Therese mirrors the empathic power of a woman, a wife, a mother. She witnesses the careful naïveté and encompassing creativity of a Christian for whom distance between faith and practice vanishes. She never loses the critical eye of a behavioral scientist: Recalling a rural vacation of her childhood on which she participated with delight in the custom of finding 40 species of wild herbs and flowers for a special blessing on the Feast of the Assumption, she asks, "Are we of the city too proud to admit our poverty?" Rural or urban, the domestic church remains the center of gravity for Therese:

> Saint Bridget of Sweden, with her saintly husband, Ulf, brought up eight children, one of whom, Saint Catherine of Sweden, even surpassed her mother in sanctity. These examples encourage us, fathers and mothers, sons and daughters of today, anxious over the woeful signs of disintegration in home and family, bearing the burden of a great responsibility. We are fortified in the possession of patrons and helpers whose

inspiring example will aid us to save our *ecclesia domestica,* our miniature church, our church in the home, living stones of the living parish and of the great church throughout all the world. ("The Christian Family and the Liturgy," National Liturgical Week, 1941)

The roster of leaders in the liturgical movement in the United States has too few laypersons and almost no married persons and parents. Franz and Therese Mueller, by word and example, brought all they could to the movement and in doing so gave it an essential dimension.

■ *James A. Wilde*

GODFREY DIEKMANN

"Man Fully Alive"

BELIEVE IN one, holy, catholic, apostolic and *changing* church!"[1] Such is Godfrey Diekmann's *credo*—and well it might be! In his 80-plus years, Diekmann, monk of St. John's Abbey in Collegeville, Minnesota, has witnessed plenty of change in the church and contributed mightily to the process that brought it about. He has been influential as editor of *Orate Fratres/Worship;* organizer and participant in national and international Liturgical Weeks; popular and gifted speaker; consultant to the Pontifical Liturgical Commission that prepared for Vatican II; Vatican II *peritus* from 1963 to 1965; member, from its founding, of the International Commission on English in the Liturgy; consultor to the Consilium for the Implementation of the Constitution on the Liturgy; preeminent teacher; sought-after retreat preacher; vigorous ecumenist; and faithful monk. And all the while, he has lived with such childlike effervescence and rock-solid faith that observers are sure it is the Spirit acting through him in each of these endeavors.

For such an array of accomplishments, Diekmann's origins seem quite modest. He grew up in Collegeville, in the heart of Stearns County, Minnesota, the sixth of eight children of John Conrad Diekmann and Rosalie Loxterkamp, German emigrés from Westphalia. His father, the local school teacher, was a man of principle, an outstanding teacher, a stern disciplinarian, an excellent musician and a great storyteller. His mother was a remarkable beauty, an excellent cook, a clever seamstress, elegant in appearance and manner, delightful, outgoing and a woman of astonishing energy. The gifts and personalities of his father and his mother are generously joined in their son. "Pechvogel"—the bad-luck bird—was Diekmann's childhood nickname for the risks he took and the scrapes he got himself into when he wasn't devouring his father's library of German classics or mastering the flute, piccolo, clarinet, oboe and English horn. "Pechvogel's" storied brushes with death in his adult years seem only a logical extension of his earlier adventures.

Teachers and Revelations

Diekmann attended St. John's as a boarding student for his last two years of high school and first two years of college. He was 17 when he crossed the threshold from college to monastery in 1926, the same year the *wunderkind* monk, Virgil Michel, just back from his European studies and thoroughly inspired by Lambert Beauduin, began to promote an American liturgical movement. During Diekmann's first year in the abbey, *Orate Fratres* was founded and The Liturgical Press began publication of its Popular Liturgical Library. One only can guess at the discussions, the chapter deliberations, the liturgical ferment and the sense of adventure that permeated St. John's Abbey and touched even fledgling monks like Diekmann. It also was during that year that he became acquainted with the concept of the Mystical Body of Christ through his novice master, Athanasius Meyer. It was like an explosion, he remembers today, and points to this discovery of a new ecclesiology with profound liturgical ramifications as a major event in his life and understanding.

When Diekmann's turn came to begin graduate studies, he, too, was sent to Europe, to pursue a Doctorate in Sacred Theology at Sant' Anselmo in Rome. Don Anselm Stolz, a gifted young systematician who also had been a student of Lambert Beauduin, was the professor who introduced him to the Fathers and particularly Tertullian, a man described by Diekmann as a violent defender of the faith who died a victim of his own zeal. Tertullian became the focus of Diekmann's doctoral dissertation and has remained the object of his intercessory prayer.

As Stolz guided his students through Matthias Scheeben's *The Mysteries of Christianity*, Diekmann formed the conviction that the effort to grasp speculative theology would be successful to the extent that it was accomplished with reverence and awe. Stolz, himself, propounded a theology of the heart that led Diekmann to sum up the theological pedagogy he learned from his mentor with the phrase: "You never know whether to do theology sitting down or to get on your knees." Here is the foundation for his extraordinarily successful career as a teacher of patristic theology, early Christianity and church history. Teaching, he contends, is a matter of contagion, of letting the sparks fly, of communicating a sense of mystery. It is no wonder that generations of students have used the expression "sometimes like a retreat" to describe what happens to them in Diekmann's classroom.

Karl Adam became another mentor after Diekmann heard him lecture at Tübingen. "The great wonder about Christianity is that you start from the top" is the way Diekmann captures Adam's message of a Christian's baptismal divinization, the act of becoming God's child, saved by the humanity of Christ. That lecture and Adam's writings, particularly *The Spirit of Catholicism* and *Christ our Brother,* profoundly challenged Diekmann's notion of Christology. So, too, did a number of brilliant lectures in sacramental theology that he heard at Maria Laach where the very atmosphere exuded Dom Odo Casel's mystery-presence and where the celebration of the liturgy, as much as the lectures of Dom Ildefons Herwegen, became highly influential in fostering his theological synthesis:

> I understood both Mystical Body and Presence. I knew that we were the Body, living members as vine and branches. But then I understood yet more. It can be summed up in a word: sacraments are not things; they are *acts*. They are acts of Christ. Christ is present and his death and resurrection become saving acts in the present so that we can take part in them.[2]

Diekmann returned from Europe in 1933. His natural dispositions, intellectual gifts and aesthetic sense had been refined through an increasing openness to culture in all its forms. Music, art and architecture, inherent curiosity about people, a beginning interest in affairs of the church and the world, the learning of several languages—all had matured him. Now he settled into the daily life of the monastery and the several full-time jobs that every monk was expected to perform.

Who Was There To Carry On?

Among his assignments, Diekmann became an assistant editor of *Orate Fratres*. He gradually assumed the lion's share of editing responsibilities, guided by Virgil Michel's constructive criticism of the finished product. This apprenticeship lasted for five years until Virgil Michel's sudden death on November 26, 1938.

Some years later, Diekmann mused about Virgil Michel in an editorial, wondering rhetorically: "After his death, who was there to carry on where Father Virgil had pioneered?"[3] Who was there, indeed! From this vantage point, it is clear that Godfrey Diekmann himself was Virgil Michel's reluctant understudy. At 30, and relying heavily on the support of his monastic community, Diekmann valiantly carried on— teaching, speaking, preaching, editing, organizing and, above all, inspiring others with the vision of liturgy as a way of life, which was the legacy of Virgil Michel.

First, there was reorganizing the staff of *Orate Fratres,* a task made far easier by securing the services of Hans Ansgar Reinhold (known to everyone as H.A.R.), a man capable of continuing Virgil Michel's breadth of interests in the column called "Timely Tracts." Diekmann also encouraged more theological articles and devoted a section of the magazine to European developments. He had a knack for anticipating new movements and new needs, inviting, in turn, regular contributions from Kathryn Sullivan (scripture), Frederick McManus (canon law) and Gerard Sloyan (catechetics). Diekmann summarized his editorial policy in a letter to subscribers: "We have stressed the essentials: praying and living with the church, for the greater honor of God. And we haven't neglected the relevance of this to the whole field of social action."[4]

Perhaps even more than his position as editor of *Orate Fratres,* it was his association with the annual Liturgical Weeks that secured his role as a key leader and spokesperson of the liturgical movement in the 1940s and the 1950s. These Weeks were launched under the auspices of the Benedictines in 1940 and sustained by the creation of the Liturgical Conference in 1943. The success of these Weeks was astounding, attracting ever greater numbers, both lay and clergy, to study and to pray together and, according to one commentator, "to find themselves laden with responsibility, rich with spiritual wealth, filled with the spirit of Christ's victory, [and] concerned with the true things of God."[5]

From the very beginning, Diekmann was active in the organization of these Weeks; from 1940 on, his presentations proved to be one of their highpoints as much because of his spirited delivery as because of his scholarship. In 1961, a collection of these talks was published under the title *Come, Let Us Worship,* its contents demonstrating that Diekmann's gift to the liturgical movement was to provide a vision of sacramental life solidly grounded in patristic sources and always oriented to the church's pastoral life.

Liturgical Weeks in the United States were modeled on those study weeks and conferences that had gathered European scholars as early as the late 1920s. In 1953, at the invitation of Johannes Wagner of Trier, Diekmann participated in the Third International Liturgical Conference in Lugano, Switzerland, the first of a number of international liturgical meetings that he would attend in the 1950s. At Lugano (1953), Louvain (1954), Assisi (1956) and Montserrat (1958), he heard groups of scholars and pastors together with representatives from the Sacred Congregation of Rites openly debating a wide range of pastoral liturgical reforms (for example, Holy Week reforms, readings in the vernacular, a three- or four-year cycle of scripture readings, extension of the practice of concelebration, vernacular recitation of the breviary, restoration of the hinge hours of Lauds and Vespers, Christian initiation and the restoration of the catechumenate).

On to the Council

Names such as Capelle, Brinkhoff, Chavasse, Fischer, Gy, Jungmann, Raes, Martimort, Roguet, Stenzel, Antonelli, Brunner, Schmidt, Robeyns, Hofinger, Botte, Crichton and McManus regularly appeared among the listing of participants at these international gatherings. Many of these scholars, including Godfrey Diekmann and Frederick McManus, were invited to serve as consultants to the Pontifical Liturgical Preparatory Commission of Vatican II. In a letter to Fred McManus in September of 1960, Diekmann wrote: "The list looks wonderful. I was able to spot only one or two obstructionists among the 46 names mentioned. And a lot of them have been outstanding in their efforts for pastoral liturgy. Some good guardian angel must have been on the job."[6]

Clearly it was not an accident of history that the liturgy schema was the first schema to be addressed at Vatican II. Most of those drafting the *Constitution on the Sacred Liturgy* (CSL) had worked together for a number of years and previously had grappled with many of the issues addressed in the schema: They had formed professional relationships over the years; they had done their homework.

Diekmann's work on the Preparatory Commission included drafting the articles on the cultural adaptation of the liturgy (CSL 37–40).[7] In retrospect, he realizes that what appeared to be a bold statement of the question of inculturation was not nearly bold enough and that diversity of rite and adaptation to given cultural structures is a precondition of meaningful reform.[8] Within the Preparatory Commission, Diekmann also lobbied tirelessly for permission to recite the breviary in the vernacular, a cause entirely consistent with his deep concern for authentic priestly piety.

Those were heady days, exhilarating days, when the hopes of the pioneers and their successors were being fulfilled. Imagine Diekmann's disappointment when he was not nominated by Bishop Bartholome of St. Cloud to serve as a *peritus* for the first session of Vatican II. His disappointment is palpable in a letter to Frederick McManus: "I would of course be forever grateful to you if you could keep me informed of what is happening, so far as your vow of secrecy allows. (Or am I still included in that as one who belonged to the Preparatory Commission?)."[9]

Diekmann's work as *peritus* began only after Archbishop Paul Hallinan arranged an appointment for him beginning with the second session. At least he was present in Rome for the final debates on the liturgy schema, the voting and the promulgation of the *Constitution on the Sacred Liturgy.* He remembers that day—December 4, 1963—vividly. A good number of participants were expressing consternation that this document did not seem like much to show for two years of work.[10] Diekmann met Dr. Albert Outler, Methodist

theologian and historian from Duke University, who said
to him:

> I am disturbed by the impatience I seem to sense among my
> Catholic colleagues that in two years you've produced only
> one document. I'm an historian, and as an historian I could
> say that I don't think in the entire history of Christianity it has
> ever happened that in two short years there has been a major
> reorientation about theological themes, such a reorientation
> that would normally require decades, if not centuries of
> maturation—and here it is in two years' time. Anything like
> impatience seems to me like a sin against the Holy Spirit.[11]

Also during the second session of Vatican II, Diekmann had
a hand in determining the outcome of the debate that raged
over the place of Mary: Should there be a separate schema
devoted to the Blessed Virgin Mary or should she be treated
within the *Dogmatic Constitution on the Church?* On the evening before a vote was to be taken on this topic, more than
800 bishops gathered to hear from four of their *periti,* Diekmann among them, speaking on the traditional treatment of
Mary in patrology. He developed his argument with one citation after another, from the Fathers about Mary, prototype of
the church, mother of the church and new Eve, and then said,
"We must look to our origins. Justin and Irenaeus have said it
all."[12] Loud applause followed. The vote the next day, one of
the closest during Vatican II, favored Mary's incorporation into
the *Constitution on the Church.*

At Home—Everywhere

During Vatican II, Godfrey Diekmann participated in the
foundation of the International Commission on English in
the Liturgy (ICEL), a group that was born in casual conversation about the need to coordinate translation efforts for inevitable
vernacular concessions. A small group of bishops and *periti*
from English-speaking countries developed a long-range plan

to establish a permanent body of translators, among them linguists and musicians, to create simple, readable, beautiful and dignified English. In the 25 years of ICEL's existence, Diekmann has served on the advisory committee. He has combined a knowledge of Latin with the ability to spot the patristic allusions in many of the texts under consideration, the patience to search for the right word and the exuberance of a child when a finished prayer text is truly pleasing.

ICEL is only one of numerous commitments that continue to occupy Diekmann's time and energies. The man is indefatigable! With the close of Vatican II, he became one of the most sought-after interpreters of its content and implications, speaking all over the country from large universities to small parochial gatherings, both within and beyond the Roman Catholic communion. In his teaching, lecturing and preaching, he continues to exhibit vitality of mind, breadth of interests, generosity of spirit and a delightful enthusiasm for whatever he is doing—combing the woods for watercress, traveling to visit his favorite cathedrals "for the last time," recording classical music since a stroke prevents his playing a wind instrument or regaling friends with a seemingly endless collection of stories.

It should surprise no one that he is a popular candidate for honorary degrees and other awards, having received 21 such recognitions over the years. An excerpt from one citation serves as fitting conclusion to this portrait of Godfrey Diekmann:

> Truly a Man for All Seasons, you are as much at ease and at home traveling the hills and vales of Stearns County in search of the elusive mushroom or in a rural kitchen preparing a supply of chokecherry preserves as you are in the lecture halls of great universities or in the sanctuary of God's house.
>
> Wherever your inspiring presence abides, you remain always and firmly the "good and faithful servant," an exemplar of what Irenaeus of Lyons meant when he wrote that the human person "fully alive is the glory of God."[13]

■ *Kathleen Hughes*

NOTES

Editor's note: This essay is excerpted from *The Monk's Tale: A Biography of Godfrey Diekmann* to be published in 1990 by The Liturgical Press.

1. Quotation found in the personal papers of Godfrey Diekmann, circa 1969.

2. G.L.D., taped interview, November 1987.

3. Godfrey Diekmann, "Ten Years of H.A.R.," *Orate Fratres* 23:6 (1948), 275.

4. Godfrey Diekmann, letter to subscribers of *Worship,* Easter 1957.

5. H. A. Reinhold, "Dosed Religion," *Orate Fratres* 15 (1940), 30–31.

6. Godfrey Diekmann, letter of Frederick R. McManus, September 2, 1960.

7. Johannes Quasten and Johannes Hofinger collaborated with Diekmann on the draft of these articles.

8. As early as 1967, Diekmann spoke of the "imperative" of ritual diversity for meaningful reform. See "Dogmatic Constitution on the Church: Commentary," Vincent A. Yzermans, *American Participation in the Second Vatican Council* (New York: Sheed and Ward, 1967), 75–76.

9. Godfrey Diekmann, letter to Frederick R. McManus, October 23, 1962.

10. It often is overlooked that the *Pastoral Instruction on the Means of Social Communication* was promulgated on the same day as the *Constitution on the Sacred Liturgy* and thus also reflects the labors of the first two sessions of Vatican II.

11. Godfrey Diekmann, taped interview, November 1987.

12. Audio tapes made during Vatican II and stored in the University Archives at St. John's University. Tape III, October 1963.

13. Excerpt from the citation accompanying the conferral of a Doctor of Letters degree, *honoris causa,* on Godfrey Diekmann, by the College of St. Thomas, May 20, 1978.

FREDERICK McMANUS
Pioneer, Peritus, Promoter

T HE ARCHDIOCESE OF BOSTON under the long sway of William Henry Cardinal O'Connell may seem an unlikely place for liturgical inspiration, but it was there that Frederick Richard McManus, born in Lynn, Massachusetts, on February 8, 1923, lived his early life. He was the first of two sons born to Frederick and Mary Toomey McManus. The senior McManus was head of the English department at the public high school in Peabody, Massachusetts. Frederick and Mary McManus passed on to their sons a commitment to education and to the service of others.

Early Work in Boston

F rederick McManus attended Boston College High School and then went on, following in another family tradition, to Holy Cross College. After two years at Holy Cross, McManus entered St. John's Seminary, Brighton, the major seminary of the archdiocese of Boston. It was there that his interest in liturgy began under the tutelage of such writers as Maurice de la Taille, Columba Marmion and Adrian Fortescue. His growing interest in liturgical topics also was sparked by his friendship with John McEneaney, then in his deacon year at St. John's and who later, as a priest of the diocese of Sioux Falls, played an important part in the American liturgical movement. McManus's interest in liturgy also was encouraged by the rector of the seminary, Monsignor Edward Murray, who appointed him seminary master of ceremonies. During his seminary years, McManus became increasingly aware of a small group of Boston priests who were active in the young American liturgical movement. He would recall later that in the archdiocese of Boston the members of this group "were in some sense outcasts but had a disproportionate local influence and tied Boston to a wider, national interest in liturgical renewal."[1] Prominent in this group of "first-generation" American liturgical pioneers were the Jesuit William Leonard and the Boston diocesan priests Thomas Carroll and Shawn Sheehan. All of them were active in the Liturgical Conference and each would occupy a prominent place in the first decades of that pivotal organization.

In addition to the inspiration of these priest promoters of liturgical renewal, McManus soon became aware of the writings and activities of the leading lay promoters from the New England area, including those of Mary Perkins Ryan and her husband John Julian Ryan. According to McManus, "the Boston liturgical people were rather defensive about the fact that, unlike the Midwesterners, they did not have much impact on liturgical song, the dialogue Mass, 'external participation,' but they prided themselves, with some reason, on being spiritually and theologically oriented toward liturgical renewal."[2]

McManus was ordained a priest on May 1, 1947. Over the next several years, he served in two parishes, St. Catherine's, Norwood, and Holy Cross Cathedral. Also in this time he served as secretary to the Metropolitan Tribunal and as master of ceremonies to Archbishop Richard J. Cushing, who had succeeded Cardinal O'Connell in 1944.

In the year that McManus was ordained, Pope Pius XII issued his encyclical *Mediator Dei*. Though in some sense a guarded opening toward liturgical renewal, it was nonetheless a landmark in the modern history of the Roman church. It gave a certain legitimacy to those already laboring for liturgical reform and was for those pioneers a welcome encouragement. Soon after ordination, McManus and a fellow Boston priest, Albert Low, developed the "Mass Demonstration" for presentation around the Boston archdiocese. This was an educational presentation of the Mass, the chief features of which were a simulated Mass celebrated in English facing the people, with an accompanying spoken explanation or commentary. The presenters made it very clear that the presentation was not a Mass nor was it meant to advocate change. Rather it was a means of making the Latin Mass more intelligible to interested Catholics. Later the presentation was published under the auspices of the National Council of Catholic Men with the imprimatur of Archbishop Cushing. A powerful western archbishop read McManus's careful presentation as a dangerous agitation for liturgical change and lost no time in decrying the publication to Archbishop Cushing. Cushing stood by his imprimatur and his priest.

McManus also was becoming involved in what was known as the Sacramental Apostolate, which published a monthly newssheet entitled *Mediator* and conducted "Liturgical Saturdays" at Holy Cross Cathedral. All of this brought McManus increasingly to the notice of the Boston people involved in liturgical activities; they soon invited him to take an active part in their own efforts and programs. McManus was drawn into the national work of the Liturgical Conference, especially through Thomas Carroll, and was introduced to two of the great figures of the American liturgical scene, Godfrey Diekmann and Michael Mathis.

In 1951, Cushing sent McManus to The Catholic University of America for graduate studies in canon law. Three years later, he finished his doctoral studies with a dissertation on the history of the Roman Congregation of Sacred Rites, established by Pope Sixtus V in 1588. After completing his doctoral studies, McManus returned to Boston where he was appointed to the faculty of St. John's Seminary to teach canon law and moral theology.

Life on the Way to Vatican II

The new liturgical attitude signaled by *Mediator Dei* continued after Pius XII and took practical form in 1951 with the restored Easter Vigil *ad experimentum.* This was followed in 1955 by the restored rites of Holy Week. McManus became a leading commentator on the new rites through his writings, especially *The Ceremonies of the Easter Vigil* (1953) and *The Rites of Holy Week* (1956). McManus gave careful explanations of the restored rites and the steps for carrying them out on the parish level. At the same time, he always was sure to point out openings in the revised order that could lead to more effective pastoral celebration and to fuller participation.

McManus's writings on liturgical and rubrical matters led Godfrey Diekmann, the editor of *Worship,* to invite McManus in 1958 to become a regular contributor to *Worship* with a column entitled "Responses." Diekmann believed that a canonist who also was an expert in liturgy could find answers to support more significant liturgical progress. In his column, McManus answered questions of liturgical law submitted to the editor. McManus's approach was greatly appreciated by readers of *Worship* and played a part in increasing pastoral liturgical awareness in the years leading up to Vatican II. Despite the overall success of the column, suspicions and criticisms of those who promoted liturgical reform continued. McManus was accused by an unsympathetic reader of "walking on canonical eggshells" and at a plenary meeting of the U.S. bishops, a future cardinal denounced McManus's writings in *Worship.*

When Father Edward Roelker, dean of the School of Canon Law at The Catholic University of America and McManus's dissertation director, died suddenly in the autumn of 1957, McManus was invited to take his place on the faculty. McManus began teaching at the university in February 1958. His role in the church in the United States became even greater once he had arrived in Washington. In 1959, he was named editor of the *Jurist,* the highly respected journal produced under the auspices of Catholic University's canon-law faculty. That same year, McManus, who had been a member of the Liturgical Conference board since the mid-1950s, was elected president of the Conference during the Liturgical Week held at Notre Dame.[3] During his student days at Catholic University, McManus had come into contact with other priests interested in liturgical reform. Some of these contacts were renewed when he joined the faculty, most notably in the case of Gerard Sloyan, a priest of the Trenton diocese and a member of the religious education department at Catholic University. Sloyan, too, played a prominent role in the Liturgical Conference and was McManus's successor as president.

Several months after McManus arrived in Washington, the U.S. bishops at their November 1958 meeting took a formal step that recognized the increasing importance of liturgy and liturgical renewal by establishing a permanent standing committee, the Bishops' Committee on the Liturgical Apostolate. Its first chairman was Archbishop Joseph Ritter of St. Louis and its first secretary was Bishop James Griffiths, auxiliary to Cardinal Spellman in his capacity of Military Vicar. Bishop Griffiths especially began to rely on McManus for assistance and advice. McManus played a major national role in 1961 when he introduced to the church in the United States the new rubrics for the Mass and Divine Office that were promulgated by Pope John XXIII in his apostolic letter *Rubricarum instructum* of July 1960. This new code of rubrics was not a liturgical advance in the same sense as the Holy Week reforms of Pius XII and it was clearly an interim measure (the convoking of

Vatican II had been announced in 1959), but the new code of rubrics did in small but telling ways point to some of the liturgical enactments of Vatican II and their subsequent implementation.

During a visit to Europe in the summer of 1953, part of which was given over to research on his doctoral dissertation, McManus met some of the staff members of the Congregation for Rites who were playing a leading role in the liturgical advances under Pius XII, particularly the future cardinal, Ferdinando Antonelli, and the Redemptorist Joseph Loew, a disciple of Pius Parsch and a scholar with an appreciation for the pastoral dimensions of liturgical reform. While in Rome, McManus also met for the first time Annibale Bugnini, the editor of *Ephemerides Liturgicae*. McManus recalls going to meet Bugnini largely because of his role in *Ephemerides Liturgicae* and completely unaware at the time of the decisive part that Bugnini had had in the liturgical reform initiatives since 1948, when Pius XII, without any public announcement, had established the Pontifical Commission for the General Liturgical Restoration. Bugnini then was already well on his way to the leading part he would play in the development of Vatican II's *Constitution on the Sacred Liturgy.*

In 1956, McManus returned to Europe as a member of the Boston delegation invited to take part in the Assisi-Rome Congress, a landmark event in preconciliar liturgical history. At that time, McManus became acquainted with a number of the European liturgical scholars with whom he would be associated at Vatican II and during the postconciliar implementation of Vatican II's decisions. Among them were Balthasar Fischer of Trier and Pierre-Marie Gy of the Institut Catholique in Paris. McManus came to know the Europeans better when he went as a stand-in for Godfrey Diekmann in July 1960 to a meeting in Munich sponsored by the European liturgical scholars just prior to the Munich Eucharistic Congress.[4] Present at that meeting were such renowned scholars as Jungmann, Pascher, Wagner, Martimort and representatives from the Congregation for Rites, including Antonelli, who gave the assembled liturgists a first but confidential look at the new rubrical reforms.

The Creation of the Constitution on the Sacred Liturgy

McManus became involved with preparations for the Council in January 1960 after the Holy See had invited pontifical faculties to submit recommendations for the conciliar agenda. The proposals submitted by the canon law faculty at Catholic University were especially farsighted and anticipated to some degree the major decisions of Vatican II, particularly in such areas as the collegiality of bishops, religious liberty and liturgical reforms. The recommendations on liturgical issues included the use of the vernacular, adaptation of rites to various cultures, restoration of the permanent diaconate, concelebration and communion under both kinds. There can be little doubt that McManus played a role in these recommendations, especially those involving the liturgy. Unfortunately, the rector of the university decided to suppress some of the recommendations of the canon lawyers, including all of those dealing with liturgical matters. That a number of the recommendations never had been sent to Rome was discovered only when Vatican II already was under way.[5]

In the late summer of 1960, McManus received a formal invitation from Cardinal Domenico Tardini, papal secretary of state, to serve as a consultor to the Pontifical Preparatory Commission on the Liturgy for the Second Vatican Council. Modestly he attributes his invitation to his acquaintance with Annibale Bugnini, who had been named secretary of the Preparatory Commission on the Liturgy. Also invited to be a consultor to this body was Godfrey Diekmann. Johannes Quasten, professor of patristics at Catholic University, was named a member of the preparatory commission. McManus attended all the preparatory meetings, beginning in November 1960 and ending with the final meeting in January 1962, nine months before the Council opened. He was particularly involved with the committees that dealt with the use of the vernacular in the liturgy and the reform of the Roman calendar.

McManus was present in Rome when Vatican II opened on October 11, 1962. He had been named a *peritus* to the Council and had been invited by Cardinal Arcadio Larraona, president of the conciliar liturgical commission. Godfrey Diekmann joined McManus as the second English-speaking *peritus* to the Commission on the Liturgy in the following year. The only American bishop voted to membership on the conciliar liturgical commission was the archbishop of Atlanta, Paul Hallinan. Hallinan had an interest in liturgical renewal, but he was not well versed in the matters at hand. He had been a Newman chaplain in his native Cleveland and a leading voice in the national Newman Association before being named a bishop in 1958. He would, however, throw himself into his new conciliar role with characteristic energy, enthusiasm and intelligence; from 1962 until his untimely death in 1968, he played a decisive role in Vatican II's liturgical decisions and in their subsequent implementation by the bishops of the United States.

During the Council, Hallinan relied heavily on McManus for liturgical information, advice and encouragement. Hallinan had known McManus from the mid-1950s and in the opening days of Vatican II they had renewed their acquaintance. They were drawn into a close friendship during the Council years;[6] this would continue afterward, particularly when Hallinan was elected chairman of the U.S. Bishops' Committee on the Liturgy in 1966. Just days before Hallinan died of a long and painful illness on March 27, 1968, he asked McManus to come to his residence in Atlanta for a last visit.

In the preparation of the *Constitution on the Sacred Liturgy,* McManus's chief role was as a member of the *coetus* (working group) responsible for Chapter III, "The Other Sacraments and the Sacramentals." He also was a member of the *coetus* that dealt with questions of liturgical law in the *Constitution* and with the overall juridical procedure for the functioning of the

Commission on the Liturgy. Like others, he was disappointed when the Council was unable to complete work on the liturgy document during the first session. He feared that the momentum achieved during the opening session might be slowed. Instead, he saw the work brought to completion and given overwhelming approval by the Fathers of the Council in late November 1963. He was present in St. Peter's Basilica for the formal ratification of the conciliar constitution.

Over and above his responsibilities in the conciliar liturgy commission, McManus had many other duties while in Rome during the four sessions of Vatican II. On a daily basis, he served as a member of the U.S. Bishops' Press Panel, which was set up by the bishops to brief reporters on each morning's happenings in the closed sessions of the Council. A number of experts took part in these briefings, but McManus, along with five or six others, was a permanent member of the panel. The briefings given by the panel and the opportunity afforded to reporters to ask questions of these experts helped to make the Council a major news event in the United States and to ensure accurate information on its deliberations and decisions. McManus also was frequently consulted by bishops and was asked to speak to groups of bishops from various countries.

The Challenge of English

During the first session of Vatican II, several English-speaking bishops, already anticipating a decision on a wider use of the vernacular, discussed informally the possibility of setting up a group of bishops to consider common concerns of English speakers when preparing liturgical texts. Among the bishops involved were Hallinan; Denis Hurley of Durban, South Africa; Guilford Young of Hobart, Australia; and Francis Grimshaw of Birmingham, England. In the second session, a formal meeting of bishops, officially representing ten conferences of bishops from countries where English is spoken, set in motion a joint episcopal body charged by the conferences with overseeing the preparation of English liturgical texts. McManus was present at the beginning of what would be the International Committee on English in the Liturgy (ICEL).

A year later, the bishop representatives of the ten conferences met again, with McManus and Godfrey Diekmann in attendance. The bishops voted to establish a body of specialists who would be responsible for preparing uniform English texts intended for the consideration and vote of each conference. McManus and Diekmann were appointed to this body, along with scholars from Australia, Canada, England and Ireland.

In the first phases of ICEL's work, McManus had many new duties. For the first two years, he was secretary to the committee of bishops. In 1965, he worked to establish the permanent secretariat of ICEL in Washington, D.C., which began functioning in September of that year.[7]

Along with other representatives from ICEL, McManus was invited to take part in the International Congress on Liturgical Translation, convened in Rome by Paul VI in November 1965 to prepare the worldwide church for the immense task of providing the needed vernacular liturgical texts.[8] McManus gave one of the principal papers at the congress. Speaking in Latin, he described a plan and program for preparing vernacular texts under the direction of the conferences of bishops, including joint commissions of bishops representing conferences sharing the same language. McManus also played a part in the elaboration of principles for preparing vernacular texts. Some of these principles were later incorporated into the Holy See's 1969 *Instruction on the Translation of Liturgical Texts,* an important theoretical and practical document that has taken a fundamental place in the development of the vernacular in the Roman church, both with texts translated from the Latin and newly composed texts.

McManus, a careful and disciplined writer with a sure knowledge of English literature and style, spoke strongly in ICEL for English liturgical texts that would be dignified and worthy of the liturgy and, at the same time, be clear, literate and contemporary. A vernacular liturgy should be capable of being clearly proclaimed by the presider and readily understood by the assembly.

Organizing the Reform

Once the Council had approved the *Constitution,* the U.S. bishops had to make prompt decisions on its implementations, especially the introduction of the vernacular. In the U.S. bishops' conference, the chief responsibility for this lay with Archbishops Hallinan and Dearden, who in 1963 had been elected chairman of the U.S. Bishops' Committee on the Liturgy. Like Hallinan, Dearden had a high regard for McManus and made him his principal adviser in preparing the many proposals on matters liturgical and requiring the study and vote of the bishops. It soon was apparent that a permanent secretariat for liturgy was necessary and this was established in January 1965 in Washington, D.C., within the structure of the bishops' conference. McManus was named first executive director of the Bishops' Committee on the Liturgy (BCL).

In the next ten years, he would work closely with Dearden, Hallinan and their successors in preparing numerous proposals and draft statements for the consideration of the body of bishops. The amount of work was staggering. Liturgical items in these years frequently took up the major share of the bishops' twice yearly meetings. As a consequence of the Council, a number of items of liturgical legislation had to be enacted by the bishops and the reformed liturgical books, prepared in English by ICEL, had to be presented to the bishops for their approval. By 1975, virtually all of the major liturgical books had been introduced in the United States, including the sacramentary (Roman Missal) and the Liturgy of the Hours. For the most part, the proposals and recommendations of the BCL overwhelmingly were accepted by the full body of bishops.

Despite increasing responsibilities in Washington at Catholic University, at the BCL, at ICEL and for a time at the Liturgical Conference,[9] McManus still spent considerable periods of time in Rome during the mid-1960s. In 1964, he had been appointed a consultor to the Consilium for the Implementation of the Constitution on the Liturgy. This body had to prepare the revised liturgical books mandated by Vatican II. McManus's chief role in the Consilium was as a member of the *coetus* that dealt with the revision of the sacramental rites apart from the Mass. He also served as a member of the central steering body of consultors for the overall work of the Consilium. He would attend meetings of the Consilium until 1970, when its task was given over to the newly established Congregation for Divine Worship.

Matters Ecumenical and Academic

During the meetings of the Consilium, McManus came into contact with leading liturgical scholars of other Christian churches. They had been invited by the Holy See to attend the meetings of the Consilium as observers. McManus later helped found the North American Consultation on Common Texts (CCT), a body composed of representatives from several Christian churches concerned with issues of liturgical renewal. Partly as a consequence of the work of the CCT, an international body of representatives of Christian churches from various English-speaking countries was formed in 1969. This new body was known as the International Committee on English Texts (ICET). Here, again, McManus worked with scholars from other churches whom he had met at the Consilium meetings. The chief result of ICET's work was *Prayers We Have in Common,* issued in final form in 1975 and containing English liturgical texts for use at the eucharistic liturgy and in the daily office. These texts were in great part accepted by the participating churches, including the 11 Roman Catholic conferences of bishops that had membership in ICEL.

In 1969, McManus was appointed a member of the U.S. Catholic-Orthodox Bilateral Consultation. This led to his appointment by Pope John Paul II in 1979 to membership on the International Joint Commission for Catholic-Orthodox Theological Dialogue. Additional ecumenical responsibilities were given to McManus in 1979 when he was appointed a consultor to the Roman Secretariat for Promoting Christian Unity. And from 1979 to 1981, McManus was president of Societas Liturgica, the international ecumenical association founded in 1967 to promote liturgical scholarship.

From 1968 to 1976, McManus was an associate editor of *Worship*. In 1974, he contributed an important article to *Worship*. This dealt with some pressing pastoral questions of liturgical law arising out of the conciliar reform. Entitled "Liturgical Law and Difficult Cases," the article was in some respects a successor for vastly changed circumstances to McManus's preconciliar "Responses" in *Worship*. The same exactness, pastoral awareness and responsible openness was evident.

McManus's dedicated and energetic service to the work of renewal in the Roman Catholic Church made him a target of Catholics unhappy with Vatican II. A 1968 issue of *Triumph* magazine pictured McManus as a giant spider at the center of a web whose multiple strands represented the many activities of church renewal in which McManus then played a part. A copy of the magazine was slipped under the door of each of the American bishops gathered in a St. Louis hotel in April of that year for a plenary meeting of the conference. More prosaic but equally biting denunciations from like-minded publications were frequent in this period. By then, McManus had been steeled by the experience of criticisms through nearly a quarter of a century and he went on determined to give what assistance and advice he could to the bishops and the local churches in their efforts to carry out Vatican II's mandate.

In 1975, with his commitments at Catholic University growing appreciably greater, McManus gave up the position of executive director of the BCL. During the previous year, he had been appointed vice-provost of the university and dean of graduate studies. McManus's involvement in the wider concerns of the university had been growing since the 1960s. He frequently was elected to university-wide academic committees and, from 1967 to 1973, he was dean of the School of Canon Law.

McManus's role in the administration of the university led to an increasing influence in American Catholic higher education. He would play a prominent part in the councils of the Association of Catholic Colleges and Universities, which he chaired from 1980 to 1982. From 1983 to 1985, McManus held the post of academic vice-president at Catholic University. After more than a decade as an administrator, he returned happily in 1985 to full-time teaching in the department of canon law.

In the 1980s and at the opening of the 1990s, McManus's liturgical activities continued through his service as staff consultant to the BCL and his membership on the advisory committee and executive committees of ICEL. McManus continued to be consulted frequently on liturgical issues nationally and internationally as well as on issues of Catholic higher education. He also was in demand as a writer and speaker on these and other topics of interest to the Christian community.

Author and Canonist

In addition to several book-length studies, McManus has written numerous articles and reviews dealing with liturgical reform, conciliar and postconciliar liturgical developments and liturgical law. These have appeared in various forms and publications but perhaps chiefly in *Worship,* the *American Ecclesiastical Review* (from the mid-1960s) and *The Jurist.* In one way or another, all of McManus's writings have aimed at encouraging and enabling the full participation of believers in the life of the church and in its sacred worship. Some sense of McManus's sure knowledge of liturgical history, liturgical law and of the conciliar and postconciliar documents can be gained by reading his *Thirty Years of Liturgical Renewal*,[10] a collection published in 1987 of all the documents on liturgical matters issued by the U.S. Bishops' Committee on the Liturgy from the 1960s to the end of the 1980s. McManus had a hand in preparing many of these statements. His introduction to the collection and his extended commentaries on each of the documents are in themselves an invaluable history and reflection on this epoch-making period in the liturgical life of the church in the United States. His own role in these developments is characteristically mentioned only in passing. McManus highlights the many steps and initiatives taken by the Roman See and the U.S. bishops to carry out Vatican II's reform. But he also is forthright in expressing disappointment about areas of the liturgical reform that he feels have not been fully put into effect and about areas where he believes there has been some later retreat on the Council's decisions.

A brief word is needed on McManus the canonist, a field in which he has had a significant and influential role in the United States and in the church worldwide. He served as a consultor to the Pontifical Commission for the Revision of the Code of Canon Law from 1967 until 1983, when the new Code went into effect. He since has played a leading part in introducing the new Code to the church in the United States. For 30 years, he has taught hundreds of canonists now working in the United States and in many other countries and through all that time he has been editor in chief of *The Jurist*. Both formally and informally, McManus has given canonical advice to countless numbers of people. He has done this as a consultant to the church nationally and internationally, as a consultant to dioceses and religious orders and as a consultant for many individuals—clergy, religious and lay. This service has been given responsibly and quietly and with enormous generosity.

After All, Integrity and Hope

Those who have participated in meetings and discussions with McManus soon have come to recognize his quick intelligence, his mastery of detail and his unerring memory. In smaller groups, they even may have come to know something of his dry, humorous asides, often delivered without the slightest change in tone or expression and not infrequently turned on himself. His ready wit and highly informed knowledge of current events and ideas in church and state, the result of prodigious reading, appear most readily in informal conversation. Those who know him well are sure to appreciate his lasting loyalties—to the church, to Catholic University, to his native Boston—and his attention and devotion to his family.

McManus's accomplishments have been acknowledged by various honors and awards, but the extent of his achievements may not be fully appreciated and understood for some time. He has accepted the special challenges and responsibilities of being an insider and yet always has remained true to himself. Godfrey Diekmann, McManus's colleague and friend of nearly 40 years, praises McManus for his personal constancy and integrity through that long and eventful period. Future students of Frederick McManus's role in the church of Vatican II will be struck by a remarkable steadiness and consistency joined to an undaunted openness and optimism. Even when faced with occasional discouragements and disappointments, he has kept to his course, waiting for a time, then coming back to plead the cause again—carefully, respectfully, with learning, faith and courage.

■ *John R. Page*

In the preparation of this essay, in addition to the works cited, the following also have been of invaluable help: *The Jurist* 48 (1988):2. This enlarged issue of *The Jurist* is a collection of articles on canonical, liturgical and ecumenical topics in honor of Frederick McManus on the occasion of his 65th birthday. For the purposes of this essay, John M. Huels's "Participation by the Faithful in the Liturgy" especially was helpful. Also of great assistance were copies of the correspondence of Frederick R. McManus and Godfrey Diekmann from 1959 to 1965. This correspondence from the archives of St. John's Abbey, Collegeville, was supplied to the author by Kathleen Hughes.

1. Letter of Frederick R. McManus to John R. Page, December 22, 1989.

2. Ibid.

3. In a note to Godfrey Diekmann sometime after the 1959 Liturgical Week McManus wrote: "Bill Leonard and I are trying to dig out from under the remains of Liturgical Week. It appears that 50% of the participants at Notre Dame think the Conference rash, imprudent and radical; 50% think it is staid, reactionary, pussy footing."

4. Through the 1950s, the European liturgical scholars held a series of important meetings and conferences at Maria Laach, St. Odile, Lugano, Mont César, Assisi, Montserrat. Munich was the last meeting before the Council. Godfrey Diekmann had attended some of the earlier meetings but was unable to go to Munich.

5. For an account of the 1960 recommendations of the canon law faculty, see John E. Lynch, "The Fulfillment of the Law," *The Catholic Historical Review* 75 (1989), 613–15.

6. See Thomas J. Shelley, *Paul J. Hallinan: First Archbishop of Atlanta* (Wilmington DE: Michael Glazier, 1989), 330 (footnote 39, chapter 14). In his important study of Hallinan, Shelley documents, especially in chapters 11 through 16, the close working relationship between Hallinan and McManus on liturgical issues.

7. The beginnings of ICEL are recounted by Frederick McManus, "ICEL, The First Years," *To Love and Serve the Lord: Essays In Honor of Archbishop Denis Hurley,* OMI (Washington DC: The Pastoral Press, expected publication, autumn of 1990).

8. At this stage there still were some restrictions on the extent to which the vernacular could be used. They would be removed by Paul VI in 1967.

9. McManus again had been elected president of the Liturgical Conference in 1964 but had to resign when he became executive director of the BCL.

10. *Thirty Years of Liturgical Renewal: Statements of the Bishops' Committee on the Liturgy,* ed. with an introduction and commentaries by Frederick R. McManus (Washington DC: Secretariat, Bishops' Committee on the Liturgy, National Conference of Catholic Bishops, 1987).

POPE PIUS XII AND PRECONCILIAR LITURGICAL REFORMS

BY 1947, THE LITURGICAL movement in Europe (and, to a lesser extent, in the United States) had been gaining momentum from the beginning of the century. Centers of liturgical study (Louvain, Trier, Paris) and the work of dynamic individuals had done much to revive popular participation in the liturgy in scores of cities and towns throughout Europe.

Interest in liturgical music had been growing for more than a century. The famous "dialogue Masses" of the period brought the entire assembly to participation. Before the war, there were already wonderful examples of new church architecture.

Activity on a more scholarly level also was increasing. Papal approval of historical biblical study led to the application of historical-critical methods to the study of the liturgy. Areas for liturgical reform were delineated and some experiments in reshaping the Easter Vigil already had taken place. Journals and other periodicals dealing with liturgy and music multiplied, as did the number of conferences and study weeks focusing on liturgical topics.

Mediator Dei

Official reaction to this liturgical ferment was mixed. By the end of World War II, the German episcopacy (urged on by those of a more conservative bent) expressed some concern over a number of practical and theological issues in a letter to Pope Pius XII. His response to this list of 17 points, "disturbing elements in the liturgical movement," was the encyclical *Mediator Dei* of November 20, 1947.

It is very much a document written "in response" and it is closely linked to the 1943 encyclical on the church, *Mystici Corporis,* in its fundamental theological affirmation. *Mediator Dei,* however, focused exclusively on the liturgy itself (the first encyclical ever to do this). In the light of the controversy brewing over the liturgical movement, it is clearly an attempt at a balanced discussion of the state of the liturgy, commending what is good and explicitly defining what is in error. Its language is most subtle and the nature of these "errors" was open to a number of contemporary interpretations.

Mediator Dei[1] begins with a vision of liturgy and ecclesiology in general. The laity not only are encouraged but are duty-bound to take part in liturgical rites (8) as well as to accept revealed truths and to obey divine law (13). Liturgy is worship rendered by the Mystical Body of Christ, head and members (20), and in it the work of redemption and its fruits are continued and given through Christ, especially in the eucharist (29).

The Christian liturgy is discussed throughout the document as primarily related to individual prayer and salvation. The Divine Office is to correspond to the individual soul's devotion (145). The church year calls all to study and imitate Christ's mysteries (the events of his life), especially his passion. Each of these mysteries is present, not in a vague way, but each with its own special grace, through the prayers of Christ for our salvation (165). Christ's suffering is the center of worship, the primary mystery of redemption as re-presented in the Mass

(164). The Christian people take an active role in the Mass through song and by offering themselves in imitation of Christ's sacrifice, uniting their intentions with those of the priest (93, 98).

The fact that the encyclical placed such stress on the importance of the liturgy in the life of the church and commended both theoretical liturgical study and practical attempts to increase lay participation (within the framework of existing laws and rubrics) was received with great satisfaction by many contemporary liturgists.[2] Indeed, *Mediator Dei* clearly expresses official papal recognition of the vital importance of the liturgy in Christian life. Despite the weaknesses of the document (its conservative stance theologically and ecclesiologically, extreme caution against any kind of liturgical experimentation, excessive fear of heresy and overwhelming focus on individual piety), *Mediator Dei* contributed a great deal to the eventual promulgation of the *Constitution on the Sacred Liturgy.*

Mediator Dei (1947), as well as the earlier important encyclical on biblical studies (*Divino Afflante Spiritu,* 1943) *Mystici Corporis* (1943), initiated a period of intense scholarly and pastoral activity to reevaluate the Roman liturgy. "The 1950s brought into the liturgical movement a sense of breathless hurry."[3]

Eugenio Maria Giuseppe Giovanni Pacelli, who became Pope Pius XII in 1939, was uniquely qualified to oversee this preconciliar period, with its urgent calls for liturgical reform and its equally vocal conservative movements urging resistance to any change. He continued to issue decrees, guide Vatican congregations and make important addresses on various liturgical topics until his death in 1958. His legal training (he held earned doctorates in both civil and canon law), as well as his extensive curial service and diplomatic experience, played important roles in setting the official Roman "policy of controlled concession"[4] on matters liturgical during the 1950s.

The Vernacular

Nowhere was this "controlled concession" more clearly seen than in the official response to the increasing demand for the use of the vernacular in the liturgy. Most of the changes made and permissions granted in this area concerned the *Rituale*. In 1947, a bilingual text of the *Rituale* was approved for use in France;[5] the need for a Ritual in the several languages of India was acknowledged in 1949; a German bilingual text was approved in 1950; and an English-language bilingual Ritual followed, for use in America (1954), Canada, Australia and New Zealand (1955). Approval for a similar Japanese text was given two months after the death of the pope in 1958.

Some eucharistic texts also were translated. The earliest permission was given for a translation of the Roman Missal into Mandarin Chinese (1949), but it appears that no text ever was actually published. The extended use of German during Sunday Mass was approved in 1953, especially in hymns and readings; although some attempts were made to restrict and modify this practice in 1954 and 1955, the permission was reconfirmed in 1958 by the Holy Office itself. In addition, vernacular readings and hymns during Holy Week were approved for use in India in 1958.

The Liturgies of Holy Week

Much of the earliest scholarly attention had been centered on the development and eventual reform of the Easter Vigil and other liturgies of the Triduum. As a result of an important address by Romano Guardini (given at the First German National Liturgical Congress in 1950), bishops from several European countries sent a request to Rome (November

1950) for permission to celebrate the Easter Vigil on Holy Saturday evening (instead of morning or early afternoon, as had been the practice). The response was close to immediate. A new *Ordo* for Holy Saturday was published in 1951 and the Easter Vigil was "restored" as a one-year experiment. This experiment was extended on a yearly basis through Holy Week, 1955; in November of that year, a revision of all Holy Week services was promulgated in the document *Maxima Redemptionis Nostrae* (with clarifications issued in 1956).

Other Reforms

One of the most important areas of discussion was the possibility of holding the celebration of the Mass in the evening. Permission for such evening Masses was given only slowly and gradually. In March of 1948, authorization for evening Masses was given to the bishops of Japan and, in August of that same year, to Poland as well (although only on a limited basis). In 1949, this permission was extended to India, along with a relaxation of the regulations concerning the eucharistic fast. Later, the apostolic constitution *Christus Dominus* (January 6, 1953) addressed both of these issues, amending the regulations for the entire church. Further extensions followed in the document *Sacram Communionem* (1957).

Other liturgical practices also were discussed during the pontificate of Pius XII. The Congregation of Rites published an important instruction on liturgy and music (September 3, 1958) that stressed the importance of active participation by all in liturgical celebration (discussed below). Liturgical rubrics officially were simplified in the decree *Cum Nostra Hac Aetate* (1955) and were modified yet again five years later with the publication of the *Codex Rubricarum* (1960). Other permissions followed in 1960: the Congregation of Rites approved the omission of the prayers after Mass in some instances and approved the afternoon distribution of communion outside of Mass, again, only in certain situations.

It appears, however, that some on the pastoral scene were quite anxious to put into practice the insights and recommendations brought to the attention of the whole church by active and enthusiastic liturgical scholars. Strict condemnation of unauthorized liturgical experimentation, especially in the *Ordo Missae*, often was the subject of official statements. In 1958, the Holy Office issued a warning "against high-handed introduction of new practices in the liturgy." A 1957 decree condemned the practice of "silent concelebration." A warning against those urging the delaying of the baptism of infants was issued in 1958.

The Arts

Liturgical art and architecture were important topics on the national and international levels. As early as 1949, the German Liturgical Commission was involved in issuing guidelines on the construction of church buildings. The Holy Office itself issued a decree on sacred art in 1952 and another on the role of the tabernacle in 1957.

In 1949, the Roman Congregation of Seminaries and Universities reiterated the importance of music training in the education of seminarians; in 1950, Rome was the host city for the First International Musical Congress. Pius XII himself wrote his longest encyclical about sacred music (*Musicae Sacrae Disciplina*, 1955), a document that had a great impact on music professionals and pastoral practice.

Much activity on the scholarly and pastoral fronts took place after the publication of *Mediator Dei*. Some idea of the range of activity and interest can be gained from this very incomplete summary.

In 1948, the Herwegen Institute for the Promotion of Liturgical Studies was founded at the abbey of Maria Laach. This abbey was already a noted center of liturgical study, not only because of the influential men who lived and worked there, but also because of its sponsorship of the journal *Jahrbuch für Liturgiewissenschaft*.

The Liturgical Institute at Trier was founded in 1947 and sponsored the first German National Liturgical Congress in 1950. It was Romano Guardini's previously mentioned address, delivered at this congress, that moved the group to directly request that their bishops urge Rome to restore the Easter Vigil to its proper form and time.

German and French liturgical scholars met together again later that same year in Luxembourg to discuss further issues in pastoral liturgy. Other German National Liturgical Congresses were held in 1955 (on the relationship between liturgy and piety), in 1957 (on the Bible and the liturgy) and in 1960 (on the missions).

In 1951, the first International Study Week was held at Maria Laach (the Center for Pastoral Liturgy in Paris also was involved in the planning). International Study Weeks would be held almost yearly through 1960 on topics such as the lectionary, the breviary, baptism/confirmation and the eucharist in East and West. The 1951 Week was important because it focused on the Roman Missal and on an agenda for the book's reform. Some of the suggestions raised at this meeting were adopted in preconciliar reforms of Holy Week and liturgical rubrics and the work of the 30 or more liturgical scholars

assembled there would have a significant impact on the composition of the reformed liturgical books mandated by
Vatican II.

The Assisi Meeting

The most significant European congress was held in 1956:
the First International Congress of Pastoral Liturgy held at
Assisi. This was essentially a retrospective look at liturgical
renewal and reform as guided by Pius XII. Six cardinals, 80
bishops and 1,200 participants from all over the world were
present. The opening address was delivered by the Prefect of
the Congregation of Rites, Gaetano Cardinal Cicognani (who
also presided at the Congress); Pius XII prepared an allocution
for the close of the meeting.[6]

In this talk, the pope noted the achievements of the liturgical
movement over the preceding 30 years. The most important
element in the pastoral area was the encouragement of "an
active and intelligent participation by the faithful in liturgical
actions."

The pope also was concerned both to legitimize and to caution the liturgical movement of 1956. He noted that "the chief
driving force . . . has come from the hierarchy" and credited
Pius X with giving "the liturgical movement a decisive impetus"
with his breviary reform in 1913. The enthusiastic response by
the laity was noted, as was the problem of liturgists encouraging "certain deviations from the right paths [which] called for
correction by ecclesiastical authority."

The remainder of the address centered on two theological
themes: the liturgy and the church and the liturgy and Christ.
The former offered significant statements to be echoed and
developed by Vatican II. The first was the centrality of liturgy
in the life of the church: "The liturgy is a vital function of the
Church as a whole." Second, every participant, cleric or lay,

must participate fully, mind and heart, as a complete person, and that the liturgical "contributions" of the hierarchy and the faithful "are not added as two separate entities, but represent the collaboration of members of the same organism which acts as a single living unit . . . one and the same body of Christ." Third, the truth of the deposit of faith (the "great mysteries of faith") found in scripture and tradition are enshrined in the liturgy. "The solemn liturgical ceremonies are . . . a profession of faith in action." The liturgy is thus a source of grace, and the eucharist is "the heart of the liturgy." Therefore, any liturgical art, architecture, furnishings or music must add to the "beauty and dignity" of the liturgy.

It is clear that such insights carried through and are given even stronger expression in the documents of Vatican II. Other subjects in this allocution seem less central (e.g., the detailed discussion of concelebration) or dated (e.g., the consideration of the relationship between the altar and the tabernacle or a suspicion of laypeople who show "a too-active desire" in the area of liturgical matters).

Active Participation and the United States

The key treatment of active participation in the liturgy was found in the *Instruction on Sacred Music and the Liturgy* issued by the Congregation of Rites on September 3, 1958. Nowhere was the impact of the document more strongly felt than in the United States.

The explosion of interest generated by the 1958 *Instruction* "gave notice of how far the day was really advanced"[7] and the resulting storm of activity surprised even the members of the Liturgical Conference itself. Only two months after the publication of the *Instruction,* for example, the American bishops instituted a national Commission for the Liturgy.

The American Liturgical Week of 1959 (at the University of Notre Dame) took the 1958 Instruction as its theme. It was the largest Week ever held to that date. The large attendance at following Weeks testified to the sustained interest in the liturgy on all levels of American Catholic life. Every talk, study group and workshop of the 1959 Week reflected in some way the overall theme of active participation by all, clergy and laity, in the liturgical life of the church. Noted liturgical scholars and "activists" delivered major addresses, among them Andrew Greeley ("Participation Problems in the Modern Parish"), Giacomo Cardinal Lercaro ("Liturgy and Social Action"), Frederick McManus ("The Law, the Liturgy and Participation") and Godfrey Diekmann ("Popular Participation and the History of Christian Piety").[8] Study groups and workshops explored the important relationship between active participation and almost every other element of church life.

The Eve of the Council

After the death of Pius XII on October 9, 1958, his successor, Pope John XXIII, continued to direct limited liturgical revisions and extend certain pastoral permissions. The entire transition period between the death of Pius XII and the beginning of Vatican II (1958–1962) centers on the papal announcement of Vatican II (January 25, 1959). The efforts of the liturgical movement during the previous half-century thus were crowned by the establishment of a liturgical commission, meeting in Rome, to prepare for Vatican II itself. This commission, to which many of the greatest minds of the liturgical movement were appointed, prepared the way for the promulgation of the *Constitution on the Sacred Liturgy (Sacrosanctum Concilium)* by the Fathers of Vatican II on December 4, 1963.

■ *Joanne Pierce*

NOTES

1. Numbers in parentheses refer to individual paragraphs of the encyclical. The text of *Mediator Dei* is available in English from a number of publishers. Perhaps the best choice is that found in *The Papal Encyclicals 1939– 1958,* ed. Claudia Carlen (McGrath Publishing Company, 1981), 119–54.

2. See Lambert Beauduin, "L'Encyclique 'Mediator Dei'," *La Maison Dieu* 13 (1948) 7–25.

3. Gerald Ellard quoted in William J. Leonard, "The Liturgical Movement in the United States," ed. William Baruna, *The Liturgy of Vatican II,* Vol. II (Chicago: Franciscan Herald Press, 1966), 307.

4. Ibid., 307.

5. For a full chronology of preconciliar liturgical activity (particularly in Europe), see Lucas Brinkhof, "Chronicle of the Liturgical Movement," *Liturgy in Development,* trans. H. Vaughan (Westminster: Newman Press, 1965), 40–67. This article is a major source for the events and dates discussed in the body of this article.

6. Several other prominent theologians and officials presented papers at the congress, including Josef Jungmann, Bernard Capelle and Giacomo Cardinal Lercaro. The collected papers may be found in *The Assisi Papers* (Collegeville: The Liturgical Press, 1957).

7. Leonard, "The Liturgical Movement," 307.

8. All talks and workshop reports are published in *Participation in the Mass: 20th North American Liturgical Week* (Washington DC: The Liturgical Conference, 1960).

ROBERT HOVDA

Conscience and Curmudgeon

OBERT HOVDA COMES BY a different route than most to be among those counted as leaders of the liturgical movement. He studied liturgy in the schools no more than the average 1940s candidate for priesthood. He has had a bit of experience as associate pastor or chaplain in parish and campus work now and then, but never got to be the beloved old pastor. He has taught liturgy to graduate students, but only briefly and he didn't much like it. He served on no official Roman or United States church commissions or boards in preparation for or in fulfillment of Vatican II.

And there is more: For two decades those who expected him to turn in a manuscript or show up and give a talk were, whether they knew it or not, taking a risk: Hovda is an alcoholic and until the mid-1970s he was drinking. And yet more: In his 40s he developed a voice problem that made it nearly always impossible for him to speak above a hoarse whisper. That is not easy to listen to.

But listen people do. This nonacademic, nonpastor has for two decades been sought after to talk with a depth and challenge rarely heard at gatherings about the liturgy. Perhaps many have found in Hovda what Woody Guthrie found and sang about in Franklin Roosevelt:

> He helped me build my union
> And he showed me how to talk.
> I could tell he was a crippled man
> But he learned my soul to walk.

Hovda has "learned" a generation how to walk. To teach would be something else, but he has "learned" the presiders and musicians, the academics and pastors, the ordinary people who prepare the liturgy in parishes.

A Convert in More Ways Than One

Robert Hovda was born in Wisconsin in 1920; a few years later, the family moved across the river and he grew up in Minnesota. His father was Methodist, his mother Lutheran. A second child was born eight years later, and soon after that came the Depression, lost job and lost home. Hovda found companions and a lifetime's direction in the Methodist youth movement in Minneapolis where speakers such as Bayard Rustin came to talk about a social gospel that the young people put into practice. In high school, he edited the school newspaper and wrote for the newsletter of the Methodist youth organization. Hovda also heard Norman Thomas several times and was a member of the Socialist Party when he left Central High School.

He also was at times in charge of worship for the youth group, and his reading took him toward Anglican authors of the day who brought together concerns for liturgy and society. Hovda found here a vision of economic reform and a case for pacifism. In his second year of college, he became an Episcopalian. He was at Hamlin College then, with a small scholarship and a night job in a refrigeration company. The next year, 1941, he left college to help support his family. He found work at a Ford plant that was being organized by the Auto Workers.

Through the pacifist Fellowship of Reconciliation, Hovda made contact with its member organization, the Episcopal Peace Fellowship. He was speaking for such a group on December 7, 1941, when the bombing of Pearl Harbor brought the United States into World War II. The next year Hovda was drafted and applied for Conscientious Objector status. Some who would not go into the armed forces went to jail, some went to camps. Most, like Hovda, were at least temporarily out of touch with their families who felt disgraced.

Hovda eventually found himself in a Civilian Public Service camp in New Hampshire, clearing away trees downed by a then long-past hurricane. The work was hard and the local people were hostile toward the pacifists, but this particular unit consisted mainly of Catholics; while they were supervised by the government, the food and clothing for the group came from Dorothy Day and the Catholic Worker. Hovda was there only three months, but many of the friendships have lasted lifetimes (including one with author Gordon Zahn).

From New Hampshire Hovda transferred to the Alexian Brothers Hospital in Chicago, hoping for more meaningful work as an orderly. That was in January of 1943. By June of that year, Hovda and others had come to feel that any cooperation with the selective service system of the government was not possible for them. Four of them walked away; they were arrested, indicted and released to await trial. Hovda expected to be sentenced to three to five years in prison. He was reading Karl Adam, a German Catholic theologian, and reached a decision to enter the Roman Catholic church before his trial and sentencing.

Hovda took instructions from a Carmelite priest, David Murphy, and was conditionally baptized on the night before his first hearing. Murphy and another priest accompanied him at his court appearances. The young lawyer who was handling the cases without charge had managed to have Hovda's case brought before a Judge Sullivan, who seemed willing to classify him as a ministry student and have charges dropped—if only he could find a seminary to accept him.

Hovda sent letters off to dozens of seminaries. Back came the answers: Thanks, but the number of seminarians we have already exceeds the needs of the diocese. But a letter from Theological College in Washington referred him to St. John's in Collegeville, Minnesota. He wrote and was accepted at once— without a bishop and without any means of support. The judicial process then brought him before another judge. Hovda prepared for the worst, but was given three years probation. The others who had walked out with him went to prison for a minimum of three years.

Years of Ferment and Service

Hovda was at Collegeville until 1949 and these were exciting years. Godfrey Diekmann was teaching, H. A. Reinhold and Maurice Lavanoux and many others were visitors, Frank Kacmarcik was working at North Central Publishing, the Young Catholic Workers and the Catholic Rural Life Movement provided opportunities to continue in the Catholic Worker tradition, and there were Liturgical Weeks and meetings of the Vernacular Society to attend.

Bishop Muensch of Fargo, while visiting Collegeville, heard Hovda's story and accepted him as a seminarian for that diocese (Muensch would later serve the church in postwar Germany and in Rome). In 1949, Hovda was ordained; his mother, who had become a Catholic, and his father were both present. His first assignment was at the Fargo Cathedral where he worked with a wonderful pastor and parish. In 1954, he was sent to serve two small parishes in rural North Dakota. He now had time for the writing he had begun in his years at the cathedral; articles were published in *Today, Amen* and *Commonweal,* along with numerous book reviews in *Worship* and *Liturgical*

Arts. There were articles on theology, scripture and spirituality as well as subjects such as the death penalty.

To Washington and Back

After ten years of parish ministry, Hovda obtained permission to explore the possibility of joining the Oratory, a community of diocesan priests. Before he could do this, however, Gerard Sloyan called from The Catholic University of America to ask if he would join the faculty. For the next three years—as Vatican II was getting underway—he taught about the church, about ecumenism, about liturgy. He enjoyed the reading this made possible but never took well to the classroom (and his voice had begun to fail him in these years). During the summers, he worked toward an STL degree. He was in Washington when the Liturgical Conference opened its first office in the early 1960s.

These years saw Hovda's first book, *Sunday Morning Crisis,* published by Helicon Press of Baltimore, a publishing house run by David McManus: They were bringing the best of European theology to the United States and were working closely with the Liturgical Conference to meet the needs of growing interest in liturgical renewal. Other Baltimore friends included Joseph Connolly, then assistant pastor at St. Gregory's parish where liturgy was celebrated each Sunday with great care and wonderful music. It was an interracial parish where Catholic activists in the civil rights movement could bring worship and zeal for justice together.

Hovda returned to North Dakota for two years, 1963–1965, to serve in campus ministry. During this time, he continued to write for the Liturgical Conference as well as for *Critic, Continuum, Emmanuel* and *Liturgical Arts.* In the summers of 1964 and 1965, Hovda was a speaker at the Liturgical Weeks in Philadelphia and St. Louis.

In the mid-1960s, with the reforms of Vatican II beginning to be implemented in every parish, the Liturgical Conference set about an ambitious publishing program to supplement the work it did through the annual Weeks. Hovda was asked to come to Washington and begin full-time work on the staff of the Conference as an editor. Over the next 13 years, he made immense contributions toward a worthy beginning for the renewal of the liturgy in American parishes.

Living Worship became his monthly letter to all who would listen, and many did as whole dioceses subscribed for their clergy. In these four pages, Hovda was at his best: taking some particular aspect of the liturgy and bringing to it a freshness that lacked nothing in scholarship, nothing in breadth. Whether he talked about music, about the entrance rite, about anointing or about the roles in liturgy, the reader would find the topic could not be hemmed in. The insights came from life, the connections were made, justice and the arts were integral to understanding. These pages hold, among other treasures, the sentences and paragraphs that eventually found their way into the United States bishops' document on *Environment and Art in Catholic Worship*.

Hovda also wrote for other periodicals published by the Conference, *Liturgy* magazine and the monthly *Homily Service*. He was instrumental in expanding the ecumenical embrace of the Conference's membership and board. Through many of these years, he belonged to the NOVA Community, a nongeographical parish in the Virginia suburbs of Washington. Hovda was able to work with others here in putting the liturgical principles he wrote about into practice; often he presided at the Sunday eucharist.

Two books that Hovda wrote during these years are especially important. When the revisions of the eucharistic liturgy were complete in the late 1960s, he prepared a book called the

Manual of Celebration. Hovda placed the sacramentary's new texts in one column and filled the other with his commentary. He also wrote introductory matter. The *Manual* sold many thousands of copies, and through this volume presiders and liturgy committees came to know and give shape to the liturgical reform in their parishes.

Strong, Loving and Wise was written near the end of Hovda's work at the Conference. It is a book for presiders, a book like no other before or since. Hovda writes about the habits that make up the art of presiding, the skills the presider needs, the way to think about this work within the church.

At Home in New York

Afterter a brief stay in Chicago where he taught at the Jesuit School of Theology, Hovda moved to New York. He lived first at St. Joseph's church in Greenwich Village where he brought support to an already fine liturgy. In 1985, he retired to an apartment in public housing on the lower east side where he continues to write (among other things, "The Amen Corner" in every issue of *Worship* magazine). He is a frequent speaker at gatherings where with eloquence he continues to summon those whose concern is liturgy to see what their work must be about:

> Becoming new persons in Christ Jesus has to mean for us making a clean break with the politics and economics of our society and of our past, so that we can really see the human scene without prejudice, freshly, newly. If the current state of the world makes it appear to us that we have to choose *either* human freedom *or* human solidarity, then it is the current state of the world that has to be challenged. The person and the community of biblical faith are pledged to both, and belief in either, by itself, is a dangerous illusion. . . .
>
> Where else [other than at eucharist] in our society are all of us—not just a gnostic elite, but everyone—called to be social

critics, called to extricate ourselves from the powers and princi-
palities that claim to rule our daily lives in order to submit
ourselves to the sole dominion of the God before whom all of us
are equal? Where else in our society are we all addressed and
sprinkled and bowed to and incensed and touched and kissed
and treated like *somebody*—all in the very same way? Where
else do economic czars and beggars get the same treatment?
Where else are food and drink blessed in a common prayer of
thanksgiving, broken and poured out, so that everybody, everybody shares and shares alike? (At Chicago's October 1981
Liturgical Conference.)

Hovda delights greatly in the theater and streets of the city.
His address book bursts with the names of hundreds of good
friends from every part of his life, names he addresses each
Christmas with a newly composed poem.

There are two definitions given for a curmudgeon. One is:
a crusty, ill-tempered, churlish old man. The other, the one that
fits Hovda in his 70s as he continues to prod against injustice
and ugliness in church and society, is this: anyone who hates
hypocrisy and pretense and has the temerity to say so; anyone
with the habit of pointing out unpleasant facts in an engaging
and humorous manner.

■ *Gabe Huck*

GERARD SLOYAN
Bridge of the Spirit

I N RESPONSE TO the Berakah Award, granted to him by the North American Academy of Liturgy in 1986, Gerard Sloyan speculated on how he would tell his life story: "If I were ever to write an autobiography it would mention, somewhat incidentally, that I got an elementary and secondary education, played all the sports indifferently and got to be an Eagle Scout, but mostly was an altar boy."[1] In fact, his immediate experiences in various liturgical roles—member of the worshiping assembly, altar boy, minister of the Triduum, priest, preacher—have grounded Sloyan's contributions to the development of liturgy in American Catholic life. He is first of all a self-described *"practicer* of the art of public worship,"[2] bringing his considerable scholarship to bear on that practice, despite his disclaimer that he is "without any formal training in [liturgy's] history or theory."

Gerard Stephen Sloyan was born in New York City on December 13, 1919, the son of Jerome James Sloyan and Marie Virginia Kelley. He grew up with his older and younger sisters, Jean and Betty, in Red Bank, New Jersey, where a third sister, Virginia, was born. His early involvement with the church's liturgy certainly left its mark, particularly a desire to be a priest, one who would take the business of worship seriously and do it well.[3]

With that goal in mind, he attended Seton Hall University in the late 1930s and then, for five years, the Immaculate Conception Seminary (Darlington), both institutions of the Archdiocese of Newark. His theological studies were concluded at The Catholic University of America, where he earned an STL in 1944. On June 3 of that year, he was ordained a priest of the diocese of Trenton, New Jersey. After pursuing doctoral studies at Catholic University (1944–1947), he served as a curate at parishes in Trenton and Maple Shade (1947–1950); his PHD was granted in 1948.

Through these years of study and early priestly ministry, Sloyan pursued an informal education in liturgy, reading *Orate Fratres* and *Liturgical Arts* as well as the patristic-oriented theology studied and presented especially by the German Benedictine scholars who had been his Darlington seminary professors, Albert von Hammenstede, Leo von Rudloff and Damasus Winzen. Others "outside Benedictine walls," such as diocesan priest-scholars Karl Adam and Matthias Scheeben and Jesuits Josef Jungmann and Emile Mersch, also were formative influences. During his years of graduate study, he dreamed with other students like James Rea, Eugene Walsh, Myles Bourke, Maurice Dingman and Joseph Konrad about a "pastoral, not monastic, liturgy that invited the people to pray in concert—knowingly, lovingly, in art forms that were simple but elegant—as Christ, head and members, singing God's praises in the Spirit."[4]

Sloyan's first experience of a National Liturgical Week came in New York City, December 27–29, 1944. This was the first week sponsored by the Liturgical Conference, heir of the Benedictine Liturgical Conference, which officially was dissolved in 1943 to be replaced by a national organization not so identified with a particular religious order. Sloyan was one of the 184 priests present out of a total attendance of 1,212.[5] Since that 1944 Liturgical Week, Sloyan affirms, his "involvement with the liturgy has been almost totally coterminous with [his] membership in the Liturgical Conference."[6]

Bringing Deep Chasms

Liturgy has been only one of Gerard Sloyan's works. He is primarily a New Testament scholar, but also an exemplary preacher, educator and ecumenist. These interests have made him a bridge across the often deep chasms that have divided liturgists from educators, practitioners from scholars, one Christian church from another and Christianity from other faiths, particularly Judaism and Islam.

His influence on religious education stems from his years as a faculty member at The Catholic University of America.[7] Sloyan returned to Washington in 1950 as an instructor in the Department of Religious Education, as it then was named. This department had been founded in 1936 to offer the MA and PhD in theology to nonclerics who could not, at the time, earn theological degrees. Sloyan introduced religious education as it is commonly understood into the department by dint of a few judicious hirings.

Sloyan moved steadily through the academic ranks of his department, eventually becoming full professor and then, in 1957, department chair. During his ten years in this position, he edited and contributed to two books on catechetics, *Shaping the Christian Message: Essays in Religious Education* (New York: Macmillan, 1958; abridged, Paulist Press-Deus Books, 1963) and *Modern Catechetics: Message and Method in Religious Formation* (New York: Macmillan, 1962). He also produced several popular introductions to theological topics as a way to help people understand the transformations taking place in Catholic theology, including the editing of an 11-book series of college textbooks for Prentice-Hall, "Foundations of

Catholic Theology." Sloyan's own volume in that series was *The Three Persons in One God* (1964).

In the early 1960s also, while Frederick R. McManus was its president, the Liturgical Conference established its first offices in Washington near the grounds of Catholic University. John B. Mannion was hired as the first full-time executive secretary.[8] Sloyan replaced McManus as president of the Conference in 1962 for a two-year term and so was in that post through Vatican II's approval of the *Constitution on the Sacred Liturgy* (1963). Those were heady times for the Conference, with huge gatherings for the annual Weeks in Philadelphia and St. Louis. Sloyan described those scenes this way: "I saw 13,000 people gather in Philadelphia and 17,000 in St. Louis . . . either apprehensively or in joyful anticipation to learn what the 'changes in the liturgy' were going to be. The chief change was one of the spirit, which many did not come prepared to hear."[9]

Because of the work involved in communicating that "change of spirit," the Liturgical Conference immediately undertook a major publishing program, to which Sloyan contributed in several ways. The weeklong planning sessions for a series of books, the first and for a long time the only aids made available to guide the celebration in the new rites, took place during the week in which President John Kennedy was shot in November 1963. The Conference's national staff and services were expanded as part of a long-range education program to help implement the decrees stemming from Vatican II.

A Focus on the Word

In the mid-1960s, Sloyan's writings began to include a new interest: preaching. In 1965, he published a collection of homilies, *To Hear the Word of God: Homilies at Mass* (New York: Herder & Herder), followed by *Nothing of Yesterday Preaches* for the same publisher (1966). This interest in homiletics and a willingness to present himself as either example or target have continued through a two-volume collection of homilies, "parochial and plain," as he describes them, *Rejoice and Take It Away: Sunday Preaching from the Scriptures* (Wilmington DE: Michael Glazier, Inc., 1984).[10]

In 1967, Gerard Sloyan left his tenured position as a department chair at Catholic University to take up a professorship in New Testament studies in an ecumenical and interfaith setting at Pennsylvania's state-related Temple University in Philadelphia. In his first years in Philadelphia, he completed a task begun through his contacts with the Catholic Biblical Association of America in Washington. Before Vatican II, the Confraternity of Christian Doctrine abandoned further revisions of existing English translations of the Bible in favor of a new translation from the original language. Three-fourths of the Hebrew Scriptures appeared in separate volumes (1955–1965) when Sloyan joined the committee as English-language editor for the New Testament portion (1966). The complete translation appeared in 1970 as the *New American Bible.*

Concerned that Catholics in the United States had a shallow understanding of the scriptures, Sloyan now directed his writing toward popular presentations reflecting the latest biblical theory. These efforts included works inserting Jesus into the Jewish milieu of his times (*Jesus on Trial: The Development of the Passion Narratives and Their Historical and Ecumenical Implications* [Philadelphia: Fortress Press, 1973]) and offering a solid analysis of the scriptural texts to be used in the Sunday assembly (*Commentary on the New Lectionary* [New York: Paulist Press, 1975]). These were followed by *Is Christ the End of the Law?* (Philadelphia: Westminster Press, 1978) and *John* in the "Interpretation" Commentary (Atlanta: John Knox Press, 1988).

Even as his publishing activity expanded, Sloyan kept in touch with other areas he considered important, making sure that the bridges he had helped build would remain strong. He was elected vice-president of the Liturgical Conference twice

(1970–1971, 1975–1980), as the Conference began to shift from a chiefly Roman Catholic to a more ecumenical and even interfaith organization, and he accepted the chair of the Conference's board of directors in 1980, a position he held until 1987. He also was a member, during these years, of the College Theology Society, the Society of Biblical Literature, the Catholic Theological Society of America (from which he received the John Courtney Murray Award in 1981) and the North American Academy of Liturgy.

Sloyan became chair of the Department of Religion at Temple University in 1970, the same year he was given the Pro Ecclesia et Pontifice medal, a papal decoration established by Leo XIII for outstanding service to the church. He held that chair until 1974 and assumed it again from 1984 to 1986. He remained professor of religion, specializing in the New Testament, until his retirement from Temple in 1990.

People and Prayer

Through the years of teaching, preaching and writing, Gerard Sloyan has held uppermost that people are worthy of respect, deserving the best tools they can be given to live the faith well. He consistently has taught that central to the practice of that faith is prayer together. These concerns were reflected in the two charges that ended his response to the Berakah Award:

> There are always *people* attached to every product, every conference, every worship office. Not all are equally gifted but all are equally people. Be terribly sensitive to the contributions of each. Try to remember the difficulty of the task, not just the quality of the product. . . .
>
> We are engaged in the one ecumenical endeavor which is likely to achieve something in the healing of a wounded church. . . . Prayer in each other's company is prelude and postlude and symphony. I say: Pray together, in the ways you know.[11]

As he has built and strengthened bridges between religious education and liturgy, liturgy and the Bible, Roman Catholics and members of other religions, scholars and practitioners, clergy and the rest of the church, Gerard Sloyan never has lost that living engagement with God, amazingly present and mysteriously remote, that gives life and spirit to the religious enterprise. His ministry and his being are filled with the freshness and delight that he still promotes in the worshiping assembly. As he reminded the members of the North American Academy of Liturgy, "The paradox we have all been called to live is the insight that prayer, that tenuous and all but impossible communion with God, is best served by old familiar forms in old familiar formularies, carried out with a freshness, a delight, an *élan* that makes them ever new."[12]

■ *Gordon E. Truitt*

NOTES

1. Gerard S. Sloyan, "Response to the Berakah Award," *Worship* 60:4 (July 1986), 308. In another context, he described himself as "a liturgical minister during the sacred Triduum in one role or another, child and adult, over a sixty-year period." Gerard Sloyan, "The Paschal Triduum: An Enduring Drama," *Pastoral Music* 13:6 (August-September 1989), 15.

2. Sloyan, "Response," 305. Italics added.

3. Ibid., 309: "The only thought that came to me and stayed was: 'This is a pretty serious business. Some priests do it better than others. I think I'd like to be in Group A.'"

4. Ibid.

5. In correspondence with the author, Sloyan notes: "My mother and my sister Betty, just out of college, were present for one night session at the Cathedral High School, but they were not registered. The war's new prosperity never reached us!"

6. Sloyan, "Response," 310.

7. In correspondence with the author, Sloyan notes, "To be a New Testament scholar is to be a religious educator. My ten years as chair of a department named religious education obscured what I was teaching all that time: the Bible and early Christianity."

8. The staff expanded fairly quickly. One month after the office was opened, Mannion hired Virginia Sloyan away from *The Pope Speaks;* within the first year he also hired Carol Campbell. Both gave years of service to the Conference.

9. Sloyan, "Response," 310.

10. Reflective of Sloyan's continuing ecumenical stance is the publication of *Worshipful Preaching* by Fortress Press in Philadelphia, traditionally a Lutheran publishing house, in the same year as *Rejoice and Take It Away* (1984).

11. Sloyan, "Response," 311.

12. Ibid., 307.

ALEXANDER SCHMEMANN

*Theologian of the
Orthodox Liturgy*

LEXANDER SCHMEMANN WAS BORN in Estonia of a
Russian family, but then moved to Paris in his early
childhood. He grew up in a large community of
Russian emigrés, which included some of the leading twentieth-century Christian thinkers, such as
N. Berdiaev and S. Bulgakov. The young Alexander pursued
studies at the University of Paris and then at the Orthodox
Theological Institute in Paris, "St. Sergius," as it generally is
known. After completing his studies, he became an instructor
in church history, first as a layman and then, in 1946, as a married priest.

Schmemann's true love was liturgy. His initiation to Orthodoxy and its spiritual life was not in the dull, compulsory
religion classes at the Russian high school *(gimnaziia)* that he
attended, but in the rich liturgical life at St. Alexander Nevskii
Cathedral on rue Daru in Paris. As a teenager, he actively participated as an altar boy, then as a subdeacon, in the services
presided over by the elderly Metropolitan Evlogii, spiritual
head of the Russian diaspora in Western Europe. The metropolitan and his clergy, while a bit "old-regime," were
enlightened and open. From these early days come Schmemann's appreciation for the importance of the liturgy, as well

as a certain love for pomp and ceremony that was to remain with him during his entire life. He always experienced the liturgy as a joyful event and this primary intuition permeated all his subsequent work.

In the Midst of Postwar Events

Intellectually, Alexander Schmemann was strongly influenced by Nicholas Afanasiev, professor of canon law and a colleague at St. Sergius. Afanasiev was the first to articulate the term "eucharistic ecclesiology"—the notion that the church is revealed and realized precisely when it celebrates the eucharist.[1] This eucharistic ecclesiology, which was to permeate Schmemann's own work throughout his career, has become popular not only among the Orthodox,[2] but recently among Roman Catholics as well.[3]

The Paris of the late-1940s was a vibrant place, not least because it became one of the chief centers of the liturgical movement. The Centre de Pastorale Liturgique (CPL) was founded there in 1943 and some of the leading twentieth-century liturgists worked within its walls—including A.-G. Martimort, Jean Daniélou and Louis Bouyer. The writings of Daniélou and Bouyer, in particular, with their emphasis on liturgiology as both a historical *and* theological discipline, had much in common with Schmemann's own views and their writings are frequently cited in his works. This period also witnessed the beginnings of the ecumenical movement. Long before Vatican II, informal gatherings between Catholics and Orthodox began to take place, often in a clandestine manner. On both Roman Catholic and Orthodox sides, liturgists were in the vanguard. Both sides drew their inspiration from the common patristic heritage and they were able to speak a common language. Schmemann took an active part in these discussions and,

through his work, was a catalyst in making the Eastern understanding of the liturgy accessible to the West. Schmemann was
later to attend Vatican II as an official observer.

Schmemann in America

In 1951, Schmemann came to America, where he joined the
faculty of St. Vladimir's Orthodox Theological Seminary in
New York. From 1962 until his death in 1983, he served as its
dean. In the United States, he was the moving force behind the
eucharistic revival within the Orthodox church. He was a pro-
lific writer[4] and a popular figure at countless campus
gatherings where he excelled as a speaker. His books were
translated into many languages and continue to be popular
and influential, not only among the Orthodox, but perhaps
even more so in the broader Christian context.

His activities were not limited to the field of liturgy. He was
very active in ecclesiastical affairs, working tirelessly for Orthodox unity in America, and he was instrumental in the establishment of the autocephalous Orthodox Church in America. For
decades, he also gave weekly sermons in Russian on "Radio
Liberty" and his name became familiar to millions of Christian
believers in Russia, whose only direct contact with the church
was through these radio broadcasts. He also was something of
a literary critic, best known for his interpretation of the writings of the Nobel laureate Alexander Solzhenitsyn, with whom
Schmemann became friends after the latter's expulsion from
the Soviet Union. Schmemann also was an influential pastor
and numerous persons from various Christian traditions count
him as their spiritual father.

Among Schmemann's most important literary works are:
For the Life of the World: Sacraments and Orthodoxy (1963);
Introduction to Liturgical Theology (1966); Great Lent (1969);
Of Water and the Spirit: A Liturgical Study of Baptism (1974);

Church, World, Mission (1979); and the posthumously published *The Eucharist: Sacrament of the Kingdom* (1988).[5] Written in an engaging, popular style, his books are targeted not so much at the scholarly world as at the general audience, to whom he consistently tries to convey his sacramental vision of the church and of creation. While in his writings Schmemann is concerned chiefly with the Byzantine liturgical tradition, his message is universal—the broad popularity of his writings certainly attests to this.

Liturgical Theology

In these and other works, Schmemann makes several important contributions to the liturgical movement. Probably the most significant is his definition of "liturgical theology," as distinct from "theology of the liturgy." Whereas previous authors have used the terms interchangeably, Schmemann made a distinction between them that has become the basis for modern terminology in the field of liturgical studies.[6] In "theology of the liturgy," the liturgy remains an *object* of theology: This includes the historical study of liturgy (which is, of course, an essential first step and without it no liturgical movement would have been possible), as well as a theological analysis either of liturgy as a whole or in its component parts—sacraments, office, liturgy of time, etc. "Liturgical theology," on the other hand, is an enterprise where the liturgy itself is the *source* of theology: It is "the elucidation of the theological meaning of worship."[7]

> Liturgical theology is therefore an independent theological discipline with its own special subject—the liturgical tradition of the church, and requiring its corresponding and special method, distinct from other methods and theological disciplines.[8]

The intuition that the liturgy is itself a source of theology is, of course, not new. Indeed, it characterized the early and the patristic churches in both East and West, only to be lost in the period of the scholastics, when liturgy was relegated to being just one of several "channels of grace," and reduced to its essential "form" and "matter." Schmemann strongly criticizes this "Western" approach, though he, of course, admits that it had its sway in the Eastern churches as well. But this change of direction evident in Schmemann's approach places him in the vanguard of the liturgical movement.

Several aspects of Schmemann's own liturgical theology also need to be mentioned. First is his emphasis on the *eschatological* nature of liturgy and closely related is his focus on eucharistic ecclesiology. Again, these ideas were inspired by his consideration of the early church's experience of the liturgy.

The liturgy, for Schmemann, is an eschatological event for it is in the liturgy that the church is realized and revealed as the reign of God in the world:

> This kingdom, which for "this world" is *yet to come* and forms the ultimate horizon of its history, is already present (revealed, communicated, given, accepted . . .) in the church. And it is the liturgy which accomplishes this presence and this parousia, and which, in this sense (in its totality) is the *sacrament of the church* and thus the *sacrament of the kingdom.*[9]

This eschatological aspect is inherent in the liturgy and, Schmemann constantly emphasizes, it is an *essential* characteristic of liturgy—just as it was an essential aspect of the life of the early church, where the eucharistic day was both the first day of the week and the Eighth Day, the Day of the Lord, on which the kingdom already is inaugurated.

In this eschatological context we place Schmemann's eucharistic ecclesiology. Assembly, eucharist, church and eschatology are not some unrelated entities in the church's life, but are different aspects of one and the same experience of the kingdom of God revealed and present here and now. The church exists to make the kingdom present and this presence is realized precisely when the church is assembled for the eucharist on the

Eighth Day and encounters the glorified Christ. This connection, so evident for the early and patristic church, generally has disappeared from the consciousness of later Christians, but it is inherent in the liturgy itself. Schmemann's major contribution was precisely to remind the liturgical movement and the church at large of this vital, theological principle.

Thus, Schmemann contributed to the liturgical movement in a number of ways. First, he was a pioneer in the development of a definition and a methodology of liturgical theology.[10] Second, his intuitions regarding both the eschatological and ecclesial dimensions of worship had a profound influence on the contemporary liturgical movement. Finally, Schmemann's theology was consistently *pastoral* in its emphasis: For him theology was not an academic discipline, but precisely the articulation within the church of the unitary aspects of Christian belief and life: eucharist, eschatology, ecclesiology—all perfectly expressed precisely in the church's *liturgical* life.

■ *Paul Meyendorff*

NOTES

1. His chief work on the subject is *Trapeza Gospodnia (Table of the Lord)* (Paris, 1952).

2. See, for example, the recent, very influential work by J. Zizioulas, *Being as Communion* (Crestwood NY: St. Vladimir's Seminary Press, 1985).

3. This notion is stressed, for example, in E. J. Kilmartin, SJ, *Christian Liturgy: Theology and Practice* I: *Systematic Theology of Liturgy* (Kansas City: Sheed and Ward, 1988).

4. His bibliography appears in *St. Vladimir's Theological Quarterly* 28 (1984) 11–26.

5. All of these are published or are available from St. Vladimir Seminary Press, Crestwood NY.

6. See T. J. Fisch, *Liturgy and Tradition: Theological Reflections by Alexander Schmemann* (Crestwood NY: St. Vladimir's Seminary Press, 1990), Introduction. This is a collection of articles in which Schmemann tackles the subject of "liturgical theology" as a specific discipline.

7. *Introduction to Liturgical Theology* (Crestwood NY: St. Vladimir's Seminary Press, 1975), 14–15.

8. Ibid., 16. See also "Liturgical Theology, Theology of Liturgy, and Liturgical Reform," *St. Vladimir's Theological Quarterly* 13 (1969) 217–24 (included as chapter 5 of *Liturgy and Tradition*).

9. A. Schmemann, "Liturgical Theology, Remarks on Method," *Liturgy and Tradition,* chapter 1.

10. See, for example, the recent work, dedicated to Schmemann, by A. Kavanagh, *On Liturgical Theology* (New York: Pueblo, 1984).

LITURGICAL ROOTS IN BOSTON

I N THE TELLING of the story, each one is free to begin wherever. Truth to tell, the liturgical movement in Boston has many roots. I think it fair to root it more than 50 years ago at the College of the Holy Cross, Worcester, Massachusetts. Jesuits and liturgy? More than a few would be surprised at the linkage. Jesuits projected an image of intellectual disciplines, detached from the softer side of ritual and art and gesture.

But a catalog of the early decades of the presidents of the National Liturgical Conference reveals quickly the Holy Cross connection: Thomas Carroll (class of 1932), Shawn Sheehan (class of 1933), John McEneaney (class of 1938), Frederick McManus (class of 1944), all priests ordained for the archdiocese of Boston. The college on the hill founded by Father Fitton fits prominently in the roots of the Catholic church in New England and has given more than its share in the birthing of the liturgical movement in New England.

These four and so many others of their era went on from Holy Cross to St. John's Seminary in Brighton where another Holy Cross alumnus, Edward G. Murray, became rector in the late 1930s. Seminary formation of those days was rigid by any standard and liturgy was not at the fore in academics or in style of celebration. What kept the flame alive at Brighton was openness to theological study.

50 Years Ago

The setting of the movement moved across Lake Street in the late 1930s and early 1940s from the Brighton seminary to the Cenacle retreat center. Regular gatherings, usually monthly, provided the arena for new insights in ecclesiology, liturgy and Christology. This was a grass-roots effort. Tom Carroll was the anchor. Authority figures were kept at a distance from these meetings: Ed Murray, the seminary rector, and John Wright, Cardinal O'Connell's secretary, were never a formal part of the Cenacle meetings. But the grass-roots movement was not unknown to the authorities. In the proceedings of the 1942 Liturgical Week, the text of a telegram from William Cardinal O'Connell is recorded designating the young Tom Carroll as official delegate from Boston.

The 1940s proved to be a time of great growth. As the National Liturgical Weeks developed from the 1940 meeting in Chicago, there always was a Boston representation, albeit small. In the first eight years, never more than a dozen were registered from Massachusetts. Then, in 1948, the week was hosted in Boston with more than 3,000 attending.

As elsewhere in the country, so in Boston, liturgy and social action were linked from early days. Tom Carroll took literally the gospel challenge of bringing sight to the blind. His efforts through many decades at Boston's Catholic Guild for the Blind now continue at the Carroll Center for the Blind. He was active from his initial days in the National Association for the Advancement of Colored People (NAACP) and the Catholic Interracial Council. When the cause escalated in the 1960s, he continued that witness not only by marching in the South but also by coordinating the march of the Catholic Interracial Council in South Boston's St. Patrick's Day parade.

With World War II, energies were redirected. The spirit of theology scholarship continued, however. The very activity of the war itself provided a new arena for these newly found interests in liturgy. Bill Leonard, a Jesuit based in Boston, has written eloquently in several essays of the pastoral experience of the liturgical movement that he and so many other Boston priests realized as military chaplains.

At the *Pilot*, Frank Moran and others fed more than a few stories about the liturgical movement into the diocesan press. Later years would see similar contributions from Connie Buckley.

Following the war, the archdiocese grew rapidly under the energetic direction of the new archbishop, Richard Cushing. Never accused of being a liturgist, he was nonetheless a pastor who read the times well and responded to the needs of the people. When Boston hosted that 1948 Liturgical Week at Mechanics Hall, Tom Carroll, Shawn Sheehan and Bill Leonard were very much at the helm, but new faces were appearing in titled roles: John Wright, honorary chairman; Charles Finn, chairman; Gus Hickey, homilist at the closing liturgy; Peter Hart, Joseph Collins, Mary Perkins Ryan on the committees.

Archbishop Cushing spoke at the opening of the week. He spoke of the need for humility and patience. And he humbled all present. And he dismissed the movement. More than a few were upset and several from the Midwest were ready to pack up and leave. But dialogue continued through the week and Archbishop Cushing offered a third virtue at the end— courage. And he bade the liturgists to reinforce their numbers. The local committee was challenged to continue: Monthly pontifical liturgies would be celebrated at the cathedral and the committee was invited to renew the cathedral's Holy Week celebrations.

Thus was born the Sacramental Apostolate. Monsignor Cornelius Sherlock held meetings at the Catholic Schools Office where each month there would be a Saturday gathering to study the literature and to celebrate the liturgy.

30 Years Ago

To appreciate the growth and the shaping of the liturgical movement in Boston in the 1950s and 1960s, one need only study the programming of the Fontbonne lectures and the Bon Secours lectures. More, perhaps, than in other large centers of the movement, in Boston the religious women and men took the movement to heart. The priests of the earlier days continued. And the laity increased especially through the gatherings at the cathedral. But the interest and commitment of the religious mushroomed. At the cathedral, at Fontbonne Academy and at Bon Secours Hospital, monthly lectures continued year by year. Sometimes big-name speakers from outside would attend, but more often soft-spoken local speakers who studied the movement and put it into practice at home would appear.

The sisters and the brothers brought the movement to the schools and to catechetics. Many contributed to this effort, but the name that endures through it all is Mary Francille Thomas, CSJ. She studied at Notre Dame under Michael Mathis and brought the fruits of her learning to the people of Boston. She visited the schools and the Confraternity of Christian Doctrine (CCD) programs in the city and in the suburbs. She brought to the catechetical movement of Boston what Mary Perkins Ryan, another New Englander prominent in liturgy and catechesis, brought to the national movement.

During these years, a local periodical called *Mediator* was published five times a year by the Sacramental Apostolate. With heady articles for serious readers and with a circulation of thousands, including all the schools and convents, Shawn

Sheehan and others brought the best of theological and historical research to focus on parish life.

The movement began to be seen in the shaping of model parishes. At St. Paul's in Cambridge, Ted Marier developed a music program that for more than 50 years has continued to be a showcase that is not embarrassed to boast of Gregorian chant even while expanding to newer repertories. One singer in that choir, Bernard Law, learned of the movement at St. Paul's while a student at Harvard. Now the archbishop of Boston, he acknowledges those roots of his own journey in liturgy. Russ Davis, music director at the seminary and in more recent years pastor at St. Paul's in Wellesley, captured that spirit and preserved it. Ed Murray, after leaving the seminary, brought the spirit of the movement to Sacred Heart parish in Roslindale where more than a few liturgists of national and international fame found hospitality when visiting Boston. At the Paulist chapel in the shadow of the statehouse, yet another model developed as new concepts of participation and ministry were studied and put into practice.

Yet another model was offered by Shawn Sheehan. After years of teaching church history at the seminary, Sheehan accepted for his first pastorate a small, poor urban parish caught in the flux of population shifts in the 1960s. Embracing the spirit of poverty and rooted strongly in the liturgy he had taught, he made St. Leo's in Dorchester a home for the migrant farm workers then settling in Boston to begin boycotts. St. Leo's rectory was a frequent gathering place for the Association of Boston Urban Priests. Liturgy and social action continued their union.

Networking increased in those days. In 1959, the New England Liturgical Committee was founded and began a round of annual or semiannual meetings. In the final days before Vatican II, everyone's activities increased. In earlier days, the accent was theological. Now the arts began to surface with Celia Hubbard and the Botolph Group, architect Willoughby Marshall, artist-theologian Adé Bethune from Newport and so many others. At St. Paul's, the music efforts developed with the formation of the Boston Archdiocesan Choir School. At Boston College, Alex Peloquin provided new melodies through the Peloquin Chorale even as he settled in at the cathedral in Providence.

New leaders of the movement were being trained. At St. John's Seminary, this was the work of Shawn Sheehan, Fred McManus, Jim O'Donohoe, Dick Quinn and many others. The New England province of Jesuits produced liturgical scholars such as Ed Kilmartin and Bob Taft. At Boston College, Bill Leonard and others trained a new generation. The archdiocese of Boston has more Catholics at college and graduate levels than many dioceses have in total population. The link between Harvard and St. Paul's parish community goes back to early days. By the late 1960s, liturgy was a priority in campus ministry, not only in the way the rites were celebrated but in the witness of social justice lived by those fed at the table.

The story of the liturgical movement in Boston gets too close to write accurately when we speak of more recent times. At the national level, the movement expanded in many directions, some would say with more discord than harmony. The simple umbrella of the Liturgical Conference now was many separate arenas, offices and organizations. The varied phases of this expanding movement were very much evident in Boston.

Yet in liturgy, music, social action, catechetics, pastoral ministry and other areas, more than a few schools of ecclesial thought and action today must trace their vitality to the roots: Tom Carroll, the Boston Liturgical Week, the Fontbonne lectures and so many others. The schools may vary, but the bond of love for the worship of the church binds closely.

■ *Richard J. Butler*

MASSEY SHEPHERD, JR.

Liturgical Renewal in the Episcopal Church

ORN MARCH 14, 1913, in Wilmington, North Carolina, Massey Hamilton Shepherd, Jr., from early
childhood enjoyed a predilection for liturgical worship. Although Shepherd's parents, who encouraged
his interest in things liturgical, were Methodists, his
paternal grandmother was an Episcopalian. Moreover, the
worship services at the Methodist church that he attended
(where as a youth he served as a substitute organist) were
rather formal; parts of each service were chanted, the eucharist
was celebrated monthly and the shape of the services was
derived from *The Book of Common Prayer.* Perhaps not surprisingly, therefore, Massey's eventual passage to the Episcopal
church was not a difficult one.

While a student at the University of South Carolina, where
he received his BA degree in 1932 and his MA one year later,
Shepherd was most influenced by Dr. G. Croft Williams, an
Episcopal priest thought by many to be a "dangerous" liberal.
In his senior year, he met Dr. Williams one evening each week
to prepare for confirmation in the Episcopal church and he
recalled that "Williams introduced me to the basics of modern
biblical criticism."

With the help of Vernon Cook, his Greek professor at USC, Shepherd was admitted to the Divinity School of the University of Chicago in 1933 to pursue graduate work in early church history. His adviser was the newly appointed dean, Shirley Jackson Case, a liberal Baptist who was published widely in the fields of early church history and New Testament studies. It was Dean Case who encouraged Shepherd's interest in liturgics and music, supervised his dissertation *(Monastic Worship in the Fourth Century)* and arranged for Shepherd to teach patristics and liturgics at the Divinity School on completion of his PHD in 1937. By his own admission, Shepherd's teaching career was "indelibly stamped" with Case's mark and methods.

Shepherd continued to teach at Chicago until 1940. During this time, he frequently visited the Berkeley School at New Haven, Connecticut, to pursue a BD degree. There, William Palmer Ladd, the dean of the Divinity School and a pioneer of the liturgical movement in the Episcopal church, introduced Shepherd (by now Shepherd had read Romano Guardini and Odo Casel and had become a convert to the ideals of the liturgical movement) to three monks of Maria Laach who had been sent to Keyport, New Jersey, to establish an American priory. One of the monks, Damasus Winzen, became a lifelong friend. "To Casel and to his disciples," Shepherd often commented, "we owe the unifying principle of the paschal mystery which has been the foundation of all liturgical revision in our time and the binding thread, if unacknowledged, of the *Constitution on the Sacred Liturgy.*"

Teaching Career

In 1940, Shepherd joined the faculty of the Episcopal Theological School in Massachusetts where he taught early and medieval church history, liturgics and church music. On Sundays, he served a church in Allerton. In 1947, he became the associate rector of St. John's Church, Roxbury Crossing, where he had ample opportunity to put liturgical principles into practice. St. John's became a leader and an example of the Associated Parishes (AP), an important organ of the liturgical movement in the Episcopal church. Incorporated on November 7, 1946, by John Patterson, John Keene, Samuel West and Massey Shepherd, AP was at first a secret organization. Its members were committed to the 1928 *Book of Common Prayer.* They believed that if Episcopalians followed its rubrics strictly, they would discover an enlivened worship that would enable them to be what the theology of the liturgical movement believed the church to be.

In 1954, Shepherd was named professor of liturgics at the Church Divinity School of the Pacific, where he taught until his retirement in 1981. "None of my work," Shepherd commented when accepting the Berakah Award of the North American Academy of Liturgy (1978), "has given me more joy than that of introducing, year to year, raw seminarians to the early church fathers and the classic liturgies of the ancient church."

In 1946, Shepherd first lectured at the University of the South in Sewanee, Tennessee, at a summer graduate school of the Episcopal church where clergy with scholarly interests gathered for spiritual and intellectual renewal. He visited Sewanee again in 1947 and 1950, becoming the director of the summer program in 1951, a position he held until 1970. Conversations following chapel services provided Shepherd with the opportunities to discuss with students the movement toward prayer-book revision. Many Episcopal priests first learned of liturgical renewal by spending their vacations at Sewanee studying with Massey Shepherd.

Despite his many scholarly responsibilities, Shepherd traveled widely to conduct teaching missions. He found these exciting for they provided him with an opportunity to address the liturgical questions that "real people" were asking. During each mission, Shepherd, accompanied by the rector of the parish, visited members of the parish who were homebound. After

1967, Shepherd also traveled extensively to annual clergy conferences to advocate the trial use of the newly authorized *Liturgy of the Lord's Supper.*

Service to the National Church

In 1947, Shepherd first became a member of the Standing Liturgical Commission of the Episcopal Church, on which he served for 30 years. Beginning in 1950, the Commission published a series of *Prayer Book Studies.* Shepherd was personally responsible for the first of these, an examination of baptism and confirmation, and he contributed to many others.

In 1964, the General Convention charged the Commission to bring to the next Convention specific proposals for prayer-book revision. At the 1967 General Convention, *The Liturgy of the Lord's Supper,* a revision of the eucharistic rite, was presented and approved for trial use. The revised rites of initiation and the daily office, plus a complete revision of the psalter, were published as *Authorized Services* in 1973. Small booklets containing alternative texts for certain rites, along with revisions of the marriage rite and of the rites for baptism and confirmation, became available in 1975. "Trial use was absolutely necessary," Shepherd commented. "Without it, we Episcopalians never would have gotten a new prayer book. As people used the proposed rites and became familiar with them, most opposition disappeared. The key was for congregations to use the new rites long enough to become comfortable with them."

At the 1976 General Convention, the full report of the Commission, entitled *The Draft Proposed Book of Common Prayer,* received the approval of the Convention. In 1979, the proposed book was approved by the Convention and eventually became the present American *Book of Common Prayer.* From 1964, when the work of revision began, until the initial approval of the book in 1976, Shepherd served as vice-chairperson of the Standing Liturgical Commission.

The revision of the prayer book was at times difficult. Throughout the lengthy process, critics attacked the proposed liturgies for compromising the faith to achieve relevance. The primary strength of the revised rites, Shepherd always maintained, is the correction of "the predominant preoccupation" of Western liturgies with concerns of sin, guilt and justification. While acknowledging that such themes are crucial, Shepherd understood redemption, the central theme of the liturgy, as bound up with creation, incarnation and eschatological hope.

A liturgical scholar with great ecumenical concern, Shepherd served as an Anglican observer during the third session of Vatican II (1964). In 1966, he was named both to the Consilium for the Implementation of the (Roman Catholic) *Constitution on the Sacred Liturgy* and to the Worship Commission of the Consultation on Church Union (COCU).

Publications and Awards

Of his many books and articles, Shepherd considered two, *The Reform of Liturgical Worship: Perspectives and Prospects* (1961) and *Liturgy and Education* (1965), to be his best. In the former, an account of the liturgical movement in the Protestant Episcopal Church of America, Shepherd proposed that churches moving toward union should work toward the production of a basically common liturgy of the eucharist before they make any definitive moves toward a common ministry. In the latter work, he suggested that worship is the source of the church's most direct knowledge of itself and of its mission.

Although much of Shepherd's teaching and writing was in the field of liturgics, he sustained throughout his life an interest in New Testament studies and the history of the early church. Not surprisingly, Shepherd received numerous awards. The honors of which he was most proud include the Berakah Award of the North American Academy of Liturgy (1978) and the Alumnus of the Year Award of the Divinity School at the University of Chicago (1978). "I count myself fortunate," he commented in accepting the first award, "to have lived, participated and agonized in a convulsive generation of liturgical reform such as the church has not known since the sixteenth century."

■ *Robert Peiffer*

THEOPHANE HYTREK
The Gift and Love of Music

THEOPHANE HYTREK WAS BORN on February 28, 1915, the daughter of Stanislaus and Mary Hytrek, in the town of Stuart, Nebraska. "I started music when I was 8 years old. It was our love at home. We had a little reed organ and later my parents bought our neighbor's piano. No one had to tell me to practice. My oldest brother learned the clarinet. My other brother and one of my sisters both played the violin. Our home became the teenage center of the neighborhood, where our friends from the school orchestra would come together and make music."[1]

The School Sisters of St. Francis staffed the parish school of St. Boniface where Sister Lily, the music teacher, taught Theophane piano. Theophane was one of 50 girls who, over the years, left Stuart and came to Milwaukee to join the School Sisters of St. Francis. When she was 13:

> My first experience of the convent choir was at early morning Mass on Corpus Christi. It was the most beautiful music I had ever heard. Right then, I had a secret desire to someday play the chapel organ.

The School Sisters of St. Francis were established in 1874. This was the same period when the Caecilian movement carried its influence to the United States through the migration of Catholic church musicians from German-speaking countries. Perhaps of greatest significance was the composer John Singenberger (1848–1934) who came to Milwaukee from Switzerland. Professor Singenberger taught music at Holy Family Normal School in Milwaukee and at various convents, including St. Joseph's motherhouse. It was in this tradition that Theophane's teachers were formed.

As a college student, Theophane showed increasing skill in the area of composition. While doing private study in advanced counterpoint at the Wisconsin Conservatory of Music (Milwaukee), she diligently explored the world of harmony and musical analysis. She remembers: "Then one day I felt I had crossed the threshold, and that I was now on the inside of a composer's laboratory—no longer on the outside looking in."

After completing an advanced degree in organ from the Conservatory in 1941, Hytrek taught music at Alverno College. For four years, she commuted once a week to DePaul University in Chicago and studied composition with Dr. Samuel Lieberson.

Organizing for Education

In 1942, Hytrek was involved with the formation of the National Catholic Music Educators Association (NCMEA). Two years later, at the first national meeting of the NCMEA in Cleveland, Harry Seitz formed a National Catholic Chorus. Hytrek was asked to be the accompanist. In the years to follow, at gatherings of the NCMEA and at the Liturgical Weeks, it was common for Hytrek to assist in the preparation of the liturgies and to serve as organist.

From 1950 to 1963, Hytrek chaired the Liturgical Committee of the NCMEA. Each diocese was encouraged to form its own local chapter of support for church musicians. Father Elmer Pfeil, longtime colleague and friend, was director of music at St. Francis Seminary in Milwaukee from 1948 to 1981. He tells of how such a chapter came about in 1951 in Milwaukee:

> Monsignor Goebel called together a dozen or so educators and challenged them to initiate programs that could be helpful to the schools and parishes of the archdiocese. Sister Theophane and I welcomed this unusual invitation and opportunity to do something positive and concrete for parish musicians. Our efforts began with a rather informal organization, called the St. Pius X Guild, that served as a framework for regular Sunday afternoon meetings. There were guest speakers on a variety of subjects, but also a heavy emphasis on demonstrations of choral and organ music. Eventually, the St. Pius X Guild published its own bulletin (known as *Gemshorn*) and sponsored a Biennial Church Music Institute at St. Francis Seminary. Sister Theophane was deeply involved in all these educational efforts, unselfishly sharing her great gifts, gently prodding and patiently encouraging the rest of us to do all we could to help church musicians grow in musical skills so that they could better serve the church.

In 1953, Hytrek began studies for a doctorate from Eastman School of Music. One of her assignments at Eastman was to write a composition imitating the style of an American composer. Having a fondness for Norman Dello Joio's music, with his frequent use of chant melodies, Hytrek wrote her "Prelude and Allegro for Oboe and Piano" in the style of Dello Joio. This piece was awarded first place in 1960 by the National Association of College Wind and Percussion Instructors. In 1976, two composers were commissioned to write musical settings of the liturgy for the Eucharistic Congress in Philadelphia: Theophane Hytrek ("Pilgrim Mass") and Norman Dello Joio

("Missa Festiva"). Over the years, dozens of Hytrek's compositions have been published and widely used.

Hytrek received her doctorate (with a major in composition)
in 1957. She was chairperson of the music department at
Alverno College from 1956 to 1968 and was a full professor
there until 1984.

Tensions after Vatican II

In the late 1950s, Hytrek assisted Irvin Udulutsch, chairperson
of the NCMEA hymn committee, in the formation of the hymnal, *Our Parish Prays and Sings*. Hytrek proofread the harmo-
nizations for this collection, contributed accompaniments of
her own and wrote the introduction. *Our Parish Prays and
Sings* became a staple resource of the Roman Catholic church
musician during the days surrounding Vatican II. It made available vernacular hymnody of liturgical and musical substance,
weaning Catholics away from less substantial hymns.

Shortly after this publication, awareness grew of the need
for Mass ordinaries designed for congregation and choir. Anxious to try her hand at such a work, Hytrek sketched the music
of her popular "Mass in Honor of Mary Immaculate." First
published in Latin in 1961, it was adapted to English in 1964.

In the early 1960s, there was a growing disenchantment
among liturgical musicians with the direction that the NCMEA
was taking. In 1964, liturgical musicians began their own organization. Meeting in Boys Town, the Church Music Association
of America was founded as a merger of the St. Cecilia Society
and the St. Gregory Society. Archabbot Rembert Weakland,
OSB, from St. Vincent's Abbey (Latrobe, Pennsylvania), was
elected the first president of the CMAA.

In August of 1966, the Fifth International Church Music
Congress took place in Chicago and Milwaukee. The program
describes the event as "an international gathering of church

musicians working with the approval of the Holy See to implement Vatican II decrees on the liturgy under the aegis of the Church Music Association of America and the Consociatio Internationalis Musicae Sacrae." Bitter polarizations were forming between those who wished to hold onto Latin chant and the polyphonic style as the "preeminent form of sacred music" and those who were willing to throw open the doors to the vernacular and the incorporation of other musical styles.

Hytrek made her own quiet but significant contribution to the meeting as the member of the program committee responsible for commissioning composers to write music for the Congress. She invited Hermann Schroeder, Daniel Pinkham, Ned Rorem and Leo Sowerby. Several weeks before the event, Hytrek wrote her "Postlude-Partita on the Old One Hundredth," which she premiered during the Congress at one of the cathedral liturgies in Milwaukee on the newly installed Noehren organ.

Later that same year (1966), the Liturgical Conference and the CMAA conducted an open forum on church music in Kansas City. Hytrek was among the speakers. In her presentation, "Facing Reality in the Liturgical Music Apostolate," she said:

> Since music is such an integral part of the liturgy, would it not be wise and fitting to give the many laborers in the musical apostolate some belated recognition by establishing a Ministry of Music in our Catholic churches. . . . Until the hierarchy and clergy recognize that the position of a music director is a highly specialized area requiring special competencies and training, music in our church will remain in a sad state of affairs.[2]

In teaching musical skills to both professional and amateur organists, Hytrek has made a lasting contribution to music in Catholic worship, not only by raising the standard of excellence in performance but also by exposing musicians to the vast field of organ literature. In doing so, Hytrek and her colleagues have led many Catholic church organists out of the musical ghetto.[3]

The years following Vatican II were a nightmare for the church musician of the Roman tradition. There was a mad dash to find and to write music in the vernacular. The demands of the new rites begged that composers experience a conversion. As Bernard Huijbers put it, composers had to learn "to love the sound of a singing congregation."[4] Hytrek became a leader in this. She gracefully bridged the troubled waters of the 1960s and early 1970s. While writing for the sound of the assembly, she never has compromised musical quality and excellence.

At the 1970 meeting of the Federation of Diocesan Liturgical Commissions in Louisville, Hytrek was instrumental in establishing the Composers Forum for Catholic Worship. She served as a member of the Forum's National Board from its inception and chaired it from 1973 to 1975. Composers were commissioned by the Forum to write music for the rites. Members received copies of the new music and were able to reproduce it for use within their worshiping communities. Although the Forum lasted only five years, it produced quality music in the vernacular and brought the kind of compositional form called for by the new rites to the attention of publishers.

A Strong and Gentle Presence

Aidan Kavanagh once lamented the fact that musicians and liturgists were working in isolation instead of collaborating their "respective crafts and gifts."[5] In the autumn of 1981, Hytrek took up this challenge. She proposed that church composers and professional liturgists from across the country be invited to Milwaukee to begin a dialogue. Archbishop Weakland wholeheartedly accepted the proposal. Since then, four symposia for church composers and liturgists have taken place.

These gatherings have stimulated much discussion and study concerning the nature of ritual music and have provided composers with a further sense of direction in their liturgical art.

In November of 1989, Hytrek was named Professor Emerita at Alverno College. She continues to teach and to accept requests to accompany liturgies and to perform in concert. She is constantly receiving commissions to write new music (which she now does with the use of a computer). Her compositions were performed at the First Annual Congress of Women Composers in 1981 in New York City and in 1984 at the American Composers Festival of the Milwaukee Symphony Orchestra.

To know Hytrek is to meet Christian simplicity, gentleness and generosity. She is humble in the truest sense: knowing her gifts so as to place them at the service of God and neighbor.

In 1990, she was the first musician and the first woman to receive the Berakah Award from the North American Academy of Liturgy. The award proclaims:

At the keyboard and in the choirloft,
In the classroom, recital hall, and for the assembly
Your teeming acoustical imagination
  has sounded *Kyrie* and thanksgiving,
    doxa and delight,
      pathos and power
        through half a century and more;
      Your love insists that organ and all instruments conjoin,
        That the music of earth and heaven combine
       Whereby every living thing may praise the Lord.

■ *Charles Conley*

NOTES

1. This article is based in large part on an interview with Sister Theophane Hytek at Alverno College, February 5, 1990.

2. Theophane Hytrek, "Facing Reality in the Liturgical Assembly Apostolate," *Crisis in Church Music?* (Washington DC: The Liturgical Conference, 1967), 99.

3. See Theophane Hytrek, "The Repertoire of the Pastoral Organist," *Pastoral Music* (October–November 1984), 23–26; see also her lecture, "Organ Literature and the Techniques of Service Playing," *Music Teaching Techniques,* ed. Richard H. Weider (Washington DC: The Catholic University of America Press, 1959), 60–74.

4. Bernard Huijbers, *The Performing Audience,* 2d ed. (Phoenix: North American Liturgy Resources, 1980), 23.

5. Aidan Kavanagh, "Beyond Words and Concepts to the Survival of Mrs. Murphy," *Pastoral Music* (April–May 1977), 20.

FRANK KACMARCIK
Artist and Designer

HEN THE LITURGICAL WEEKS began in this country
in 1940, many liturgists believed the United States
was at least 20 years behind Europe in liturgical
renewal. This was especially true regarding the environment for worship. Much of the progress that has
been made in architecture and the arts in this country can be
attributed to Frank Kacmarcik: artist, designer, calligrapher,
liturgical consultant, lecturer, collector of fine art and
manuscripts.

Frank Kacmarcik was born on March 15, 1920, in St. Paul,
Minnesota. His parents were devout Catholics, who attended
church regularly, said the rosary as a family (Frank has four
younger sisters) and sang hymns during the day. His father had
been a cowherd from the village of Landok in Poland. When
he came to the United States, he worked as a furniture uphol-
sterer and refinisher. Frank's mother was a homemaker, who
enjoyed working in the garden. She had been lame until, at the
age of 11, she was cured on a pilgrimage to the shrine of our
Lady of Czestochowa.

Studies and Influences

Kacmarcik did not pursue any formal training in art until after he had finished high school. In 1938, he won a scholarship to the Minneapolis College of Art and Design where he studied under Alexander Masley, a painter and designer, "a good teacher who knew how to ask questions, not necessarily give answers." From another professor, Frank Kofron, Kacmarcik learned "a profound appreciation for the printed word, for the beauty of type, and for the book as an object of art."[1]

For a short time, Kacmarcik was a novice at St. John's Abbey. Here he was exposed to the work of the saintly monk and artist, Clement Frischauf, one of the last painters of the Beuronese school, which was Benedictine in its simplicity and eclectic in its methodology.

Kacmarcik eventually joined the army and was stationed in Europe during World War II. He served as a surgical technician and chaplain's assistant—and he visited many cathedrals, museums and bookstores. After his discharge from the military, he went through the "typical academic training in painting" at the Academie de la Grand Chaumiere and he studied religious art and church decoration at the Centre d'Art Sacre. While in Europe, he developed his eclectic appreciation for good art, especially his love for icons, Byzantine art, Beuronese art and the various periods of church architecture.

The Bauhaus movement, which had developed in Germany in the 1920s, aimed at creating a simple and functional object that would become an extension and expression of the person using it.[2] Kacmarcik's goal of designing a "total atmosphere" that would integrate architecture, furnishings, artwork, vestments, vessels and landscaping is due partly to the influence of the Bauhaus. So, too, is his emphasis on simplicity (simple clarity) and functionality of form.

In 1928, architect Rudolf Schwarz proposed a liturgical arrangement (floor plan) for the feast hall of Schloss

Rothenfels-am-Main, the castle whose chaplain happened to be the famed liturgist Romano Guardini.

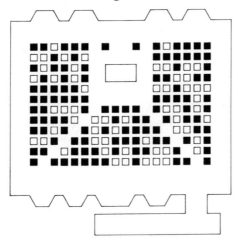

Note the placement of the altar on the long wall, the use of 90-degree angle seating.[3] This liturgical arrangement is one that Kacmarcik would employ and would develop with great sophistication.

St. John's and <u>Worship</u>

When Kacmarcik returned to the United States in 1950, he became professor of art at St. John's University. In 1953, Abbot Baldwin Dworschak hired architect Marcel Breuer to build the abbey's new church. Kacmarcik worked with Breuer (on this and other projects) and credits him with influencing his designs on altars and furnishings. Kacmarcik's strong opinions about the design of the abbey church, however, eventually led to his leaving St. John's in the later part of 1954.

During this second period at St. John's, Kacmarcik became close friends with Michael Marx, OSB, whose Christian wisdom, liturgical understanding, monastic attitude and common sense have greatly influenced Kacmarcik through the years.

With Marx's encouragement and guidance, Kacmarcik has deepened his skills as a calligrapher and designer.

In 1951, Kacmarcik began to design the covers for *Worship* magazine. At first, these designs were quite controversial. His designs were supported by Godfrey Diekmann and others at The Liturgical Press, who were committed to exposing people to new methods of capturing the essence of our faith. Obviously, their confidence was well founded. The covers of *Worship* have won critical acclaim and many other publishers have sought Kacmarcik's services.

Creating the Role of Design Consultant

In the later part of 1954, Kacmarcik left St. John's to pursue a career as a full-time consultant in church design, in printing and in the graphic arts. Kacmarcik adopted as models for his role as consultant architects Augustus Welby Pugin and Ralph Adams Cram and artist Eric Gill.[4] We see their influence in Kacmarcik's eclecticism, in his integration of the various arts in a total environment and in his ban on decoration for the sake of decoration ("Never allow anyone to put something into the building because 'I thought that would look nice.' Let the building's proportions and materials be its beauty.").

When Kacmarcik began his full-time work as a consultant in design, in printing and the graphic arts, his vocation became more clarified:

> In the economy of salvation the sacred artist is to serve as a spokesman and minister of the Christian mystery, to provide a prophetic and priestly mediation of God's truth to God's people. His principal mission is the manifestation of the mystery of redemption in all its breadth and depth. He is to penetrate it first in contemplation, then to announce it vitally—not by words, but by visual media.[5]

Kacmarcik takes seriously the norms of *Environment and Art in Catholic Worship* and places his emphasis on quality furnishings and materials as well as on liturgical design for human interaction and active participation. He challenges the pastor to realize that he is a

> temporary custodian of community property. The pastor's taste is not a matter of general interest. He is building a church which must function spiritually as a church for that ever-changing Christian community as long as the building lasts.[6]

Kacmarcik addresses one of the key problems facing the church today when he states his belief that we don't give a priority to good art, that artists aren't hired and trained to create this kind of artwork, that the church hasn't nourished them. Instead, he says, amateur dabbling is substituting for the work of professional artists.

Evoking the Redeemer's Presence

Kacmarcik is convinced that the environment of a church should "evoke the Redeemer's presence as sovereign Lord *(Kyrios)* of the worshiping assembly."[7] In ancient and medieval times, this was accomplished artistically by apse mosaics of Christ the Good Shepherd, Christ the Messianic Sovereign, Christ the Pantokrator or the exalted Christ seen as a jeweled cross.

Kacmarcik has attempted to evoke the Redeemer's presence as sovereign Lord by making use of an approach known as "visual silence." The source of this approach is Romano Guardini, who spoke of the need to identify the forces that influence us, the need to be "sensitive to the elements, to the earth and the world, to materials as signs. It means being concerned with simplicity, welcoming visual silence."[8] He says that this silence is "like being in a prairie and seeing the sky. Today people are used to surrounding themselves with visual noise, to avoiding themselves."

He designs a church as an environment in which people can find themselves in silence, an environment in which materials and furnishings and overall design challenge the whole assembly to be part of the action. In this effort, our arts and environment must call the church to reach out to serve beyond its walls. If all one experiences when coming to church is the comfortable feeling of being alone with God, if nothing readies a person to interact with the assembly, then the design of the church hasn't served the mission of the church.

His Work

A study of Kacmarcik's churches reveals the following elements: an almost square, slightly off-center altar; a central and prominent presidential chair; a substantial pulpit; freestanding altar candles; a well-lighted sanctuary; skylights over the seats of the assembly; benches and not pews; wide aisles, especially along the walls of the nave; sloped (raked) floors; a large baptismal pool, preferably in the "commons" or else in the nave; a large paschal candle standing near the baptismal pool; a large narthex or "commons" gathering space; a minimal number of devotional statues in the main body of the church; a small eucharistic reservation chapel; a separate daily Mass chapel; and several reconciliation chapels. Of course, not all these elements are found in every building. Nonetheless, Kacmarcik has endeavored to employ as many of these elements as possible to create the optimum environment for worship.

Obviously a strong advocate of the needs of the contemporary liturgy, Kacmarcik respects the treasures of the past. In such buildings, he restores, preserves and adapts the interior so that it can serve the needs of the contemporary liturgy. For example, sometimes he has restored an old reredos by stripping away decades of paint and dirt to return the reredos to its original beauty.

A prominent feature in many of Kacmarcik's churches is the immovable furniture. Usually the altar, the presidential chair and the ambo are made of granite. He says that this is because granite is available in Minnesota, because it has the quality of something eternal, that little sparkle of transcendence, the sense of the timeless. The immovable nature of these furnishings also is insurance that people without liturgical expertise will not ruin the arrangement and interaction of the major furnishings.

Kacmarcik has pioneered the ministry of liturgical design consultants. While not an architect, he has facilitated a parish's working with its architect to design a worship space suitable for the needs of the contemporary church. Much of his effort is devoted to educating people about what a church is and how it should be constructed to do its job. Usually, this is accomplished at a "town-hall meeting" where people have a chance to talk, but no vote is taken. Decisions, he believes, are best left to the committee.

Frank Kacmarcik is undoubtedly one of the finest ministers of visual environment working in the church today. Many of his churches have won architectural awards for their excellence; he received the Berakah Award from the North American Academy of Liturgy in 1981. The churches he has helped to build or renovate are simple and elegant, challenging in their use of quality materials and furnishings, appropriate in their seating arrangement and beautiful in a very natural and earthy way. His designs challenge a community to become the "living words, the living gestures, the living sacrifice, the living meal."[9] They are not for everyone. Yet, those communities that have chosen him to be their consultant have found him to be an extraordinary educator, one who truly understands and respects the way the environment serves and shapes the liturgical assembly.

■ *Robert L. Tuzik*

NOTES

1. Frank Kacmarcik, "The Berakah Award for 1981," *Worship* 55 (1981), 360.

2. See James Notebaart, "The New Design: A Synthesis of Design Trends in the Twentieth Century," *Liturgy* 21 (1976), 104: "The movement tried to bring this [creating a simple and functional object] about by integrating the arts rather than dissociating them, by including the human in the project, rather than presenting the human being as alienated from technology."

3. See Frederic Debuyst, *Modern Architecture and Christian Celebration* (Richmond: John Knox Press, 1968), 61: "The liturgical arrangement of Schloss Rothenfels was probably 'optimal,' the best possible solution for an active participation of the faithful in word and sacrament."

4. Kacmarcik describes Pugin as "the great researcher who turned the church toward the Medieval, restored eclectic gothic attitudes, and integrated the various sciences: architecture, design of furnishings, vestments, chalices." He describes Cram as the "scholar-architect, who wrote plays and who, like Pugin, also integrated the various arts into a highly unified design."

5. Frank Kacmarcik, "The Bible and Creative Imagination," *Liturgical Arts* 32 (1963–1964), 65.

6. Frank Kacmarcik, lecture at a Conference on Church Architecture, February 23–25, 1965, sponsored by the Liturgical Conference and quoted in *Church Architecture, the Shape of Reform* (Washington DC: Liturgical Conference, 1965), 75.

7. Frank Kacmarcik, "The Visualization of Christ's Coming in Glory," *Liturgical Arts* 31 (1962–1963), 43.

8. Kacmarcik, "The Berakah Award for 1981," 364.

9. *Environment and Art in Catholic Worship*, 29.

ALEXANDER PELOQUIN
OMER WESTENDORF
CLARENCE RIVERS

Music for the Movement

THE MUSIC HISTORIAN delights in assigning a landmark piece to substantiate the claim that a new period of music history has begun. Claudio Monteverdi's opera, *Orfeo,* is said to be the major direction change from the Renaissance to the Baroque. The move from the Classical to the Romantic is blamed on Beethoven's symphonies. These landmarks are important—if one assumes that developments and evolutions do occur and that creative effort is not just one big bang after another in history.

Five hundred years from now students of music and liturgy are going to have a field day grappling with the flotsam and jetsam that suggest enormous change in the efforts toward postconciliar reforms. Looking only at the musical implementation of the reformed liturgical documents, they will see musicians faced with an overwhelming challenge: The documents call for *participatio actuoso,* but they provide no established musical repertory to do that.

The enormous adjustment in liturgical music in the last generation has been about musicians breaking from the "choir only" model of the solemn high Mass and constructing musical forms to provide a way for the assembly to make sounds out loud that express the liturgical moment. Music was to allow ministers and assembly to have their parts to sing. So the church musicians needed to think about different relations in musical dialogue, musical expression and the musical language that permits all of that without sacrificing musical integrity. All of this meant stress for composers, most of whom had little liturgical expertise. It was like a liturgical/musical dialectic: old ideas invaded by new ideas and the struggle to form something new. It was not exactly what Monteverdi experienced with Renaissance polyphony and Baroque rhythms, but the anxiety must have been similar. All point to a shift in music history.

Those historians will come across three names that will strike them as somewhat musical: Peloquin, Westendorf and Rivers. Here are three composers who took on the challenge to develop solutions to the problems of "What shall we sing?" and "When shall we sing it?" With questions as large as those, it is a wonder that anything was written at all. These three took on the need for new language for worship, both musical and textual.

Alexander Peloquin

Alexander Peloquin was born at the threshold of the 1920s with all its social changes and the new prosperity. His native New England and its strongly immigrant church enjoyed the growing strength of its members taking their places in politics and society as most first- and second-generation American Catholics were cultivating their modest existences as members of the middle class. They valued home life and some comforts like music. For the Peloquins that meant a piano, voice lessons and singing in the church choir.

Peloquin's intense music training (including a piano concerto performance under the direction of Leonard Bernstein) brought him in 1950, at the age of 31, to be director of music at the Cathedral of Sts. Peter and Paul in Providence, Rhode

Island. He quickly established himself as a force in the church music scene not only in New England but throughout the United States. Vocal and instrumental artists joined in a group called the Peloquin Chorale; it was a testing ground for new music. Peloquin also directed the Boston University Chorus, whose members frequently augmented the strength of the Chorale.

The music in Providence's cathedral was an oasis for church musicians and all who could rejoice in the old and new treasures of church music. Worshipers heard the great repertory of sacred music in the context of the liturgy. As part of the music ministry, masterpieces such as Verdi's *Requiem* were performed as a *concert spirituel*.

Peloquin made music and he talked about music. He was a familiar figure at the Liturgical Weeks and, later, at the meetings of the National Association of Pastoral Musicians. His droll and illuminating lecture-demonstrations brought real and · much-needed knowledge about music history to the Catholic musicians.

Peloquin's place at the front of the new period of singing the liturgy in English was assured when he directed the choir and assembly at the first sung Mass in English in the United States in 1964 at the Liturgical Week in St. Louis. That event initiated a new era in the history of the church's music. Not only did the assembly sing the liturgy in English, they sang in both traditional hymnody and in the new compositions of Clarence Rivers who led them in "God is love," a successful blend of black gospel and blues.

Peloquin's own composition began in the Latin liturgy and has continued to grow. His compositional technique manifests rhythmical characteristics that he has perfected. For example, the six-eight meter that is found in many of his works is displaced by a shift of accent that creates this pattern: 1-2-3, 1-2-3, 1-2, 1-2 (not unlike "America" in *West Side Story*). In his growing attention to rhythms, Peloquin composed *"Missa a la*

Samba" with South American meters and instrumental accompaniment that suggested the use of bongo drums. Clearly rhythmical complexity was no longer an avant-garde element or an expression belonging only to the African-American church. Peloquin made it part of the common vocabulary. Music was never to be dull; he saw to that.

Less rhythmically erratic was his "Mass of the Bells" in 1972. The Gloria became the Catholic anthem of the decade. Its power is derived from an immediate appeal with the antiphon based on the intonation ("Gloria in excelsis Deo") of chant Mass 8 *(Missa de Angelis).* The pentatonic melody falling and rising is irresistible. The relentless six-eight meters give it fluidity. Two other elements are important in the popularity of this piece. It is a text of the liturgy: Catholics—everyone in the assembly—could sing the liturgical text at the appropriate time. And it is reminiscent of the Latin liturgy: most American Catholics of the 1970s remembered singing the Mass of the Angels. It was a bond. In form, this Gloria was verse/refrain. It provided an approachable method that placed no unusual demands on the assembly. Hardly new to the liturgy, the refrain approach as used in this Gloria showed its worth once again as a way to congregational song.

Many believe Peloquin's *Lyric Liturgy,* published in 1974, to be his most effective use of singable congregational lines and rhythmical energy. Not devoid of extravagance, the work begins with a gathering song, "God of the heights, God of the depths" (in 1979, this seemed to become something of an unofficial papal entrance song during the visit of John Paul II to the United States).

In his *American Liturgy,* Peloquin used the Russian choral tradition the communion song, "In memory of you." Russian pieces are frequently found in his concerts and he has shown a remarkable understanding of that style. "In memory of you" alternates the Gregorian chant *"Ave verum corpus"* with a sonorous antiphon, "Lord Jesus, you are here with us. This we do in memory of you." Peloquin successfully achieves the mysterious detachment the Russian style excites.

In 1990, Peloquin celebrated his 40th anniversary as music director of the Providence cathedral. It has been a vocation marked by dedication. His place in the ferment of these decades remains to be seen, but from today's vantage point one must reckon with the proliferation of his music: From "Gloria of the Bells" to the two collections of the *Songs of Israel*, his music swept into the repertory of Catholic parishes and holds there a secure place.

Omer Westendorf

When the appropriate parish committee gathers to deliberate on the selection of a hymnal or missalette or worship aid, they have an abundance of resources to consider. They have their work cut out for them, and it's all Omer Westendorf's fault. He did the furrow work when he circulated the *People's Mass Book* in the late 1950s from his young music company, The World Library of Sacred Music.

The format of that first edition was spiral-bound with a blue cardboard cover. It included radical choices such as "Praise to the Lord"—a Protestant hymn! From this beginning would come several editions from 1964 onward of the *People's Mass Book*.

Westendorf completed his advanced degree in music in 1950 at the University of Cincinnati, his native city. That same year he started his music company. Its elegant title would imply elegant surroundings and a fine, engraved catalog. Nothing could be further from the truth: "When I opened World Library in 1950, my mother had what I guess you would call a tenement house, an old house, a real long, single room, narrow in width. Real ramshackle. When the music came from Europe I stacked it on the floor; there were no shelves. The front door of the house couldn't be opened because the floorboards were so warped. I was the staff. I answered the phone and took the orders."

Westendorf became interested in beginning World Library from his experience as music director of St. Bonaventure Church in Cincinnati, a job he began at age 20. During World War II, he had been an infantryman in the European battlefield. While in Europe, he occasionally rummaged around the choir lofts and organ galleries of churches to discover what music was being used. When the war ended, he continued to be interested in the European musical scene and imported music to be used with his choir. This led him to the founding of the World Library. Relying heavily on the Dutch composers, Westendorf was able to offer American Catholic musicians an alternative to the then common fare.

Thus he positioned himself for the coming explosion in the Catholic church. In 1958, the Liturgical Week was held in Cincinnati and Westendorf created a music book. Drawing on the music being used at liturgies celebrated at Theological College in Washington, D.C., he also prepared four hymns on cards to be used at the Week.

The 1964 edition of the *People's Mass Book* listed some unknown writers and composers, among them J. Clifford Evers, Mark Evans and Paul Francis. These were pseudonyms for Westendorf. There are 40 of his texts in that volume, including, "Where charity and love prevail" and "Sent forth by God's blessing." Even in these first published texts, he could sometimes startle: "The warrior's spear and lance / are splintered by his glance. / The guns and nuclear might / stand withered in his sight" (his rendition of "A mighty fortress"). He produced a charming text for the tune of Ashgrove, "Let all things now living." Its second stanza carried a rollicking phrase that fits the tune admirably: "Our faith ever sharing, / in love ever caring, / we claim as our neighbor / all those of each race." In his version of Psalm 150 to Vermulst's tune, he gave the psalm a majestic swing. Another Westendorf masterpiece is his translation of the "Ubi caritas": "Where charity and love prevail." With Benoit's tune this has provided countless parishes with a supple and satisfying setting; simple and dignified, the text is a natural companion to the chantlike setting.

Westendorf's writing of texts reached a high point in 1976 when he composed the text that became the official hymn for the International Eucharistic Congress in Philadelphia. "You satisfy the hungry heart . . ." began his "Gift of Finest Wheat." It was set to a tune by Robert Kreutz and was instantly successful. Unabashedly Romantic, the tune and text made a significant contribution to the first stage of composing and writing to follow Vatican II.

With the proliferation of missalettes and the scourge of illegally copied music, hard times fell on World Library. Westendorf's company was absorbed as World Library Publications into the J. S. Paluch Company. Westendorf's influence continues as shown in the series of high-quality choral work entitled the "Omer Westendorf Series." In the last decade, some of Westendorf's best-known texts have appeared in the standard Protestant hymnals as well as in many Catholic hymnals. In a way, things have come full circle from Westendorf's introduction of Protestant hymnody to Catholics in the early 1960s.

Westendorf has been active in the Hymn Society of America and other organizations. He was given an honorary doctorate in 1988 by Alvernia College in Reading, Pennsylvania.

Still a resident of Cincinnati, Westendorf can muse over a career that was shaped by a church in need of a language to use at worship: simple, intelligent and dignified to accompany the new rites initiated by Vatican II. His texts have nourished that church.

Clarence Rivers

In 1988, "A Festival of Hymns" celebrated the publication of *Lead Me, Guide Me*, the African-American Catholic Hymnal.

St. Agnes Church, Cincinnati, hosted the event. During the celebration, the following citation was presented to Clarence Joseph Rufus Rivers:

> CLARENCE—light-bearing, shining, darkness-dispelling
>
> JOSEPHUS—dreamer and visionary, exiled and homeward bound
>
> RUFUS—aflame with creative spirit, passionate prophet proclaiming
>
> RIVERS—ever-flowing, restoring, running waters in weary wilderness and dry desert
>
> We salute you, son of Africa in African-American diaspora, brother, friend, priest in the world-embracing Catholic Christian Community. In your unique pilgrim's progress a way for us has been shown to break bonds of cultural constraint, to cross boundaries and religious divisions, to build bridges over ideological chasms. We honor and acclaim you, renowned liturgist and melodist, first among many to devote artistic genius to inculturation in worship. May your name go forth with these volumes of worshipful songs. May every voice be lifted in spirit-filled harmony and in thankful, soulful praise. May the gift of Negritude, generously shared, enliven one great human family bound by love throughout the whole wide earth.

It was fitting that such a presentation be made in the city that has been home to Clarence Rivers for most of his life, even if his relation to its people has often resembled that of the prophet to his homeland. Clarence was born on September 9, 1933, to Clarence Rivers, Sr., and Lorraine Echols Rivers in Selma, Alabama. The family moved to Cincinnati just before World War II, and Clarence and his brother Elliot were enrolled in St. Ann's School in the West End. Before he finished grade school, Clarence had become a Catholic, and after one year at Elder High School he entered St. Gregory's Preparatory Seminary.

Following his ordination in 1956, Rivers was assigned to Purcell High School as a full-time faculty member, with residence at St. Joseph Parish in the West End. The interest in drama sparked during college studies led him to found a semi-professional theater company, "The Queen's Men," specializing in the works of Shakespeare. During this decade of high school teaching, he continued to pursue graduate studies in English and American literature at Xavier University and Yale and in drama at The Catholic University of America.

Throughout his student days, Rivers had always been an avid singer and participant in choral activities. No one was surprised when he responded with his own composition to the requests of the teachers at St. Joseph School for music that would interest the children. These songs became more widely known, particularly through the interest of the women of Grailville, near Cincinnati. People turned to Rivers as a resource for the new music that would be needed as liturgical changes were implemented. Archbishop Alter appointed him early in 1964 to the expanded Archdiocesan Liturgical Commission and its music subcommittee.

Rivers involved himself both locally and nationally in the liturgical apostolate. His expertise in drama gave him insight on the poor liturgical practices that caused so much complaint. He made a proposal to begin a National Institute of Ritual and Drama, but his archbishop requested that he first pursue graduate studies in liturgy at the Institut Catholique in Paris. He returned to found Stimuli, a nonprofit corporation that seeks to apply media presentations, the performing arts and particularly black culture to the needs of education and celebrations (both civic and religious). This organization provided the umbrella under which Rivers took on a great variety of commissions and invitations.

Such activities included Rivers' work in founding and directing for four years the Department of Culture and Worship in the National Office for Black Catholics (NOBC). He organized national and international gatherings, small seminars and workshops like NOBC's annual Workshop in Music and Worship. He designed and organized the Black Heritage Program of the International Eucharistic Congress in Philadelphia in 1976 and has been involved in television and film projects as a writer, producer or consultant.

In the 1970s, Rivers' presence and participation helped launch several new organizations and associations. He consolidated his own professional preparation by acquiring a PHD in Black Culture and Religion from the Union Graduate School of Cincinnati. His work there is published in *The Spirit in Worship*. Previously published books are *Celebration, Reflections,* and *Soulfull Worship*.

Recently, Rivers has taken a less visible role of consultant, confidant, even intermediary. On the national and local level, he has played a significant part in the church, especially among its African-American members. He continues to be passionately committed to the provision of truly "soulfull worship" through the education and formation of artist-leaders.

■ *Fred Moleck (on Peloquin and Westendorf)*

■ *Giles Pater (on Rivers)*

NOTES ON AUTHORS

Gerard Austin (PIERRE-MARIE GY) is the director of the liturgical studies program at The Catholic University of America. Austin's doctoral work was directed by Gy.

Richard J. Butler (LITURGICAL ROOTS IN BOSTON) is pastor of Sacred Heart Parish in Lexington, Massachusetts.

Charles Conley (THEOPHANE HYTREK) is the pastor of St. Robert Bellarmine Parish in Union Grove, Wisconsin.

Mary Pierre Ellebracht (MARTIN HELLRIEGEL) ministers in the Assumption Parish catechumenate in O'Fallon, Missouri.

Virgil Funk (JOSEPH GELINEAU) lives in Washington, D.C., and is the founder and president of the National Association of Pastoral Musicians.

Dennis Geaney (BERNARD LAUKEMPER) is associate pastor at St. Victor Parish in Calumet City, Illinois.

Daniel Grigassy (J. D. CRICHTON) teaches at Christ the King Seminary in East Aurora, New York. Crichton was the subject of his doctoral dissertation.

Charles Gusmer (BALTHASAR FISCHER) teaches at Immaculate Conception Seminary in Newark, New Jersey. His dissertation was directed by Fischer.

Gabe Huck (ROBERT HOVDA) is the director of Liturgy Training Publications in Chicago, Illinois. He worked with Hovda at the Liturgical Conference for several years.

Kathleen Hughes (GODFREY DIEKMANN) is professor of liturgy at Catholic Theological Union in Chicago.

Robert Kennedy (GERALD ELLARD, MICHAEL MATHIS) is assistant professor of liturgy at St. Bernard Institute in Rochester, New York.

Frances Krumpelman (JOSEPH STEDMAN, JUSTINE WARD) is an assistant to several professors at Catholic Theological Union in Chicago and is a part-time retreat director.

Regina Kuehn (ROMANO GUARDINI) is an artist and liturgical consultant in Oak Park, Illinois. Guardini was an advisor for her doctoral thesis.

Michael Kwatera (PROSPER GUÉRANGER, PIUS PARSCH) is a monk of St. John's Abbey, Collegeville, Minnesota, and a doctoral student at the University of Notre Dame.

Richard Leggett (LAMBERT BEAUDUIN, EDMUND BISHOP, WALTER HOWARD FRERE, EVELYN UNDERHILL) teaches liturgics at Vancouver School of Theology in Vancouver, British Columbia.

Patrick Malloy (ODO CASEL, VIRGIL MICHEL) teaches liturgy at St. John's University in Collegeville and is a PHD candidate at the University of Notre Dame.

Marchita Mauck (FREDERIC DEBUYST) is an art historian and liturgical consultant. She teaches at Louisiana State University.

Paul Meyendorff (ALEXANDER SCHMEMANN) is assistant professor of liturgical theology at St. Vladimir's Orthodox Theological Seminary in Crestwood, New York.

Fred Moleck (OMER WESTENDORF, ALEXANDER PELOQUIN) is associate professor of fine arts at Seton Hill College.

John Page (FREDERICK MCMANUS) is the executive secretary of the International Commission on English in the Liturgy in Washington, D.C. He has worked with McManus in that capacity.

Giles Pater (CLARENCE RIVERS) is pastor of St. Agnes Church in Cincinnati, Ohio.

Robert Peiffer (JOSEF JUNGMANN, MASSEY SHEPHERD) is a doctoral candidate at the University of Notre Dame and campus minister at Bloomsburg University.

Joanne Pierce (PIUS XII AND PRECONCILIAR LITURGICAL REFORMS) teaches liturgy at Barry University in Miami.

Grant Sperry-White (LOUIS BOUYER, WILLIAM BUSCH, GREGORY DIX) is a doctoral student at the University of Notre Dame.

Judith Stoughton (ADÉ BETHUNE) is retired and lives in St. Paul, Minnesota.

John Sullivan (BERNARD BOTTE) is the provincial of the Washington Province of the Discalced Carmetlie Friars. Botte directed Sullivan's doctoral studies.

Gordon Truitt (GERARD SLOYAN) is editor of *Pastoral Music,* the magazine of the National Association of Pastoral Musicians, in Washington, D.C. He was on the editorial staff of the Liturgical Conference when Sloyan was on the board.

Robert Tuzik (REYNOLD HILLENBRAND, FRANK KACMARCIK, H. A. REINHOLD) teaches liturgy at Mundelein Seminary and is the liturgical consultant in the Office for Divine Worship in Chicago, Illinois. Hillenbrand's contribution to the liturgical movement was the subject of his doctoral dissertation.

Susan White (MAURICE LAVANOUX) is a lecturer in liturgy and worship at Westcott House in Cambridge, England. The Liturgical Arts Society was the subject of her doctoral dissertation.

James A. Wilde (THERESE AND FRANZ MUELLER) is a freelance author, editor and translator in Oak Park, Illinois.